The increase in debt around the world, and in particular in emerging market economies, is one of the most important global developments in recent years. It is also one of the main sources of risk to global financial stability and economic growth. *Global Waves of Debt* is an important contribution to understanding the process of rapid debt accumulation and its risks. It draws lessons from the experience of previous waves of debt buildup through an outstanding comparative approach. Although the postcrisis wave is very different from previous ones, sudden and large changes in risk appetite or global interest rates could nonetheless have severe negative repercussions in many economies. Policy makers must take the necessary steps to ensure that the consequences from this wave are also different from previous ones, and the insights from this book are of great help in this regard.

José de Gregorio
Dean of the School of Economics and Business
The University of Chile
Former Governor of the Central Bank of Chile

This timely and important book documents the global experience of the four waves of public and private debt accumulation from 1970 to the present. The authors skillfully surf through the data, dissecting the cross-country experience from each episode with a focus on emerging and developing economies. They extract the key lessons from the thoroughly documented experience of the first three waves and map these into the current wave, which began in 2010. The rigorous exploration yields a better understanding of the fourth wave and possible future scenarios. The previous waves of debt ended in crises in many countries. The authors expertly explore whether the implications of the current wave could be different and what role policy can play. This book is an essential resource for anyone interested in the history and prospects of national, regional, and global public and private debt.

Warwick McKibbin
Professor and Director of the Centre for
Applied Macroeconomic Analysis
Australian National University

As debt levels surge around the world, a comprehensive and systematic examination of previous episodes of debt accumulation—and how they end—is just the sort of analysis for these times. How the current experience compares against previous episodes, and the special conditions that currently prevail—including extremely low real interest rates—is examined in detail. Those who read the book thinking they already know the postwar history of debt will be surprised, and enlightened.

Menzie Chinn
Professor of Public Affairs and Economics
University of Wisconsin

Just as it is easy for economies to get flooded by waves of debt, so it is easy for readers to drown in a sea of books and articles on debt. But this time the experience is different. *Global Waves of Debt* not only provides a very well researched analysis of the history of debt over the last five decades with many new insights into its good and bad consequences, but it does so in an easy read. While it leaves one worried in light of the current, ongoing wave of debt, one will enjoy the ride.

Stijn Claessens
Head of Financial Stability Policy and
Deputy Head of the Monetary and Economic Department
Bank for International Settlements

This book is a timely contribution to the debate on the implications of global borrowing for economic performance. Taking a historical perspective, Kose, Nagle, Ohnsorge, and Sugawara provide a clear articulation of the potential vulnerabilities raised by the exceptionally large and rapid current buildup of global indebtedness. The book documents well how current indebtedness positions are an artifact of our low interest rate environment and illustrates the extent to which borrowing nations would face challenges given an abrupt change in global conditions. It closes with an inspection of how pursued policies have affected historical outcomes in the wake of disruptive shocks to borrowing capacities and discusses the implications of these experiences for current policy. Arguments in the narrative are supported by a large array of empirical evidence that will be of use to researchers and practitioners alike. I would recommend this book most highly to anyone interested in international financial issues.

Mark M. Spiegel
Senior Policy Adviser, Economic Research
Federal Reserve Bank of San Francisco

Global Waves of Debt has done a signal service by reminding us that this time may be no different. In the current environment of low growth rates and interest rates, which are expected to remain low for the foreseeable future, and monetary policy at a seeming dead end globally, calls for fiscal stimulus and increased debt are becoming the flavor of the day in both advanced and emerging markets. The authors' painstaking work reveals that the increase in debt globally has already been larger, faster, and more broad based since the Great Financial Crisis than in the previous three waves. This should be seen as a leading indicator for the possibility of financial crises ahead and shake up the complacency that is evident in macroeconomic policy making today with regard to increasing levels of both public and private debt. Kudos to the authors for their fine analytical work in putting together this unprecedented volume that puts the current situation in comparable historical perspective.

Rakesh Mohan
Senior Fellow, Jackson Institute for Global Affairs
Yale University
Former Deputy Governor of the Reserve Bank of India

Global Waves of Debt

Global Waves of Debt

Causes and Consequences

M. Ayhan Kose, Peter Nagle, Franziska Ohnsorge,
and Naotaka Sugawara

ISBN (paper): 978-1-4648-1544-7
ISBN (electronic): 978-1-4648-1545-4
DOI: 10.1596/978-1-4648-1544-7

Cover design: Quinn Sutton, World Bank Group. Further permission required for reuse.

Library of Congress Control Number: 2020914229

Summary of Contents

Contents

Figures

Tables

Foreword

Waves of debt accumulation have been a recurrent feature of the global economy over the past 50 years. In emerging market and developing economies, there have been four major debt waves since 1970. The first three waves ended in financial crises—the Latin American debt crisis of the 1980s, the Asian financial crisis of the late 1990s, and the global financial crisis of 2007-09.

A fourth wave of debt began in 2010, and debt has reached $55 trillion in 2018, making this wave the largest, broadest, and fastest growing of the four. Although debt financing can help meet urgent development needs such as basic infrastructure, much of the current debt wave is taking riskier forms. Low-income countries are increasingly borrowing from creditors outside the traditional Paris Club lenders, notably from China. Some of these lenders impose nondisclosure clauses and collateral requirements that obscure the scale and nature of debt loads. There are concerns that governments are not as effective as they need to be in investing the loans in physical and human capital. In fact, in many developing countries, public investment has been falling even as debt burdens rise.

The debt buildup also warrants close analysis because of slower growth during the current wave. In comparison with conditions before the 2007-09 crisis, emerging market and developing economies have been growing more slowly even though debt has been growing faster. Slower growth has meant weaker development outcomes and slower poverty reduction.

Global Waves of Debt presents the first in-depth analysis of the similarities and differences in the post-1970 waves of debt accumulation. It also features a comprehensive examination of more than 500 individual episodes of government and private debt surges that have occurred in 100 emerging market and developing economies over the past five decades. The study reports that roughly half of those debt surges ended in financial crises.

The latest debt surge in emerging market and developing economies has been striking: in just eight years, total debt climbed to an all-time high of roughly 170 percent of gross domestic product (GDP). That marks an increase of 54 percentage points of GDP since 2010—the fastest gain since at least 1970. The bulk of this debt increase was incurred by China (equivalent to more than $20 trillion). The rest of the increase was broad based—involving government as well as private debt—and observable in virtually every region of the world.

The study shows that simultaneous buildups in public and private debt have historically been associated with financial crises that resulted in particularly prolonged declines in per capita income and investment. Emerging market and developing economies already are more vulnerable on a variety of fronts than they were ahead of the last crisis: 75 percent of them now have budget deficits, their foreign-currency-denominated corporate debt is significantly higher, and their current account deficits are four times as large as they were in 2007. Under these circumstances, a sudden rise in risk premiums could precipitate a financial crisis, as has happened many times in the past.

Clearly, it's time for course corrections. The study identifies several concrete steps that policy makers can take to lower the probability and severity of a crisis. Better debt management can help them lower borrowing costs and improve debt sustainability. Greater debt transparency—by governments as well as creditors—can make it easier to identify and remedy the biggest risks. By removing uncertainty, it can also help speed up investment flows. Pursuing alternatives to public debt accumulation can also help: governments should encourage private sector investment and work to expand the tax base in ways that encourage growth.

Towering though it may seem, the latest global wave of debt can be managed. Across the world, interest rates are at historic lows, moderating the costs of the debt. But leaders need to recognize the danger and move countries into safer territory in terms of the quality and quantity of investment and debt—sooner rather than later.

David Malpass
President
World Bank Group

Acknowledgments

We are privileged to have superb colleagues, many of whom have contributed to the work presented in this book. We are grateful to Carlos Arteta, Justin-Damien Guénette, Jongrim Ha, Alain Kabundi, Sergiy Kasyanenko, Patrick Kirby, Wee Chian Koh, Franz Ulrich Ruch, Ekaterine Vashakmadze, Dana Vorisek, Collette M. Wheeler, Sandy Lei Ye, and Shu Yu for their contributions to background research and literature reviews. The book is a product of the Prospects Group and was produced under the general guidance of Ceyla Pazarbasioglu, former Vice President for Equitable Growth, Finance and Institutions of the World Bank Group.

This study would not have been possible without insightful comments from Eduardo Borensztein, Kevin Clinton, Antonio Fatas, Erik Feyen, Graham Hacche, Catiana Garcia Kilroy, Ugo Panizza, Fernanda Ruiz-Nunes, Anderson Caputo Silva, Christopher Towe, and Igor Esteban Zuccardi.

We owe a debt of gratitude to many colleagues who provided useful suggestions on earlier drafts and discussed our findings: Mahama Samir Bandaogo, Kevin Barnes, Sebastian Franco Bedoya, Robert Beyer, Cesar Calderon, Kevin Carey, Stijn Claessens, Francesca de Nicola, Asli Demirgüç-Kunt, Dinara Djoldosheva, Doerte Doemeland, Sebastian Michael Essl, Marcello Estevao, David Gould, Birgit Hansl, Elena Ianchovichina, Ergys Islamaj, Gerard Kambou, Megumi Kubota, Hans Peter Lankes, Daniel Lederman, William Maloney, Andrew Mason, Aaditya Mattoo, Nadir Mohammed, Lili Mottaghi, Ha Nguyen, Rolande Pryce, Rong Qian, Martin Rama, Frederico Gil Sander, Shakira Sharifuddin, Max Rudibert Steinbach, Temel Taskin, Hans Timmer, Christina Wood, Albert Zeufack, and Fan Zhang.

We are particularly thankful to Shijie Shi and Jinxin Wu for their outstanding research support. Excellent research assistance was also provided by Vanessa Arellano Banoni, Yushu Chen, Zhuo Chen, Khamal Antonio Clayton, Shihui Liu, Julia R. R. Norfleet, Vasiliki Papagianni, Jankeesh Sandhu, Xinyue Wang, Heqing Zhao, and Juncheng Zhou.

We would like to thank our colleagues who worked on the production and dissemination of the book. Adriana Maximiliano and Quinn Sutton assembled the print publication. Graeme Littler provided editorial and website support. Joseph Rebello and Alejandra Viveros managed media relations and dissemination.

About the Authors

M. Ayhan Kose is Director of the World Bank Group's Prospects Group. He previously worked in the Research and Western Hemisphere Departments of the International Monetary Fund. He is a Nonresident Senior Fellow at the Brookings Institution, a Research Fellow at the Centre for Economic Policy Research, a Dean's Fellow at the University of Virginia's Darden School of Business, and a Research Associate at the Center for Applied Macroeconomic Analysis.

Peter Nagle is an Economist in the World Bank Group's Prospects Group. Previously, he worked at the Institute of International Finance and the International Directorate at the Bank of England.

Franziska Ohnsorge is Manager of the World Bank Group's Prospects Group. Before joining the World Bank, she worked in the Office of the Chief Economist of the European Bank for Reconstruction and Development and in the African, European, and Strategy and Policy Review Departments of the International Monetary Fund. She is a Research Fellow at the Centre for Economic Policy Research and a Research Associate at the Centre for Applied Macroeconomic Analysis.

Naotaka Sugawara is a Senior Economist in the World Bank Group's Prospects Group. Previously, he worked in the Research Department of the International Monetary Fund and the Office of the Chief Economist for Europe and Central Asia in the World Bank.

Abbreviations

ARA	Assessing Reserve Adequacy
BIS	Bank for International Settlements
CAC	collective action clauses
CLOs	collateralized loan obligations
CRFB	Committee for a Responsible Federal Budget
DSAs	debt sustainability analyses
EAP	East Asia and Pacific
ECA	Europe and Central Asia
EMDEs	emerging market and developing economies
EU	European Union
FBR	foreign bank reliance
FDI	foreign direct investment
FDIC	Federal Deposit Insurance Corporation
FRED	Federal Reserve Economic Data
FSB	Financial Stability Board
G20	Group of Twenty (Argentina, Australia, Brazil, Canada, China, France, Germany, India, Indonesia, Italy, Japan, Republic of Korea, Mexico, Russian Federation, Saudi Arabia, South Africa, Turkey, United Kingdom, United States, and European Union)
GDP	gross domestic product
GFC	global financial crisis
HIPC	Heavily Indebted Poor Countries (initiative)
IDA	International Development Association
IFAWG	International Financial Architecture Working Group
IIF	Institute of International Finance
IMF	International Monetary Fund
IPVAR	interacted panel vector autoregression
LAC	Latin America and the Caribbean
LICs	low-income countries
LMICs	lower middle-income countries
MDRI	Multilateral Debt Relief Initiative
MNA	Middle East and North Africa
MTDs	medium-term debt management strategies
NEXGEM	next generation emerging markets
OECD	Organisation for Economic Co-operation and Development
SAR	South Asia
SDGs	Sustainable Development Goals
SSA	Sub-Saharan Africa
SVAR	structural vector autoregression
UNCTAD	United Nations Conference on Trade and Development
USAID	United States Agency for International Development

Another global wave of debt underway...

The global economy has experienced four waves of broad-based debt accumulation over the past 50 years. In the latest wave, underway since 2010, global debt has grown to an all-time high of 230 percent of gross domestic product (GDP) in 2018. The debt buildup was particularly fast in emerging market and developing economies (EMDEs). Since 2010, total debt in these economies has risen by 54 percentage points of GDP to a historic peak of about 170 percent of GDP in 2018. Following a steep fall during 2000-10, debt has also risen in low-income countries to 67 percent of GDP ($268 billion) in 2018, up from 48 percent of GDP (about $137 billion) in 2010.

Why this study?

The size, speed, and reach of the postcrisis debt buildup in EMDEs raises concerns about its potential consequences for macroeconomic and financial stability. To shed light on these consequences, this study presents the first in-depth analysis of four waves of debt accumulation, puts the current debt wave into historical perspective, analyzes national episodes of debt accumulation, examines the links between debt accumulation and financial crises, and draws policy lessons. The study employs a wide range of approaches, including event studies, econometric models, country case studies, and a detailed review of historical episodes.

Three historical waves: All ended with crises

Before the current wave, EMDEs experienced three waves of broad-based debt accumulation. The first wave spanned the 1970s and 1980s, with borrowing primarily accounted for by governments in Latin America and the Caribbean region and in low-income countries, especially in Sub-Saharan Africa. The combination of low real interest rates in much of the 1970s and a rapidly growing syndicated loan market encouraged these governments to borrow heavily.

The first wave culminated in a series of crises in the early 1980s. Debt relief and restructuring were prolonged in the first wave, ending with the introduction of the Brady Plan in the late 1980s for mostly Latin American countries. The Plan provided debt relief through the conversion of syndicated loans into bonds, collateralized with U.S. Treasury securities. For low-income countries, substantial debt relief came in the mid-1990s and early 2000s with the Heavily

Indebted Poor Countries initiative and the Multilateral Debt Relief Initiative, spearheaded by the World Bank and the International Monetary Fund.

The second wave ran from 1990 until the early 2000s as financial and capital market liberalization enabled banks and corporations in the East Asia and Pacific region and governments in the Europe and Central Asia region to borrow heavily, particularly in foreign currencies. It ended with a series of crises in these regions in 1997-2001 once investor sentiment turned unfavorable.

The third wave was a run-up in private sector borrowing in Europe and Central Asia from European Union headquartered "mega-banks" after regulatory easing. This wave ended when the global financial crisis disrupted bank financing in 2007-09 and tipped several economies in Europe and Central Asia into recessions.

Historical waves: Many similarities but some differences as well

The three waves of debt began during periods of low real interest rates and were often facilitated by financial innovations or changes in financial markets that promoted borrowing. The waves ended with widespread financial crises and coincided with global recessions (1982, 1991, and 2009) or downturns (1998 and 2001). These crises were typically triggered by shocks that resulted in sharp increases in investor risk aversion, risk premiums, or borrowing costs, followed by sudden stops of capital inflows and deep recessions. The financial crises were usually followed by reforms designed to lower vulnerabilities and strengthen policy frameworks. Many EMDEs introduced inflation targeting, greater exchange rate flexibility, fiscal rules, or more robust financial sector supervision in the aftermath of crises.

There are some important differences among the first three waves. The financial instruments used for borrowing have evolved as new instruments or financial actors have emerged. The nature of EMDE borrowers in international financial markets has changed, with the private sector accounting for a growing share of debt accumulation through the three waves. The severity of the economic damage done by the financial crises that ended the waves varied among them, and across regions. Output losses were particularly large and protracted in the wake of the first wave, when the majority of debt accumulation had been by governments. Meanwhile, in many EMDEs, improvements in policy frameworks after the first two debt waves played a role in mitigating the adverse impact of the global financial crisis that marked the end of the third wave.

The fourth wave: Similar to previous waves but larger, faster, and broader

The latest wave of debt accumulation began in 2010 and has already seen the largest, fastest, and most broad-based increase in debt in EMDEs in the past 50 years. The average annual increase in EMDE debt since 2010 of almost 7 percentage points of GDP has been larger by some margin than in each of the previous three waves. In addition, whereas previous waves were largely regional in nature, the fourth wave has been widespread with total debt rising in almost 80 percent of EMDEs and rising by at least 20 percentage points of GDP in just over one-third of these economies.

The current wave of debt accumulation bears many similarities to the previous three waves. Global interest rates have been very low since the global financial crisis and the ensuing search for yield by investors has contributed to narrowing spreads for EMDEs. Some major changes in financial markets have again boosted borrowing, including through a rise of regional banks, growing appetite for local currency bonds, and increased demand for EMDE debt from the expanding nonbank financial sector. As in the earlier waves, vulnerabilities have mounted in EMDEs as the current wave has proceeded amid slowing economic growth.

National episodes of debt accumulation: Debt distress more likely

At the individual country level, EMDEs have historically undergone recurrent surges of rapid debt accumulation. When these episodes took place in many economies, they collectively formed the global waves of debt discussed above. A closer examination of national episodes offers a more granular perspective on the causes and consequences of debt accumulation.

Since 1970, there have been 519 national episodes of rapid debt accumulation in 100 EMDEs, during which government debt typically rose by 30 percentage points of GDP and private debt by 15 percentage points of GDP. The typical episode lasted about eight years. About half of these episodes were accompanied by financial crises, which were particularly common in the first and second global waves, with severe output losses compared to countries without crises. Crisis countries typically registered larger debt buildups, especially for government debt, and accumulated greater macroeconomic and financial vulnerabilities than did noncrisis countries.

Although financial crises associated with national debt accumulation episodes were typically triggered by external shocks such as sudden increases in global interest rates, domestic vulnerabilities often amplified the adverse impact of these shocks. Crises were more likely, or the economic distress they caused was more severe, in countries with higher external debt—especially short-term—and lower international reserves.

Unsustainable policies: A recipe for debt distress

Most EMDEs that experienced financial crises during debt accumulation episodes employed various combinations of unsustainable macroeconomic policies and suffered structural and institutional weaknesses. Debt buildup had often funded import substitution strategies, undiversified economies, or inefficient sectors that did not raise export earnings or had poor corporate governance. Many of these economies had severe weaknesses in their fiscal and monetary policy frameworks, including poor revenue collection, widespread tax evasion, public wage and pension indexing, monetary financing of fiscal deficits, and substantial use of energy and food subsidies. In addition, crisis countries often borrowed in foreign currency and managed their exchange rates, while regulation and supervision of banks and other financial institutions were frequently weak. Several EMDEs that experienced crises also suffered from protracted political uncertainty.

End of the current wave: Will history repeat itself?

Although EMDEs have gone through periods of volatility in the current wave of debt accumulation, they have not experienced widespread financial crises. The exceptional size, speed, and reach of debt accumulation in EMDEs during the fourth wave, however, should give policy makers in EMDEs pause. Despite the sharp rise in debt, these economies have experienced a decade of repeated growth disappointments and are now facing weaker growth prospects in a fragile global economy. In addition to their rapid debt buildup, they have accumulated other vulnerabilities, such as growing fiscal and current account deficits and a shift toward a riskier composition of debt. Thus, despite exceptionally low real interest rates, and prospects for continued low rates in the near-term, the current wave of debt accumulation could follow the historical pattern and culminate in financial crises in these economies.

A sudden global shock, such as a sharp rise in interest rates or a spike in risk premiums, could lead to financial stress in more vulnerable economies. Among low-income countries, the rapid increase in debt and the shift from concessional toward financial market and non-Paris Club bilateral creditors have raised concerns about debt transparency and collateralization. Elevated debt in large EMDEs could amplify the impact of adverse shocks and trigger a downturn in these economies, posing risks to global and EMDE growth.

Policies matter!

Although there is no magic bullet of a policy prescription to ensure that the current debt wave proceeds smoothly, the experience of past waves of debt points to the critical role of policy choices in determining the outcomes of these episodes. Specific policy priorities ultimately depend on country circumstances, but four broad strands of policies can help reduce the likelihood that the current debt wave will end in crisis and, if crises were to take place, to alleviate their impact: policies to manage the composition of debt, strong macroeconomic and financial policy frameworks, sound financial sector policies, and robust business environments and institutions.

First, higher government or private debt and a riskier composition of debt (in terms of maturity, currency denomination, and type of creditor) are associated with a higher probability of crisis. Hence, sound debt management and debt transparency will help reduce borrowing costs, enhance debt sustainability, and contain fiscal risks. Creditors, including international financial institutions, can spearhead efforts in this area by encouraging common standards, supporting capacity building, and highlighting risks and vulnerabilities through timely analytical and surveillance work.

Second, robust monetary, exchange rate, and fiscal policy frameworks can safeguard EMDEs' resilience in a fragile global economic environment. The benefits of stability-oriented and resilient monetary policy frameworks cannot be overstated. Flexible exchange rates can discourage a buildup of substantial balance sheet mismatches and reduce the likelihood of large exchange rate misalignments. Fiscal rules can help prevent fiscal slippages, ensure that revenue windfalls during times of strong growth are prudently managed, and manage and contain risks from contingent liabilities. Revenue and expenditure policies can be adjusted to expand fiscal resources for priority spending.

Third, proactive financial sector regulation and supervision can help policy makers identify and act on emerging risks. Financial market deepening can help mobilize domestic savings, which may be a more stable source of financing than foreign borrowing.

Fourth, in several crisis cases, it became apparent that borrowed funds had been diverted toward purposes that did not raise export proceeds, productivity, or potential output. Apart from effective public finance management, policies that promote good corporate governance can help ensure that debt is used for productive purposes. Sound bankruptcy frameworks can help prevent debt overhangs from weighing on investment for prolonged periods.

PART I

Setting the Stage

[T]he notion that additional debt is a free lunch is foolish. High debt levels make it more difficult for governments to respond aggressively to shocks.

Kenneth Rogoff (2019)
Thomas D. Cabot Professor of Public Policy and Professor
of Economics at Harvard University

CHAPTER 1
Debt: Evolution, Causes, and Consequences

The global economy has experienced four waves of debt accumulation over the past 50 years. The first three ended with financial crises in many emerging market and developing economies. During the current wave, which started in 2010, the increase in debt in these economies has already been larger, faster, and more broad-based than in the previous three waves. Current low interest rates—which markets expect to be sustained into the medium term—appear to mitigate some of the risks associated with high debt. However, emerging market and developing economies are also confronted by weak growth prospects, mounting vulnerabilities, and elevated global risks. A menu of policy options is available to reduce the likelihood of the current debt wave ending in crises and, if crises were to take place, to alleviate their impact.

Motivation

Waves of debt accumulation have been a recurrent feature of the global economy over the past 50 years, involving both advanced economies and emerging market and developing economies (EMDEs). Since the global financial crisis, another wave has been building, with global debt reaching an all-time high of roughly 230 percent of global gross domestic product (GDP) in 2018 (figure 1.1).

Total (public and private) EMDE debt also reached a record high of almost 170 percent of GDP ($55 trillion) in 2018, an increase of 54 percentage points of GDP since 2010. Although China accounted for the bulk of this increase—in part due to its sheer size—the debt buildup was broad-based: In about 80 percent of EMDEs, total debt was higher in 2018 than in 2010. Excluding China (where the rapid debt buildup was mostly domestic), the increase in debt in EMDEs was in almost equal measure accounted for by external and domestic debt. In low-income countries (LICs), following a steep fall between 2000 and 2010, total debt also increased to 67 percent of GDP ($270 billion) in 2018, up from 48 percent of GDP (about $137 billion) in 2010.

In contrast, in advanced economies, total debt has remained near the record levels reached in the early aftermath of the global financial crisis, at about 265 percent of GDP in 2018 ($130 trillion). Whereas government debt has risen, to a high of 104 percent of GDP ($50 trillion), private sector debt has

FIGURE 1.1 **Evolution of debt**

Global debt has trended up since 1970, reaching about 230 percent of GDP in 2018. Debt has risen particularly rapidly in EMDEs, reaching a peak of about 170 percent of GDP in 2018. Much of the increase since 2010 has occurred in the private sector, particularly in China. Debt in low-income countries has started to rise after a prolonged period of decline following debt-relief measures in the late 1990s and 2000s. Advanced economy debt has been broadly flat since the global financial crisis, with increased government debt more than offsetting a mild deleveraging in the private sector.

A. Global debt

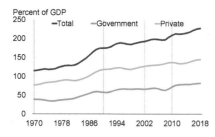

B. Debt in EMDEs

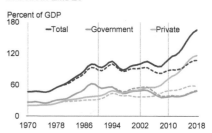

C. Debt in low-income countries

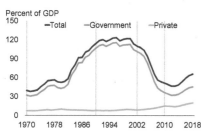

D. Debt in advanced economies

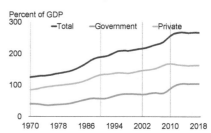

Sources: International Monetary Fund; World Bank.
Note: Aggregates calculated using current U.S. dollar GDP weight and shown as a 3-year moving average. Gray vertical lines represent start of debt waves in 1970, 1990, 2002, and 2010. EMDEs = emerging market and developing economies.
B. Dashed lines refer to EMDEs excluding China.

fallen slightly amid deleveraging in some sectors. Total debt has fallen since 2010 in two-fifths of advanced economies.

Debt accumulation in EMDEs has not followed a linear process. Different EMDE regions and sectors have experienced diverse debt developments since 1970. Before the current wave of debt accumulation, EMDEs experienced three waves of broad-based debt accumulation over the period 1970-2009: 1970-89, 1990-2001, and 2002-09. Although each of these waves of rising debt had some unique features, they all shared the same fate: they ended with financial crises and subsequent substantial output losses in many countries.

The current environment of low interest rates, combined with subpar global growth, has led to a lively debate about the benefits and risks of further government debt accumulation to finance increased spending (World Bank 2019).[1] Although the focus of this debate has been mainly on advanced economies, it is also of critical importance for EMDEs. Borrowing can be beneficial for EMDEs, particularly in economies with substantial development challenges, if it is used to finance growth-enhancing investments in areas such as infrastructure, health care, and education. Government debt accumulation can also be appropriate temporarily as part of countercyclical fiscal policy, to boost demand and activity in economic downturns.

High debt carries significant risks, however, particularly for EMDEs because it makes them more vulnerable to external shocks. The rollover of debt can become increasingly difficult during periods of financial stress, potentially resulting in a crisis. High government debt can also limit the size and effectiveness of fiscal stimulus during downturns, and dampen long-term growth by weighing on productivity-enhancing private investment.

EMDEs have been navigating dangerous waters as the current debt wave has coincided with multiple challenges for these economies (figure 1.2). They have experienced a decade of repeated growth disappointments and are now confronted by weaker growth prospects in a fragile global economy (Kose and Ohnsorge 2019). In addition to their rapid debt buildup during the current wave, these economies have accumulated other vulnerabilities, such as growing fiscal and current account deficits, and a compositional shift toward short-term external debt, which could amplify the impact of shocks. By 2018, the share of EMDE government debt held by nonresidents had grown to 43 percent and foreign currency-denominated EMDE corporate debt had risen to 26 percent of GDP; by 2016, the share of nonconcessional LIC government debt had risen to 55 percent.

Thus, despite current exceptionally low real interest rates, including at long maturities, the latest wave of debt accumulation could follow the historical pattern and eventually culminate in financial crises in EMDEs. A sudden global shock, such as a sharp rise in interest rates or a spike in risk premiums,

---

[1] Blanchard (2019); Blanchard and Summers (2019); Blanchard and Tashiro (2019); Blanchard and Ubide (2019); Eichengreen et al. (2019); Furman and Summers (2019); Krugman (2019); and Rachel and Summers (2019) discuss reasons for additional borrowing in advanced economies, and the United States in particular. Alcidi and Gros (2019); Auerbach, Gale, and Krupkin (2019); CRFB (2019); Eichengreen (2019); Mazza (2019); Riedl (2019); Rogoff (2019a, 2019b); and Wyplosz (2019) caution against adding to debt.

FIGURE 1.2 Postcrisis debt accumulation, growth, and interest rates

Despite a very fast debt buildup since 2010, EMDE growth has slowed. The current environment of low interest rates mitigates immediate concerns about debt accumulation.

A. Growth and debt in EMDEs

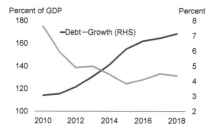

B. Long-term interest rates

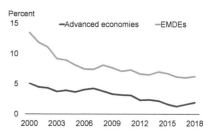

Sources: International Institute of Finance; World Bank.
Note: EMDEs = emerging market and developing economies.
A. Total debt (in percent of GDP) and real GDP growth (GDP-weighted at 2010 prices and exchange rates).
B. Average long-term nominal government bond yields (with 10-year maturities) computed with current U.S. dollar GDP weights, based on 36 advanced economies and 84 EMDEs.

could lead to financial stress in more vulnerable economies. These risks were illustrated by the recent experiences of Argentina and Turkey, which witnessed sudden episodes of sharply rising borrowing costs and severe growth slowdowns. Among LICs, meanwhile, the rapid increase in debt and the shift from concessional toward financial market and non-Paris Club creditors have raised concerns about debt transparency and collateralization. Elevated debt in major EMDEs, including China, could amplify the impact of adverse shocks and trigger a sharp slowdown in these economies, posing risks to global and EMDE growth.

Against this challenging backdrop, this study compares the current wave of debt accumulation to previous episodes, analyzes national episodes of rapid debt accumulation, examines the links between elevated debt levels and financial crises, and offers a menu of policy options.

Contributions to the literature

An extensive literature has explored various aspects of debt accumulation, especially in the context of government and private debt crises. This study adds to this literature in five dimensions.

Analysis of global debt waves. The study provides the first in-depth analysis of the similarities and differences among the four distinct waves of broad-based debt accumulation in EMDEs since 1970. Each wave contains episodes that have been widely examined in the literature (for example, the Latin American debt crisis and the Asian financial crisis), but they have rarely been put into a common framework. The construct of waves puts national and regional episodes of rapid debt buildup into a common context that takes into account global developments. It also provides a comparative perspective across waves, and facilitates a unified analysis of these episodes that takes into account the interaction of global drivers, such as global growth and financial market developments, with country-specific conditions. Earlier work has typically examined developments in a longer historical perspective and focused mainly on debt developments in advanced economies, usually based on case studies.[2] For EMDEs, previous studies have often analyzed certain periods of debt distress, or crises in individual countries.[3]

Current wave in historical context. Although many studies have documented the recent increase in debt in EMDEs, none has presented developments since the global financial crisis in comparative analysis with previous debt waves. In contrast to other recent work, the study thus puts the current (fourth) wave of debt accumulation in EMDEs into historical perspective.[4]

Detailed study of national episodes of rapid debt accumulation. Spurts of debt buildups are common in EMDEs and, when they coincide, form global waves of debt. The separate analysis of individual episodes offers key insights into the macroeconomic consequences, at the country level, of debt accumulation. The study undertakes the first comprehensive empirical analysis of a large number of individual episodes of rapid government and private debt accumulation in 100 EMDEs since 1970. Earlier work has examined developments in government and private debt markets separately, or focused on a smaller group of (mostly advanced) economies or regions.[5]

---

[2] Several studies have examined the impact of mounting government debt in advanced economies (BIS 2015; Cecchetti, Mohanty, and Zampolli 2011; Eberhardt and Presbitero 2015; Eichengreen et al. 2019; Mbaye, Moreno-Badia, and Chae 2018; OECD 2017; Panizza and Presbitero 2014; Reinhart, Reinhart, and Rogoff 2012).

[3] For example, contagion from the Asian crisis has been examined by Baig and Goldfajn (1999); Chiodo and Owyang (2002); Claessens and Forbes (2013); Glick and Rose (1999); Kaminsky and Reinhart (2000, 2001); Kawai, Newfarmer, and Schmukler (2005); Moreno, Pasadilla, and Remolona (1998); and Sachs, Cooper, and Bosworth (1998).

[4] The recent debt accumulation, without the historical context, has been discussed in IMF (2016, 2019) and World Bank (2015, 2016, 2017).

[5] Government debt crises have been discussed in Kindleberger and Aliber (2011); Reinhart, Reinhart, and Rogoff (2012); Reinhart and Rogoff (2011); and World Bank (2019). Private debt accumulation episodes (credit booms) have been examined in Dell'Arricia et al. (2014, 2016); Elekdag and Wu (2013); Jordà, Schularick, and Taylor (2011); Mendoza and Terrones (2008, 2012); Ohnsorge and Yu (2016); and Tornell and Westermann (2005).

Analysis of the links between debt accumulation and financial crises. The study employs an eclectic set of approaches to identify the most frequent triggers of crises and the country-level vulnerabilities that contribute to or exacerbate crises.[6] In addition, it considers selected country cases to illustrate the consequences of rapid debt accumulation that end in crisis.

Menu of policies. Armed with insights from an extensive analysis of the global and national waves of debt accumulation and the empirical links between elevated debt and financial crises, as well as the earlier literature, the study distills lessons and presents a rich menu of policy options that can help EMDEs boost resilience to future crises.

Key findings and policy messages

The book offers a range of analytical findings and policy messages but has three recurring themes.

Unprecedented debt buildup. The postcrisis wave of debt buildup has been unprecedented in its size, speed, and reach in EMDEs. Similar waves in the past half-century led to widespread financial crises in these economies. Accordingly, policy makers must remain vigilant about the risks posed by record-high debt levels.

Precarious protection of low interest rates. Continued low global interest rates provide no sure protection against financial crises. The historical record suggests that borrowing costs could increase sharply—or growth could slow steeply—for a wide range of reasons, including heightened risk aversion and rising country risk premiums. A sudden increase in borrowing costs and associated financial pressures would take place against the challenging backdrop of weak growth prospects, mounting vulnerabilities, and elevated global risks.

Policies matter. Robust macroeconomic, financial, and structural policies can help countries strike the right balance between the costs and the benefits of debt accumulation. Such policies are also critical to help reduce the likelihood of financial crises and alleviate their impact, if they erupt. Although many EMDEs have better policy frameworks now than during previous debt waves, there remains significant room for improvement.

---

[6] The econometric model builds on an extensive literature on early warning systems. See Chamon and Crowe (2012); Frankel and Saravelos (2012); and Kaminsky, Lizondo, and Reinhart (1998) for reviews of the early warning literature. Berg, Borensztein, and Patillo (2005) review the performance of early warning models.

FIGURE 1.3 **Debt in EMDEs**

The region and sector of debt accumulation have varied substantially over the four debt waves (1970-1989, 1990-2001, 2002-09, and since 2010). The latest wave of debt began in 2010 and has already seen the largest, fastest, and most broad-based increase in debt in EMDEs. It reached across almost all EMDE regions and encompassed both government and private borrowing.

A. Government debt

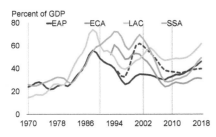

B. Private Debt

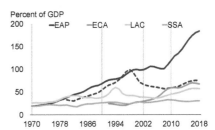

C. Change in total debt

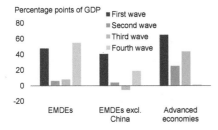

D. Average annual change in total debt

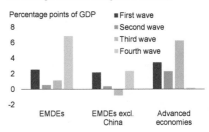

Sources: International Monetary Fund; World Bank.
Note: EAP = East Asia and Pacific; ECA = Europe and Central Asia; EMDEs = emerging market and developing economies; LAC = Latin America and the Caribbean; SSA = Sub-Saharan Africa.
A.B. Averages computed with current U.S. dollar GDP as weight and shown as a 3-year moving average. Dashed lines for EAP refer to EAP excluding China. Lines for ECA start in 1995 because of smaller sample size before that year. Vertical lines in gray are for years 1970, 1990, 2002, and 2010.
C.D. First wave covered the period 1970-89; second wave from 1990 to 2001; third wave from 2002 to 2009; and fourth wave from 2010 onward. EMDEs includes 147 economies.
C. Change in total debt from the start to the end of each wave.
D. Rate of change calculated as total increase in debt-to-GDP ratios over the duration of a wave, divided by the number of years in a wave.

Previous global waves of debt: Similar yet different

The buildup of EMDE debt to record-high levels in 2018 has not been a linear process. Different EMDE regions and sectors have experienced diverse debt developments. Four waves of broad-based debt buildup have occurred in EMDEs since 1970 (figure 1.3). The first (1970-89) occurred mainly in Latin America and the Caribbean (LAC) and LICs, especially in Sub-Saharan Africa (SSA); the second (1990-2001) was concentrated in East Asia and Pacific (EAP) but also involved some EMDEs in Europe and Central Asia

(ECA) and LAC; and the third (2002-09) occurred chiefly in ECA. The fourth wave (2010 onward), in contrast, has covered all EMDE regions.

The three previous waves displayed several significant similarities. They all began during prolonged periods of very low real interest rates and were often facilitated by changes in financial markets that contributed to rapid borrowing. The three past waves all ended with widespread financial crises and coincided with global recessions (1982, 1991, and 2009) or downturns (1998 and 2001). These crises were often triggered by shocks that resulted in a sharp increase in borrowing cost stemming from either an increase in investor risk aversion and risk premiums or a tightening of monetary policy in advanced economies. These crises typically featured sudden stops of capital flows. They usually led not only to economic downturns and recessions but also to reforms designed to lower external vulnerabilities and strengthen policy frameworks. In many EMDEs, inflation-targeting monetary policy frameworks and greater exchange rate flexibility were introduced, fiscal rules were adopted, and financial sector regulation and supervision were strengthened.

These similarities notwithstanding, the waves differed in some fundamental dimensions. The financial instruments used for borrowing shifted over time as new instruments or financial actors emerged. The nature of EMDE borrowers on international financial markets has changed, with the private sector accounting for a growing share of borrowing through the first three waves. The severity of the economic damage done by the financial crises that ended the first three waves also varied across the waves, and across regions. Output losses were particularly large in the first wave, when the majority of debt accumulation was in the government sector and debt resolution was protracted.

The current wave: Biggest, with vulnerabilities

The debt accumulation in EMDEs since 2010 has already been larger, faster, and more broad-based than in the previous three waves (figure 1.3). Since 2010, EMDE debt has risen by almost 7 percentage points of GDP per year, on average. The debt buildup in China has accounted for the bulk of the average EMDE debt increase, was much faster than that in the third wave, and was predominantly (more than four-fifths of the total debt buildup) in the private sector. Whereas previous waves were considerably more pronounced in some regions than in others, the fourth wave has been global, with total debt rising in about 80 percent of EMDEs and by at least 20 percentage points of GDP in just over one-third of EMDEs. In the current wave, most national episodes of debt accumulation have involved both government and private debt accumulation, in contrast to the previous three waves, when the buildup was concentrated in one of the two sectors.

In other aspects, the current wave of debt accumulation bears resemblances to the earlier ones. As in the previous waves, interest rates have been very low during the current wave, and the search-for-yield environment has contributed to falling spreads for EMDEs. Some major changes in financial markets have again boosted borrowing: they include a growing role of regional banks, a growing appetite for local currency bonds, and increased demand for EMDE debt from the expanding shadow banking sector. As in earlier waves, vulnerabilities have mounted during the current one, with a shift to riskier debt instruments, including greater reliance on financial markets and non-Paris Club bilateral lenders (particularly in LICs).

National debt buildups: Harbinger of crises?

Spurts of debt buildup are common in EMDEs, and when they coincide they form the global waves of debt discussed previously. Separate from the global waves of debt, the national episodes of debt accumulation offer a wealth of insights into macroeconomic developments during periods of rapid debt accumulation. Since 1970, there have been 519 national episodes of rapid debt accumulation in 100 EMDEs (figure 1.4).[7] The duration of a typical debt accumulation episode is seven to eight years. The median debt buildup from the beginning of the episode to peak debt is twice as large for government debt (30 percentage points of GDP) as for private debt (15 percentage points of GDP).

About half of these national episodes were associated with a financial crisis, with sizeable economic costs. Eight years after the beginning of a *government* debt accumulation episode, output in episodes with crises was about 10 percent lower than in episodes without a crisis, whereas investment was 22 percent lower. Similarly, eight years after the beginning of a *private* debt accumulation episode, output was 6 percent and investment 15 percent lower in episodes with crises than in those without a crisis. Thus, crises associated with rapid *government* debt buildups tended to feature larger output losses than crises associated with rapid *private* debt buildups.

Although financial crises were often triggered by external shocks, such as sudden increases in global interest rates, during rapid debt accumulation

---

[7] A national episode of rapid debt accumulation is defined as a period during which the government debt-to-GDP ratio or the private sector debt-to-GDP ratio rises from trough to peak by more than one (country-specific) 10-year rolling standard deviation.

FIGURE 1.4 **Debt and financial crises**

Financial crises have been a recurrent feature of rapid debt accumulation episodes—in EMDEs, more than half of the episodes have involved a crisis, at substantial macroeconomic cost.

A. Share of EMDEs in rapid debt accumulation episodes

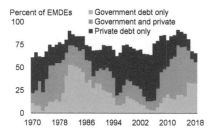

B. Crises during debt waves

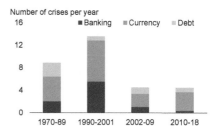

C. Duration of rapid debt accumulation episodes in EMDEs

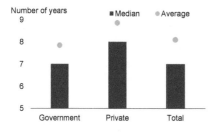

D. Change in debt during rapid debt accumulation episodes in EMDEs

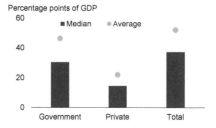

E. Outcomes of rapid government debt accumulation episodes after eight years

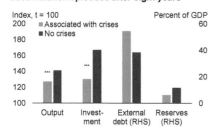

F. Outcomes of rapid private debt accumulation episodes after eight years

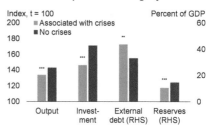

Sources: Federal Reserve Economic Data; International Monetary Fund; Laeven and Valencia (2018); World Bank.
Note: EMDEs = emerging market and developing economies.
A. Share of EMDEs which are in rapid debt accumulation episodes.
B. Number of crises in a specific wave divided by the number of years in a wave.
E.F. Median based on balanced samples. Year "t" refers to the beginning of rapid government debt accumulation episodes (Appendix A). Episodes associated with crises are those that experienced financial crises (banking, currency, and debt crises) during or within two years after the end of episodes. The information on crises is taken from Laeven and Valencia (2018). "*", "**", and "***" denote that medians between episodes associated with crises and those with no crises are statistically different at 10 percent, 5 percent, and 1 percent levels, respectively, based on Wilcoxon rank-sum tests.

episodes, domestic vulnerabilities often increased the likelihood of crises and amplified their adverse impact. Most countries where crises erupted suffered from unsustainable combinations of inadequate fiscal, monetary, or financial policies. Crises were more likely, and the economic distress they caused was more severe, in countries with higher external debt—especially short-term—and lower levels of international reserves. When both government and private debt rose together—as they have in the current wave—the likelihood of a currency crisis was higher than when government or private debt accumulated individually.

Looking forward: Will history repeat itself?

The current wave has already seen a substantial increase in debt in many EMDEs (figure 1.5). In one-quarter of EMDEs, the buildups of government or private debt in the current wave have already exceeded those of the typical historical episode. In some EMDEs, private debt has risen more than twice as much (by 30 percentage points of GDP) as in the median historical episode.

EMDEs need to chart a course through troubled waters as the current debt wave evolves. They face weaker growth prospects because of multiple structural headwinds. They also have pressing investment needs to achieve development goals and improve living standards. The challenge for EMDEs is to find the right balance between taking advantage of the present low interest rate environment and avoiding the risks posed by excessive debt accumulation.

On the upside, the current financial environment appears to alleviate some risks associated with the ongoing debt wave. In particular, global interest rates are very low, and are expected to remain low for the foreseeable future. In addition, many EMDEs have better fiscal, monetary, and financial sector policy frameworks now than they had during the previous debt waves. A wide range of reforms has been undertaken since the crisis to make the global financial system more resilient. The global financial safety net has also expanded over the past decade.

However, in addition to their historically large debt buildup during the current wave, EMDEs have accumulated other vulnerabilities that could amplify the adverse impact of financing shocks and cause debt distress. A sizable number of EMDEs now have not just higher total debt but also higher external debt, higher short-term debt, and lower reserves, as well as wider fiscal and current account deficits, than at the peak of the third wave of debt accumulation.

FIGURE 1.5 **Prospects and vulnerabilities in EMDEs**

Long-term growth prospects have slowed substantially from precrisis rates. Since 2010, fiscal and current account balances have weakened in EMDEs while debt has risen above or near levels in past episodes of rapid debt accumulation.

A. Consensus long-term growth forecasts

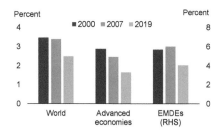

B. Current account and fiscal balances

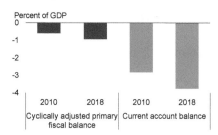

C. Current levels of government debt versus previous rapid debt accumulation episodes

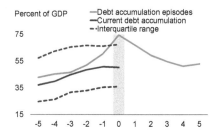

D. Current levels of private debt versus previous rapid debt accumulation episodes

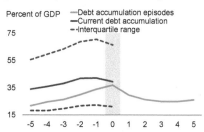

Sources: Consensus Economics; International Monetary Fund; Laeven and Valencia (2018); World Bank.
Note: EMDEs = emerging market and developing economies.
A. Bars show long-term (10 years ahead) average annual growth forecasts surveyed in respective years. Sample comprises 38 economies—20 advanced economies (AEs) and 18 EMDEs—for which Consensus forecasts are consistently available during 1998-2018. Aggregate growth rates calculated using constant 2010 U.S. dollar GDP weights.
B. Unweighted averages for current account balance and cyclically adjusted primary balance based on data for 152 EMDEs.
C.D. Median levels of debt during debt accumulation episodes, as defined in Appendix A. t=0 indicates the peak of debt accumulation episodes that were completed before 2018. For current debt accumulation, t=0 indicates 2018.

Debt distress could be triggered by unexpected, sustained jumps in global interest rates or in risk premiums. In a highly uncertain global environment, EMDEs face a wide range of risks, including the possibility of disruptions in advanced economy financial markets, steep declines in commodity prices, increased trade tensions, and a sudden deterioration in corporate debt markets in China. If any of these risks were to materialize, they could lead to a sharp rise in global interest rates or risk premiums or weakening growth and, in turn, trigger debt distress in EMDEs. Furthermore, one of the lessons from previous crises is that shocks tend to come from unexpected sources. Thus, low or even falling global interest rates provide only a precarious protection against financial crises.

Although EMDEs have gone through periods of volatility during the current wave of debt accumulation, they have not experienced widespread financial crises. A multitude of factors will determine the future evolution of the current wave. The key unknown is whether the current wave will end in financial crises in many EMDEs, as previous waves did, or whether EMDEs have learned the lessons from the previous waves and will prevent history from repeating itself.

Policies: They matter!

Although no magic bullet of a policy prescription exists to ensure that the current debt wave proceeds smoothly, the experience of past waves of debt points to the critical role of policy choices in determining the outcomes of these episodes. A menu of policy options is available to reduce the likelihood that the current debt wave will end, if crises were to take place, to alleviate their impact.

First, higher government or private debt and a riskier composition of debt (in terms of maturity, currency denomination, and creditors) are associated with a higher probability of crisis. Hence, sound debt management and debt transparency will help reduce borrowing costs, enhance debt sustainability, and contain fiscal risks. Creditors, including international financial institutions, can spearhead efforts in this area by encouraging common standards and highlighting risks and vulnerabilities through timely analytical and surveillance work.

Second, strong monetary, exchange rate, and fiscal policy frameworks can safeguard EMDEs' resilience in a fragile global economic environment. The benefits of stability-oriented and resilient monetary policy frameworks cannot be overstated. Flexible exchange rates can discourage a buildup of large currency mismatches and reduce the likelihood of large exchange rate misalignments. Fiscal rules can help prevent fiscal slippages, ensure that revenue windfalls during times of strong growth are prudently managed, and contain and manage risks from contingent liabilities. Revenue and expenditure policies can be adjusted to expand fiscal resources for priority spending.

Third, robust financial sector regulation and supervision can help recognize and act on emerging risks. Financial market deepening can help mobilize domestic savings that may provide more stable sources of financing than foreign borrowing.

Fourth, in several crisis cases, it became apparent that borrowed funds had been diverted toward purposes that did not raise export proceeds or productivity or potential output. Apart from effective public finance management, policies that promote good corporate governance can help ensure that debt is used for productive purposes. Sound bankruptcy frameworks can help prevent debt overhangs from weighing on investment for prolonged periods.

Synopsis

Chapter 2 briefly reviews the literature on the costs and benefits of debt accumulation. Chapter 3 presents a global perspective of debt accumulation, examining the three historical waves of broad-based debt accumulation in EMDEs and documenting differences and similarities across these waves. Chapter 4 puts the current wave in historical perspective. Chapter 5 employs multiple approaches to explore the links between debt accumulation and financial crises. Chapter 6 concludes with a discussion of the potential trajectory of the current debt wave, the main lessons and policy messages, and areas for future research.

The remainder of this introductory chapter summarizes each subsequent chapter: it presents that chapter's motivation and contribution to the literature, main questions it explores, and its main findings.

Chapter 2. Benefits and Costs of Debt: The Dose Makes the Poison

Amid record-high global debt, low interest rates and subpar growth have led to an intense debate on whether the recent rapid increase in debt is reason for concern. Some argue that countries, especially those that issue reserve currencies, should take advantage of low interest rates to borrow more to finance priority expenditures.[8] Others caution that high debt weighs on long-term growth, by increasing the risk of crises, limiting the scope for countercyclical fiscal stimulus, and dampening private investment.[9]

Although the focus of this debate has been mainly on advanced economies, EMDEs face similar issues. Many of these economies have also borrowed heavily and, in many cases, hard-won reductions in public debt ratios before

---

[8] Blanchard (2019); Blanchard and Summers (2019); Blanchard and Tashiro (2019); Blanchard and Ubide (2019); Eichengreen et al. (2019); Furman and Summers (2019); Krugman (2019); and Rachel and Summers (2019) discuss reasons for additional borrowing in advanced economies, and the United States in particular.

[9] Alcidi and Gros (2019); Auerbach, Gale, and Krupkin (2019); CRFB (2019); Eichengreen (2019); Mazza (2019); Riedl (2019); Rogoff (2019a, 2019b); and Wyplosz (2019) caution against adding to debt.

FIGURE 1.6 **Potential benefits and costs of debt**

EMDEs have large investment needs to meet development goals, which can be financed by debt; however, high debt levels limit the ability of governments to support economic activity during recessions and blunt the effectiveness of fiscal stimulus. High debt is also associated with high interest payments.

A. Investment needs in EMDEs

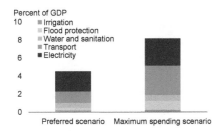

B. Investment needs, by EMDE region

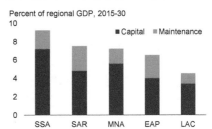

C. Fiscal multipliers after two years

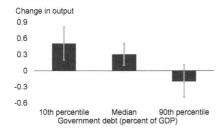

D. Government debt and interest payments in EMDEs, 2018

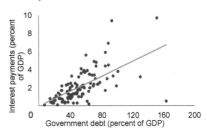

Sources: Huidrom et al. (2019); Rozenberg and Fay (2019); World Bank.
Note: EAP = East Asia and Pacific; EMDEs = emerging market and developing economies; LAC = Latin America and the Caribbean; MNA = Middle East and North Africa; SAR = South Asia; SSA = Sub-Saharan Africa.
A. Bars show average annual aggregate spending needs during 2015-30. "Preferred scenario" is constructed assuming ambitious goals and high spending efficiency, and "maximum spending scenario" assuming ambitious goals and low spending efficiency. Country sample includes low- and middle-income countries.
B. Bars show average annual spending needs during 2015-30. Estimates are generated using policy assumptions that cap investment needs at 4.5 percent of lower-middle-income countries' GDP per year (that is, the "preferred scenario" in panel A).
C. Bars show the conditional fiscal multipliers for different levels of government debt after two years. Fiscal multipliers are defined as cumulative change in output relative to cumulative change in government consumption in response to a 1-unit government consumption shock. They are based on estimates from the interacted panel vector autoregression model, where model coefficients are conditioned only on government debt. X-axis values correspond to the 10th to 90th percentiles in the sample. Bars represent the median, and vertical lines are the 16-84 percent confidence bands.
D. Total (external and domestic) government debt versus total (external and domestic) government interest payments (both in percent of GDP), in 2018.

the global financial crisis have largely been reversed over the past decade. The trade-offs EMDEs face are actually even starker, in light of their histories of severe debt crises even at lower levels of debt than in advanced economies and their more pressing spending needs to achieve development goals and improve living standards (figure 1.6).

Chapter 2 briefly reviews the literature on debt to provide a basis for assessing the merits of additional debt accumulation in EMDEs. Specifically, it addresses three questions:

- What are the benefits of debt accumulation?

- What are the costs associated with debt accumulation?

- What is the optimal level of debt?

The chapter brings together the main themes of theoretical and empirical studies on both government and private debt to provide answers to the three questions. Although it cannot do justice to the rich literature on debt, the chapter sets the stage for the discussion in subsequent chapters that describe the evolution of global waves of debt, puts the current debt wave into historical context, and examines the relationship between debt buildups and financial crises.

Chapter 2 reports two main findings. First, debt accumulation offers both benefits and costs. The benefits depend heavily on how productively the debt is used, the cyclical position of the economy, and the extent of financial market development. The costs of debt include interest payments, the possibility of debt distress, constraints that debt may impose on policy space and effectiveness, and the possible crowding out of private sector investment.

Second, there is no generally applicable optimal level of debt, either for advanced economies or for EMDEs. Optimal levels of debt depend on country characteristics, financial market conditions, the behavior of governments and private agents, and the multiple functions of debt.

Chapter 3. Global Waves of Debt: What Goes up Must Come Down?

Total (domestic and external) debt of public and private nonfinancial sectors in EMDEs has increased dramatically over the past half-century. The trajectory of debt accumulation, however, has not been smooth. Individual countries have frequently undergone episodes of rapid debt accumulation, by either the public sector or the private sector or both. These episodes sometimes ended in financial crises, which were followed by prolonged periods of deleveraging. Similarly, the characteristics of debt have changed over time, with the importance of external debt waxing and waning, and the types of debt instruments used also evolving.

Different EMDE regions and sectors have experienced diverse debt developments since 1970. In some regions, there have been waves of debt buildups where many countries simultaneously saw sharp increases in debt, often followed by crises and steep declines in debt ratios. For example, government debt increased sharply in LAC and SSA in the 1970s and 80s, but peaked in the late 1980s in LAC and in the late 1990s in SSA, before falling. By contrast, the EAP region (excluding China) saw a buildup in private debt in the 1990s, which unwound from 1997 onward. In the aftermath of the global financial crisis, the EAP region (this time mainly driven by China) has once again seen a rapid accumulation of private debt.

Chapter 3 examines the evolution of debt in EMDEs and identifies "waves" of rising debt—periods in which growth in debt has been broad-based across many countries in one or more regions. The waves of rising debt in EMDEs occurred in the periods 1970-89, 1990-2001, 2002-09, and the current period, beginning in 2010.

The identification of the waves meets some basic criteria. The end of a wave is broadly defined as the year when the total debt-to-GDP ratio in the region or country group concerned peaks and is followed by two consecutive years of decline. The dating of the end of waves is also approximately consistent with the timing of policies to resolve the financial crises that they engendered. In principle, waves could be overlapping (indeed, developments in LIC debt reached across all three waves), but there are visible surges followed by plateaus or declines in regional EMDE debt. The identification of the waves takes these turning points as convenient starting and end points for the episodes.

Using the framework of global waves of debt, the chapter answers the following questions in the context of the first three, completed waves of debt buildup:

- How did the three historical waves of debt evolve?

- What were the similarities between the waves?

- How did the waves differ?

The chapter provides the first in-depth analysis of the similarities and differences among the three historical waves of broad-based debt accumulation in EMDEs since 1970. It identifies the following debt waves in EMDEs before the current wave.

- The first wave spanned the 1970s and 1980s, with borrowing primarily accounted for by governments in LAC and LICs, especially in SSA. The combination of low real interest rates in much of the 1970s and a rapidly growing syndicated loan market encouraged EMDE governments to

FIGURE 1.7 **The first wave of debt**

The 1970s were a period of rapid growth for many LAC, but external debt grew sharply to unsustainable levels. The debt-to-GDP ratio in LICs also rose steadily from the 1970s to the early 1990s. As debt levels and interest payments became unsustainable, many LICs fell into arrears and requested rescheduling.

A. LAC: Growth

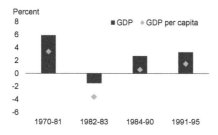

B. LAC: External debt

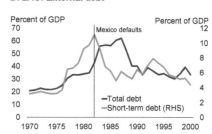

C. LIC: External debt

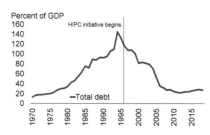

D. Cumulative debt relief in LICs

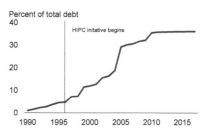

Sources: Haver Analytics; International Monetary Fund; Organisation for Economic Co-operation and Development; World Bank.
Note: HIPC = Heavily Indebted Poor Countries (Initiative); LAC = Latin America and the Caribbean; LICs = low-income countries.
A. GDP weighted average across 32 LAC countries.
B. Short-term debt has maturity of less than 12 months. Sample includes 24 countries.
C. Sample includes 29 LICs, defined as countries with a gross national income per capita of $1,005 or less in 2016.
D. Cumulative debt relief since 1990, as a share of total debt in 1996, when the HIPC initiative began.

borrow heavily (figure 1.7). This debt buildup culminated in a series of crises in the early 1980s. Debt relief and restructuring were prolonged in this wave, ending with the introduction of the Brady plan in the late 1980s, mostly for LAC countries, and debt relief in the form of the Heavily Indebted Poor Countries initiative and Multilateral Debt Relief Initiative in the mid-1990s and early 2000s for LICs.

- The second wave ran from 1990 until the early 2000s as financial and capital market liberalization enabled banks and corporations in EAP and governments in ECA to borrow heavily; it ended with a series of crises in these regions in 1997-2001 (figure 1.8).

FIGURE 1.8 **The second and third waves of debt**

In the second wave, external debt soared in EAP in the early to mid-1990s, particularly private sector debt, often at short maturities. In the third wave, benign financing conditions and financial sector deregulation in advanced economies fueled cross-border lending and precrisis credit booms, particularly in ECA.

A. EAP: Growth in external debt

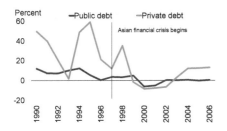

B. EAP: Sectoral distribution of external debt

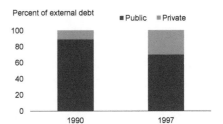

C. ECA: External debt

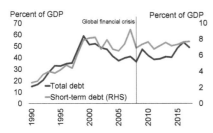

D. Cross-border lending to EMDEs

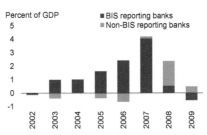

Source: World Bank.
Note: BIS = Bank for International Settlements; EAP = East Asia and Pacific; ECA = Europe and Central Asia; EMDEs = emerging market and developing economies; IMF = International Monetary Fund.
A.B. Includes long-term external debt only.
A. Negative values indicate declining external debt in U.S. dollar terms.
D. Offshore financial centers are excluded. Based on data for 86 EMDEs excluding China. BIS data are from the BIS locational banking statistics and represent changes in stock of claims on EMDEs. Lending by non-BIS banks is calculated as total bank loans and deposits from the IMF Balance of Payment Statistics minus cross-border lending by BIS reporting banks. Cross-border lending flows as a percentage of GDP are shown as total for all countries in the sample divided by their aggregate GDP.

- The third wave was a runup in private sector borrowing in ECA from European Union-headquartered "mega-banks" after regulatory easing. This wave ended when the global financial crisis and the euro area debt crisis disrupted bank financing in 2008-09 and tipped several ECA economies into deep (albeit short-lived) recessions.

The chapter distills similarities among these three debt waves. The three waves of debt began during prolonged periods of low real interest rates, and were often facilitated by financial innovations or changes in financial markets that promoted borrowing. The waves ended with widespread financial crises and coincided with global recessions (1982, 1991, and 2009) or downturns (1998 and 2001). These episodes were typically triggered by shocks that resulted in sharp increases in investor risk aversion, risk premiums, or borrowing costs, followed by sudden stops of capital inflows. The financial crises were generally costly. They were usually followed by reforms designed to lower financial vulnerabilities and strengthen policy frameworks. In some EMDEs, various combinations of inflation targeting, greater exchange rate flexibility, and fiscal rules were introduced, and financial sector supervision was strengthened.

The chapter also points to important differences among the three completed waves. The financial instruments used for borrowing have evolved as new instruments or financial actors have emerged. The nature of EMDE borrowers in international financial markets has changed, with the private sector accounting for a growing share of debt accumulation through the three waves. The severity of the economic damage done by the financial crises that ended the waves varied among them, and across regions. Output losses were particularly large in the wake of the first wave, when most debt accumulation had been by government sectors.

Chapter 4. The Fourth Wave: Ripple or Tsunami?

The current global wave of debt, which started in 2010, has already seen the largest, fastest, and most broad-based increase in debt in EMDEs in the past 50 years. Despite the recent prolonged period of very low interest rates, there is a risk that the latest wave of debt accumulation may follow the historical pattern of its predecessors and result in widespread financial crises.

Chapter 4 examines the current wave and puts it in historical context by considering the following questions:

- How has debt evolved in the fourth wave?

- What factors have contributed to debt accumulation during the fourth wave?

- What are the similarities and differences between the fourth wave and the previous waves over the past half-century?

In contrast to earlier studies, chapter 4 puts the current wave of broad-based debt accumulation in EMDEs into historical perspective. Earlier work has recognized the steep postcrisis increase in debt in certain regions or groups of countries. For example, some studies have examined mounting government debt in advanced economies. There has also been considerable interest in the postcrisis increase in debt in EMDEs, including low-income and lower-middle-income countries (Essl et al. 2019; World Bank and IMF 2018a, 2018b). Again, however, these studies have documented the postcrisis growth of debt without the historical lens of the global waves framework.

The chapter reports three major results. First, the latest wave began in 2010 and has already seen the largest, fastest, and most broad-based increase in debt in EMDEs in the past 50 years. The average annual increase in EMDE debt since 2010, of almost 7 percentage points of GDP, has been larger by some margin than in each of the previous three waves. Also, whereas previous waves were largely regional in nature, the fourth wave has been global, with total debt rising in about 80 percent of EMDEs and by at least 20 percentage points of GDP in more than one-third of EMDEs (figure 1.9).

Second, the current wave of debt accumulation bears many resemblances to the three previous waves. Interest rates in advanced economies have been very low since the global financial crisis, and search for yield by investors has contributed to narrowing spreads for EMDEs. Some major structural changes in financial markets have again boosted borrowing, including through a rise of regional banks, growing appetite for local currency bonds, and increased demand for EMDE debt from the expanding shadow banking sector. As in the earlier waves, mounting vulnerabilities have become apparent as the current wave has proceeded, with a shift to riskier debt instruments and an increasing reliance on non-Paris Club bilateral lenders, particularly in LICs. In addition, fiscal and external deficits have increased in many EMDEs since 2010.

Third, the fourth wave has been different from the previous episodes in terms of the size, speed, and reach of debt accumulation in EMDEs. Meanwhile, multiple reforms have increased the resilience of the international financial system, and global financial safety nets have been expanded and strengthened since the global financial crisis. Many EMDEs have improved their macroeconomic and prudential policy frameworks over the past two decades. In contrast to previous waves, the current wave has been set against a backdrop of broadly stable advanced economy debt ratios.

Chapter 5. Debt and Financial Crises: From Euphoria to Distress

EMDEs experience recurrent episodes of rapid debt accumulation. When they take place in tandem in many economies, these national episodes turn into global waves of debt. Whereas the two earlier chapters examined global waves of debt, this chapter turns its attention to the implications of rapid

FIGURE 1.9 **The fourth wave of debt**

The fourth wave has seen the most broad-based increase yet in debt across regions and borrowing sectors. Both government and private debt have shifted toward riskier funding sources. The increase in government debt has been accompanied by a growing share of nonresident investors, whereas corporations increased borrowing in foreign currencies.

A. Countries with increase in government debt, by region

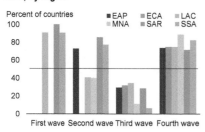

B. Countries with increase in private debt, by region

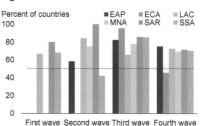

C. Average maturity and nonconcessional debt in EMDEs

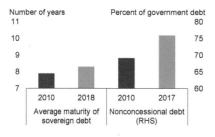

D. Nonresident share of government debt, foreign currency share of corporate debt

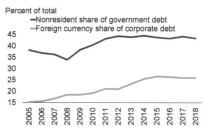

Sources: Bank for International Settlements; Institute of International Finance; International Monetary Fund; World Bank.
Note: EAP = East Asia and Pacific; ECA = Europe and Central Asia; EMDEs = emerging market and developing economies; LAC = Latin America and the Caribbean; MNA = Middle East and North Africa; SAR = South Asia; SSA = Sub-Saharan Africa.
A.B. Charts show the share of countries where the debt-to-GDP ratio increased over the duration of the wave. Regions are excluded if available country-level data cover less than one-third of the full region.
C. Median of 35 EMDEs.
D. Nonresident share of government debt is average for 45 EMDEs, with a smaller sample size for earlier years. Foreign currency share of corporate debt of average for 21 EMDEs.

debt accumulation at the country level. Rising or elevated debt levels increase a country's vulnerability to financing shocks, which can culminate in financial crises, with large and lasting effects on economic activity.

Chapter 5 provides a more granular perspective on the causes and consequences of debt accumulation by addressing the following questions:

- What are the main features of national episodes of rapid debt accumulation?

- What are the empirical links between debt accumulation and financial crises?

- What are the major institutional and structural weaknesses associated with financial crises?

The chapter makes several novel contributions to an extensive literature on the links between debt and financial crises, as reviewed in chapter 2. First, the chapter undertakes the first comprehensive empirical study of a large number of national rapid government and private debt accumulation episodes in a large number of EMDEs since 1970. It not only considers what happens during the financial crises associated with rapid debt accumulation episodes but also examines how macroeconomic and financial aggregates evolve over the entire debt accumulation episode.

Second, the chapter expands on earlier empirical studies of the correlates of crises by analyzing the links between debt accumulation and financial crises in a single empirical framework and by extending the horizon of analysis to cover the four global waves of debt accumulation. Finally, it presents a comprehensive review of country case studies of rapid debt accumulation episodes associated with financial crises. Based on a literature review that extracts common themes from a large set of country case studies, this complementary qualitative approach helps identify the major structural and institutional weaknesses associated with financial crises.

Chapter 5 presents five main results. First, since 1970, there have been 519 national episodes of rapid debt accumulation in 100 EMDEs. These episodes have been common, because three-quarters of EMDEs were in either a government or a private debt accumulation episode or both in the average year. The duration of a typical government debt accumulation episode is seven years and private debt episode is about eight years. The median debt buildup during a government debt accumulation episode (30 percentage points of GDP) tended to be considerably larger than that during a private debt episode (15 percentage points of GDP).

Second, about half of the national debt accumulation episodes were accompanied by a financial crisis (figure 1.10). Crises were particularly common during the first and second global waves: of all episodes that concluded in these two waves, almost two-thirds were associated with crises. National debt episodes that coincided with crises were typically associated with greater debt buildups, weaker economic outcomes, and larger macroeconomic and financial vulnerabilities than were noncrisis episodes. Crises during rapid government debt buildups featured significantly larger output losses than crises during rapid private debt buildups: in the case of government (private) debt, after eight years, the level of GDP in episodes with crises was about 10 (6) percent lower than in episodes without crisis and investment was 22 (15) percent lower.

FIGURE 1.10 **Debt and financial crises**

About half of all episodes of government and private debt accumulation during 1970-2018 were associated with financial crises, typically multiple types of crises. Episodes associated with financial crises featured significantly larger government debt increases (by 4 percentage points of GDP). Eight years after the start of the rapid government debt accumulation episode, episodes associated with financial crises had lower output (by 11 percent).

A. Government debt accumulation episodes associated with crises

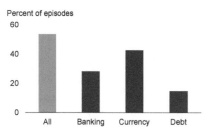

B. Private debt accumulation episodes associated with crises

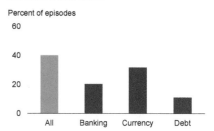

C. Debt during government debt accumulation episodes

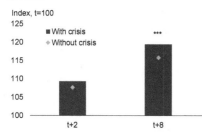

D. Output and per capita output during government debt accumulation episodes

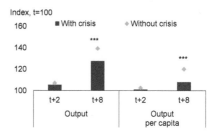

Sources: International Monetary Fund; Laeven and Valencia (2018); World Bank.

A.B. Episodes associated with crises are those that experience financial crises (that is, banking, currency, and debt crises, as in Laeven and Valencia 2018) during or within two years after the end of episodes. For definition of episodes and sample, see Appendix A.

C.D. Medians for pooled government and private episodes with data available for at least 8 years from the beginning of the episode. Year "t" refers to the beginning of rapid private or government debt accumulation episodes. All variables are scaled to 100 at t=0. Episodes associated with crises are those that experience financial crises (that is, banking, currency, and debt crises, as in Laeven and Valencia 2018) during or within two years after the end of episodes. *, **, and *** denote that medians between episodes associated with crises and those with no crises are statistically different at 10 percent, 5 percent, and 1 percent levels, respectively, based on Wilcoxon rank-sum tests.

C. Cumulative change in government debt in percentage points of GDP, rebased to 100 at the start of the government debt accumulation episode (t).

D. Based on cumulative real growth rates for output and output per capita from the start of the government debt accumulation episode.

Third, an increase in debt, either government or private, was associated with a significantly higher probability of crises in the following year. Over and above this increase, combined accumulation of both government and private debt resulted in a higher likelihood of a currency crisis compared to debt increases that were solely government or solely private.

Fourth, although external shocks, such as sudden increases in global interest rates, typically triggered financial crises during national debt accumulation episodes, domestic vulnerabilities often amplified the adverse impact of these shocks. Crises were more likely, or the economic distress they caused was more severe, in countries with higher external debt—especially short-term—and lower levels of international reserves.

Fifth, most EMDEs that experienced financial crises during debt accumulation episodes employed an unsustainable combination of macroeconomic policies, and suffered structural and institutional weaknesses. Many of them had severe fiscal weaknesses, including poor revenue collection, widespread tax evasion, public wage and pension indexing, monetary financing of fiscal deficits, and substantial use of energy and food subsidies. Many of the crisis countries borrowed in foreign currency, employed managed exchange rate regimes, and sustained weakly regulated banks. Debt buildup often funded import substitution strategies or undiversified economies, or borrowed funds were channeled into sectors that were inefficient, did not raise export earnings, or had poor corporate governance. Several of them also suffered from protracted political uncertainty.

Chapter 6. Policies: Turning Mistakes into Experience

As documented in chapter 4, the wave of global debt accumulation since 2010, the fourth during the past 50 years, has already been larger, faster, and more broad-based than the three previous episodes. The preceding three global waves ended with financial crises in many EMDEs, which raises the question of whether the current wave will end in a similar way.

Several factors are likely to shape the trajectory of the current wave of debt, including prospects for global interest rates and economic growth. Although EMDEs are not in full control of some of these factors, they would benefit from using the lessons from their own experiences with rapid debt accumulation to avoid the mistakes of the past.

The previous chapters examined the causes and consequences of global and national episodes of rapid debt accumulation. Chapter 6 focuses on the likely evolution of the current wave and presents a summary of the main lessons and policy messages based on the analysis in earlier chapters. In particular, it addresses the following questions:

- What forces will shape the evolution of the current debt wave?

- What are the lessons to be drawn from previous episodes of rapid debt accumulation?

- What policies can lower the likelihood and cost of future debt crises?

The chapter makes three contributions to an already-rich policy debate. First, it discusses the likely evolution of the current wave of debt accumulation from the perspective of EMDEs. It also considers the recent debate about the merits of debt accumulation in the current era of low interest rates. Previous work has mostly focused on the consequences of debt accumulation for advanced economies, as reviewed in chapter 2. Second, the chapter offers a compilation of salient lessons about the consequences of rapid debt accumulation based on the analysis of the global and national episodes of debt accumulation presented in the earlier chapters.[10] Third, the chapter offers a comprehensive set of policy prescriptions that can help lower the likelihood of debt-related financial crises and mitigate their effects when they materialize.

The chapter presents the following findings.

Striking the right balance. In the current debt wave, many EMDEs have both accumulated a record amount of debt and experienced a persistent growth slowdown. Some of these economies now also share a wide range of external and domestic vulnerabilities that have historically been associated with a higher likelihood of financial crises. In addition, EMDEs are confronted by a wide range of risks in an increasingly fragile global context. As a result, despite currently record-low global interest rates, stronger policy frameworks in some EMDEs, and a strengthened international safety net, the latest wave of debt accumulation could follow the historical pattern and result in financial crises (figure 1.11). The study of past waves shows the critical importance of policy choices in reducing the likelihood of the current debt wave ending in crisis and, if crises were to take place, mitigating their impact.

Lessons from experience. Debt accumulation is unlikely to be benign unless it is well-spent to finance truly output-enhancing purposes and it is resilient (in terms of maturity, currency, and creditor composition) to economic and financial market disruptions. These conditions require not only prudent

---

[10] For studies on general lessons from the global financial crisis, see Dabrowski (2010) and IMF (2018); for specific policy areas such as financial supervision and regulation or corporate governance, see Buiter (2009); Claessens et al. (2010); Claessens, Kose, and Terrones (2010); Dewatripont, Rochet, and Tirole (2010); King (2018); and Liang, McConnell, and Swagel (2018).

FIGURE 1.11 **Risks and policy implications**

Since the 1990s, many EMDEs have introduced fiscal rules and inflation-targeting monetary policy regimes and allowed greater exchange rate flexibility and central bank transparency. Policy frameworks that are more resilient may help mitigate some of the risks arising from growing corporate debt and deteriorating sovereign credit ratings.

A. EMDEs with fiscal rules

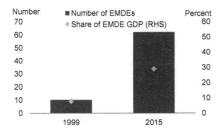

B. EMDEs with inflation targeting

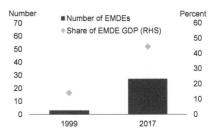

C. EMDEs with flexible exchange rates

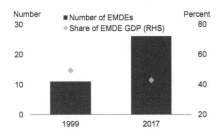

D. EMDE central bank transparency

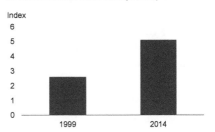

E. Sovereign credit ratings

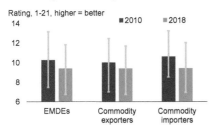

F. Nonfinancial corporate debt

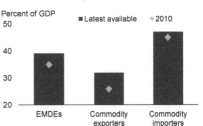

Sources: Dincer and Eichengreen (2014); Ha, Kose, and Ohnsorge (2019); Huidrom et al. (2019); International Monetary Fund; Kose et al. (2017); World Bank.

Note: EMDEs = emerging market and developing economies; IMF = International Monetary Fund.

A. EMDE implementing one or more fiscal rules on expenditure, revenue, budget balance or debt.

B. Inflation targeting as classified in the IMF *Annual Report of Exchange Arrangements and Exchange Restrictions*.

C. Flexible exchange rate are defined as those classified as "Floating" or "Free Floating" in the IMF *Annual Report of Exchange Arrangements and Exchange Restrictions*.

D. As classified in Dincer and Eichengreen (2014).

E. Unweighted averages of foreign currency sovereign credit ratings for 49 EMDE commodity exporters and 40 EMDE commodity importers. Whiskers denote interquartile ranges.

F. Based on data for 40 EMDEs. Latest available datapoint is 2019Q2 for Argentina, Brazil, Chile, China, Colombia, Hungary, India, Indonesia, Malaysia, Mexico, Poland, Russian Federation, Saudi Arabia, South Africa, Thailand, and Turkey; 2017 for the rest. Unweighted average of nonfinancial corporate debt in 21 EMDE commodity exporters and 19 EMDE commodity importers.

government debt management but also robust financial system regulation and supervision and sound corporate governance. It is critical to respond effectively to external shocks especially when there are domestic vulnerabilities. Private debt can quickly turn into public debt during periods of financial stress. Once debt distress materializes, prompt resolution is critical to avoid a prolonged period of weak economic activity.

Policy options. Although specific policy priorities depend on country circumstances, four broad strands of policy options can help contain the risks associated with debt accumulation. First, governments need to put in place mechanisms and institutions that help them strike the proper balance between the benefits and costs of additional debt. These mechanisms include sound debt management and high debt transparency. International creditors can support sustainable borrowing by implementing prudent lending standards (including in terms of transparency), appropriately distributing risk, and ensuring the productive use of debt.

Second, the benefits of stability-oriented and resilient fiscal and monetary policy frameworks cannot be overstated. Third, financial sector policies need to be designed to foster responsible private sector borrowing. This design includes robust supervisory and regulatory frameworks as well as corporate and bank bankruptcy frameworks that allow prompt debt resolution to limit the damage from debt distress. Fourth, it is essential to have strong corporate governance practices and effective bankruptcy and insolvency regimes.

References

Alcidi, C., and D. Gros. 2019. "Public Debt and the Risk Premium: A Dangerous Doom Loop." VoxEU.org, May 22, 2019. https://voxeu.org/article/public-debt-and -risk-premium.

Auerbach, A. J., W. G. Gale, and A. Krupkin. 2019. "If Not Now, When? New Estimates of the Federal Budget Outlook." Brookings Report, February 11, Brookings Institution, Washington, DC.

Baig, T., and I. Goldfajn. 1999. "Financial Market Contagion in the Asian Crisis." *IMF Staff Papers* 46 (2): 167-95.

Berg, A., E. Borensztein, and C. Pattillo. 2005. "Assessing Early Warning Systems: How Have They Worked in Practice?" *IMF Staff Papers* 52 (3): 462-502.

BIS (Bank for International Settlements). 2015. "Debt." BIS Papers 80, Bank for International Settlements, Basel.

Blanchard, O. J. 2019. "Public Debt and Low Interest Rates." *American Economic Review* 109 (4): 1197-229.

Blanchard, O. J., and L. H. Summers. 2019. *Evolution or Revolution? Rethinking Macroeconomic Policy After the Great Recession.* Cambridge: MIT Press.

Blanchard, O. J., and T. Tashiro. 2019. "Fiscal Policy Options for Japan." PIIE Policy Brief 19-7, Peterson Institute for International Economics, Washington, DC.

Blanchard, O. J., and A. Ubide. 2019. "Why Critics of a More Relaxed Attitude on Public Debt Are Wrong." PIIE Realtime Economic Issues Watch (blog), July 15, 2019. https://www.piie.com/blogs/realtime-economic-issues-watch/why-critics-more-relaxed -attitude-public-debt-are-wrong.

Buiter, W. H. 2009. "Lessons from the Global Financial Crisis for Regulators and Supervisors." Financial Markets Group Discussion Paper, London School of Economics and Political Science, London, U.K.

Cecchetti, S., M. Mohanty, and F. Zampolli. 2011. "The Real Effects of Debt." BIS Working Paper 352, Bank for International Settlements, Basel.

Chamon M., and C. Crowe. 2012. "Predictive Indicators of Crises." In *Handbook in Financial Globalization: The Evidence and Impact of Financial Globalization*, edited by G. Caprio, 499-505. London: Elsevier.

Chiodo, A., and M. Owyang. 2002. "A Case Study of a Currency Crisis: The Russian Default of 1998." *Federal Reserve Bank of St. Louis Review* 84 (6): 7-18.

Claessens, S., and K. Forbes, eds. 2013. *International Financial Contagion.* Berlin: Springer.

Claessens, S., M. A. Kose, and M. Terrones. 2010. "The Global Financial Crisis: How Similar? How Different? How Costly?" *Journal of Asian Economics* 21(3): 247-64.

Claessens, S., M. L. Laeven, D. Igan, and M. G. Dell'Ariccia. 2010. "Lessons and Policy Implications from the Global Financial Crisis." IMF Working Paper 10/44, International Monetary Fund, Washington, DC.

CRFB (Committee for a Responsible Federal Budget). 2019. "Why Should We Worry About the National Debt?" Budgets & Projections paper, April 16, Committee for a Responsible Federal Budget, Washington, DC.

Dabrowski, M. 2010. "The Global Financial Crisis: Lessons for European Integration." *Economic Systems* 34 (1): 38-54.

Dell'Ariccia, G, D. Igan, L. Laeven, and H. Tong. 2014. "Policies for Macrofinancial Stability: Dealing with Credit Booms and Busts." In *Financial Crises: Causes, Consequences, and Policy Responses*, edited by S. Claessens, M. A. Kose, L. Laeven, and F. Valencia. Washington, DC: International Monetary Fund.

Dell'Ariccia, G, D. Igan, L. Laeven, and H. Tong. 2016. "Credit Booms and Macrofinancial Stability." *Economic Policy* 31 (86): 299-355.

Dewatripont, M., J. C. Rochet, and J. Tirole. 2010. "Balancing the Banks: Global Lessons from the Financial Crisis." Princeton, NJ: Princeton University Press.

Dincer, N., and B. Eichengreen. 2014. "Central Bank Transparency and Independence: Updates and New Measures." *International Journal of Central Banking* 10 (1): 189-259.

Eberhardt, M., and A. F. Presbitero. 2015. "Public Debt and Growth: Heterogeneity and Non-Linearity." *Journal of International Economics* 97 (1): 45-58.

Eichengreen, B. 2019. "The Return of Fiscal Policy." *Project Syndicate*, May 13, 2019. https://www.project-syndicate.org/commentary/return-of-fiscal-policy-by-barry-eichengreen-2019-05.

Eichengreen, B., A. El-Ganainy, R. Esteves, and K. J. Mitchener. 2019. "Public Debt through the Ages." NBER Working Paper 25494, National Bureau of Economic Research, Cambridge, MA.

Elekdag, S., and Y. Wu. 2013. "Rapid Credit Growth in Emerging Markets: Boon or Boom-Bust?" *Emerging Markets Finance and Trade* 49 (5): 45-62.

Essl, S., S. Kilic Celik, P. Kirby, and A. Proite. 2019. "Debt in Low-Income Countries: Evolution, Implications, Remedies." Policy Research Working Paper 8794, World Bank, Washington, DC.

Frankel, J. A., and G. Saravelos. 2012. "Can Leading Indicators Assess Country Vulnerability? Evidence from the 2008-09 Global Financial Crisis." *Journal of International Economics* 87 (2): 216-31.

Furman, J., and L. H. Summers. 2019. "Who's Afraid of Budget Deficits? How Washington Should End Its Debt Obsession." *Foreign Affairs* 98: 82-94.

Glick, R., and A. K. Rose. 1999. "Contagion and Trade: Why Are Currency Crises Regional?" *Journal of International Money and Finance* 18 (4): 603-17.

Ha, J., M. A. Kose, and F. Ohnsorge. 2019. *Inflation in Emerging and Developing Economies: Evolution, Drivers and Policies*. Washington, DC: World Bank.

Huidrom, R., M. A. Kose, J. J. Lim, and F. Ohnsorge. 2019. "Why Do Fiscal Multipliers Depend on Fiscal Positions?" *Journal of Monetary Economics*. Advance online publication. https://doi.org/10.1016/.

IMF (International Monetary Fund). 2016. *Analyzing and Managing Fiscal Risks—Best Practices*. Washington, DC: International Monetary Fund.

IMF (International Monetary Fund). 2018. *Global Financial Stability Report. A Decade after the Global Financial Crisis: Are We Safer?* Washington, DC: International Monetary Fund.

IMF (International Monetary Fund). 2019. *Global Financial Stability Report. Lower for Longer*. October. Washington, DC: International Monetary Fund.

Jordà, Ò., M. Schularick, and A. M. Taylor. 2011. "Financial Crises, Credit Booms, and External Imbalances: 140 Years of Lessons." *IMF Economic Review* 59 (2): 340-78.

Kaminsky, G. L., S. Lizondo, and C. M. Reinhart. 1998. "Leading Indicators of Currency Crises." *IMF Staff Papers* 45 (1): 1-48.

Kaminsky, G. L., and C. M. Reinhart. 2000. "On Crises, Contagion, and Confusion." *Journal of International Economics* 51 (1): 145-68.

Kaminsky, G. L., and C. M. Reinhart. 2001. "Bank Lending and Contagion: Evidence from the Asian Crisis." In *Regional and Global Capital Flows: Macroeconomic Causes and Consequences*, edited by T. Ito and A. O. Krueger, 73-99. Chicago: University of Chicago Press.

Kawai, M., R. Newfarmer, and S. Schmukler. 2005. "Crisis and Contagion in East Asia: Nine Lessons." *Eastern Economic Journal* 31 (2): 185-207.

Kindleberger, C. P., and R. Z. Aliber. 2011. *Manias, Panics and Crashes: A History of Financial Crises.* London: Palgrave Macmillan.

King, M. 2018. "Lessons from the Global Financial Crisis." *Business Economics* 53 (2): 55-9.

Kose, M. A., S. Kurlat, F. Ohnsorge, and N. Sugawara. 2017. "A Cross-Country Database of Fiscal Space." Policy Research Working Paper 8157, World Bank, Washington, DC.

Kose, M. A., and F. Ohnsorge, eds. 2019. *A Decade after the Global Recession: Lessons and Challenges for Emerging and Developing Economies.* Washington, DC: World Bank.

Krugman, P. 2019. "Perspectives on Debt and Deficits." *Business Economics* 54 (3): 157-59.

Laeven, L., and F. Valencia. 2018. "Systemic Banking Crises Revisited." IMF Working Paper 18/206, International Monetary Fund, Washington, DC.

Liang, N., M. M. McConnell, and P. Swagel. 2018. "Responding to the Global Financial Crisis: What We Did and Why We Did It." Preliminary Discussion Draft. https://www.brookings.edu/wp-content/uploads/2018/08/15-Outcomes-Prelim-Disc-Draft-2018.12.11.pdf.

Mazza, J. 2019. "Is Public Debt a Cheap Lunch?" *Bruegel* (blog), January 21, 2019. https://bruegel.org/2019/01/is-public-debt-a-cheap-lunch/.

Mbaye, S., M. Moreno-Badia, and K. Chae. 2018. "Bailing Out the People? When Private Debt Becomes Public." IMF Working Paper 18/141, International Monetary Fund, Washington, DC.

Mendoza, E. G., and M. E. Terrones. 2008. "An Anatomy of Credit Booms: Evidence from Macro Aggregates and Micro Data." NBER Working Paper 14049, National Bureau of Economic Research, Cambridge, MA.

Mendoza, E. G., and M. E. Terrones. 2012. "An Anatomy of Credit Booms and their Demise" NBER Working Paper 18379, National Bureau of Economic Research, Cambridge, MA.

Moreno, R., G. Pasadilla, and E. Remolona. 1998. "Asia's Financial Crisis: Lessons and Policy Responses." Pacific Basin Working Paper Series 98-02, Federal Reserve Bank of San Francisco.

OECD (Organisation for Economic Co-operation and Development). 2017. *OECD Economic Outlook*. November. Paris: Organisation for Economic Co-operation and Development.

Ohnsorge, F., and S. Yu. 2016. "Recent Credit Surge in Historical Context." Policy Research Working Paper 7704, World Bank, Washington, DC.

Panizza, U., and A. F. Presbitero. 2014. "Public Debt and Economic Growth: Is There a Causal Effect?" *Journal of Macroeconomics* 41 (September): 21-41.

Rachel, L., and L. H. Summers. 2019. "On Falling Neutral Real Rates, Fiscal Policy, and the Risk of Secular Stagnation." BPEA Conference Draft, March 7-8, Brookings Institution, Washington, DC.

Rajan, R. 2019. "Is Economic Winter Coming?" *Project Syndicate*, November 12, 2019. https://www.project-syndicate.org/commentary/trump-recession-risks-by-raghuram-rajan-2019-11.

Reinhart, C., V. Reinhart, and K. Rogoff. 2012. "Public Debt Overhangs: Advanced-Economy Episodes Since 1800." *Journal of Economic Perspectives* 26 (3): 69-86.

Reinhart, C. M., and K. S. Rogoff. 2011. "From Financial Crash to Debt Crisis." *American Economic Review* 101 (5): 1676-706.

Riedl, B. 2019. "Yes, We Should Fear Budget Deficits." *Economics 21* (blog), February 8, 2019. https://economics21.org/yes-we-should-fear-budget-deficits.

Rogoff, K. 2019a. "Risks to the Global Economy in 2019." *Project Syndicate*, January 11. https://www.project-syndicate.org/commentary/global-economy-main-risks-in-2019-by-kenneth-rogoff-2019-01.

Rogoff, K. 2019b. "Government Debt Is Not a Free Lunch." *Project Syndicate*, December 6, 2019. https://www.project-syndicate.org/commentary/government-debt-low-interest-rates-no-free-lunch-by-kenneth-rogoff-2019-11.

Rozenberg, J., and M. Fay. 2019. *Beyond the Gap: How Countries Can Afford the Infrastructure They Need While Protecting the Planet*. Washington, DC: World Bank.

Sachs, J. 1985. "External Debt and Macroeconomic Performance in Latin America and East Asia." *Brookings Papers on Economic Activity* 1985 (2): 523-73.

Tornell, A., and F. Westermann. 2005. *Boom-Bust Cycles and Financial Liberalization*. Cambridge, MA: MIT Press.

World Bank. 2015. *Global Economic Prospects Report: Having Fiscal Space and Using It*. January. Washington, DC: World Bank.

World Bank. 2016. *Global Economic Prospects: Divergences and Risks.* June. Washington, DC: World Bank.

World Bank. 2017. *Global Economic Prospects: A Fragile Recovery.* June. Washington, DC: World Bank.

World Bank. 2018. *Global Economic Prospects: The Turning of the Tide.* June. Washington, DC: World Bank.

World Bank. 2019. *Global Economic Prospects: Heightened Tensions, Subdued Investment.* June. Washington, DC: World Bank.

World Bank and IMF (International Monetary Fund). 2018a. "Debt Vulnerabilities in Emerging and Low-Income Economies." October 2018 Meeting of the Development Committee, World Bank, Washington, DC.

World Bank and IMF (International Monetary Fund). 2018b. "G-20 Note: Strengthening Public Debt Transparency: The Role of the IMF and the World Bank." World Bank, Washington, DC.

Wyplosz, C. 2019. "Olivier in Wonderland." Vox CEPR Policy Portal, June 17, 2019. https://voxeu.org/content/olivier-wonderland.

Yared, P. 2019. "Rising Government Debt: Causes and Solutions for a Decades-Old Trend." *Journal of Economic Perspectives* 33 (2): 115-40.

Yu, B., and C. Shen. 2019. "Environmental Regulation and Industrial Capacity Utilization: An Empirical Study of China." *Journal of Cleaner Production.* Advance online publication. https://www.sciencedirect.com/science/article/pii/S0959652619338569.

Yu, S. 2016. "The Effect of Political Factors on Sovereign Default." *Review of Political Economy* 28 (3): 397-416.

Of course, at some point, growth will slow or interest rates will rise, and liquidity will tighten. Whenever that happens, financial assets will suffer significant price declines, and corporations will find it hard to roll over debt.

Raghuram Rajan (2019)
Katherine Dusak Miller Distinguished Service
Professor of Finance at the University of Chicago
Booth School of Business

Considering currently subdued investment and low interest rates, additional government borrowing might appear to be an attractive option for financing growth-enhancing initiatives such as investment in human and physical capital. The literature on debt, however, calls for caution: the cost of rolling over debt can increase sharply during periods of financial stress and result in costly crises; high debt can limit the ability of governments to provide fiscal stimulus during downturns; and high debt can weigh on investment and long-term growth.

Introduction

Amid record-high global debt, low interest rates and subpar growth have led to an intense debate on whether the recent rapid increase in debt is reason for concern. Some argue that countries, especially those that issue reserve currencies, should take advantage of low interest rates to borrow more to finance priority expenditures.[1] Others caution that high debt weighs on long-term growth by increasing the risk of crises, limiting the scope for countercyclical fiscal stimulus, and dampening private investment.[2]

Although the focus of this debate has been mainly on advanced economies, similar issues are also faced by emerging market and developing economies (EMDEs). Many of these have also borrowed heavily, and in many cases hard-won reductions in public debt ratios before the global financial crisis have largely been reversed over the past decade. The trade-offs EMDEs face are actually even starker, in light of their histories of severe debt crises, even at lower levels of debt than in advanced economies, and their more pressing spending needs to achieve development goals and improve living standards.

This chapter briefly reviews the literature on debt to provide a basis for assessing the merits of additional debt accumulation in EMDEs. Specifically, it addresses three questions:

- What are the benefits of debt accumulation?

---

[1] Blanchard (2019); Blanchard and Summers (2019); Blanchard and Tashiro (2019); Blanchard and Ubide (2019); Eichengreen et al. (2019); Furman and Summers (2019); Krugman (2019); and Rachel and Summers (2019) discuss reasons for additional borrowing in advanced economies, and the United States in particular.

[2] Alcidi and Gros (2019); Auerbach, Gale, and Krupkin (2019); CRFB (2019); Eichengreen (2019); Mazza (2019); Riedl (2019); Rogoff (2019a, 2019b); and Wyplosz (2019) caution against adding to debt.

- What are the costs associated with debt accumulation?

- What is the optimal level of debt?

The chapter brings together the main themes of theoretical and empirical studies on both government and private debt to provide answers to the three questions. Although it cannot do justice to the rich literature on debt, the chapter sets the stage for the discussion in subsequent chapters that describe the evolution of global waves of debt, puts the current debt wave into historical context, and examines the relationship between debt buildups and financial crises.

Main findings. The chapter's findings, in summary, are as follows:

- *Benefits and costs of debt.* Debt accumulation offers both benefits and costs. The benefits depend heavily on how productively the debt is used, the cyclical position of the economy, and the extent of financial market development. The costs of debt include interest payments, the possibility of debt distress, constraints that debt may impose on policy space and effectiveness, and the possible crowding out of private sector investment.

- *Optimal level of debt.* There is no generally applicable optimal level of debt, either for advanced economies or for EMDEs. Optimal levels of debt depend on country characteristics, financial market conditions, the behavior of governments and private agents, and the multiple functions of debt.

The following two sections review the literature on the benefits and costs of debt. The literature attempts to weigh some of these benefits and costs to isolate the factors that determine the optimal level of debt, as summarized in the subsequent section. The final section concludes with a summary.

Benefits of debt

Additional debt accumulation by EMDEs could be justified because of their need to invest in growth-enhancing projects, such as infrastructure, health, and education, and to protect vulnerable groups. During periods of weak growth, it may also be appropriate to borrow in order to employ expansionary fiscal policy to stimulate activity.

Promoting long-term growth. Government investment in physical and human capital can provide an important foundation for stronger growth over the long term. Such investments have taken on greater urgency in light of the expected further slowdown in potential gross domestic product (GDP) growth—the rate of growth an economy can sustain at full employment and capacity—over the next decade (World Bank 2018). In EMDEs, in particular, annual potential GDP growth is expected to slow by 0.5 percentage point to 4.3 percent during 2018-27, well below the average annual rate of 6.7 percent during 2002-07. To the extent that debt-financed investment spending stems the slowdown in potential growth, it also helps preserve the revenues required to service this debt (Fatás et al. 2019).

Despite substantial progress over the past two decades in many areas, several Sustainable Development Goals (SDGs) remain well out of reach (Vorisek and Yu 2020).[3] To meet the SDGs, EMDEs have large investment needs: low- and middle-income countries face aggregate investment needs of $1.5 trillion-$2.7 trillion per year—equivalent to 4.5-8.2 percent of annual GDP—between 2015 and 2030 to meet infrastructure-related SDGs, depending on the effectiveness of this investment, accompanying policy reforms, and the degree of ambition in meeting the SDGs (Rozenberg and Fay 2019; figure 2.1).[4] Infrastructure investment can have particularly large growth benefits if it connects isolated communities with markets, allows companies to realize economies of scale by increasing market size, or increases competitive pressures (Calderón and Servén 2010; Égert, Kozluk, and Sutherland 2009).

These estimates of global investment needs build on a significant body of work on investment needs at the regional level. In some regions and countries, the investment needed to meet infrastructure-related goals exceeds the 4.5-8.2 percent of GDP estimated at the global level.[5] For example, Africa's infrastructure needs have been estimated at about $93 billion per

---

[3] Eleven percent of the global population still lives in extreme poverty, defined as $1.90 per day or less. Out of every 1,000 of the world's infants, 29 still perish before they reach their first birthday. Twelve percent of the global population still have either restricted or no access to safe water, according to the World Bank's SDG Atlas. More than 500 million people still live in fragile security situations.

[4] Similarly, UNCTAD (2014) discusses the need for additional spending of $1.6 trillion to $2.5 trillion per year between 2015 and 2030 to achieve the goals related to economic infrastructure (that is, power, transport, telecommunications, and water and sanitation). The additional annual investment needed to meet the SDG on health in low- and middle-income countries is found to be about $370 billion (Stenberg et al. 2017).

[5] These estimates are based on a variety of costing exercises that are often not directly comparable (Vorisek and Yu 2020). They use different country samples and time periods; differ in their definitions of the targets to be achieved with investment (for example, SDGs or other policy goals) and inclusion of maintenance costs; and do not always attempt to estimate optimal plans for meeting future investment needs in light of the historical, and possibly constrained, relationship between infrastructure, income level, population, and urbanization (Fay et al. 2017).

FIGURE 2.1 **Potential benefits of debt**

EMDEs have large investment needs to meet development goals, which could be financed by debt. Fiscal policy in many EMDEs has become less procyclical since the mid-2000s. Debt-financed countercyclical fiscal support is particularly effective when an economy is in a recession.

A. Spending needs in EMDEs

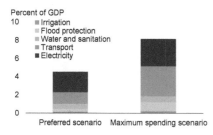

B. Spending needs, by EMDE region

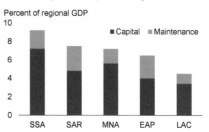

C. Response of output to government consumption increase in EMDEs

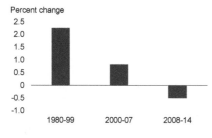

D. Fiscal multipliers, by business cycle phase

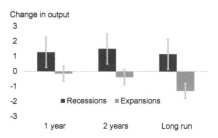

Sources: Huidrom et al. (2019); Rozenberg and Fay (2019); World Bank.
Note: EAP = East Asia and Pacific; EMDEs = emerging market and developing economies; LAC = Latin America and the Caribbean; MNA = Middle East and North Africa; SAR = South Asia; SSA = Sub-Saharan Africa.
A. Bars show average annual aggregate spending needs during 2015-30. "Preferred scenario" assumes ambitious goals and high spending efficiency, and "maximum spending scenario" assuming ambitious goals and low spending efficiency. Country sample includes low- and middle-income countries.
B. Bars show average annual spending needs during 2015-30. Estimates are generated using policy assumptions that cap investment needs at 4.5 percent of lower-middle-income countries' GDP per year (that is, the "preferred scenario" in panel A).
C. Bars show impulse response of the cyclical component of real GDP to a 1 percent positive shock to cyclical component of real government spending (in percent) using a panel structural vector autoregressive model for 15 EMDEs during 1980-2014.
D. Chart shows the conditional fiscal multipliers during recessions at select horizons (Huidrom et al. 2019). These are based on estimates from an interacted panel vector autoregression model, where model coefficients are conditioned only on the phase of the business cycle. Recessions are determined by the Harding-Pagan (2002) business cycle dating algorithm. Bars represent the median responses, and error bands are the 16-84 percent confidence bands.

year, or about 15 percent of annual regional GDP.[6] Even if major potential efficiency gains are captured, the region will still face an infrastructure funding gap of $31 billion per year, mainly for power. In Latin America and

---

[6] For estimates in the context of Africa, see African Development Bank (2010); Blimpo and Cosgrove-Davies (2019); Calderon, Cantú, and Chuhan-Pole (2018); and Foster and Briceño-Garmendia (2010).

the Caribbean between 2008 and 2013, investment in infrastructure averaged 2.7 percent of GDP a year, lower than the 4-5 percent of GDP average estimate of infrastructure investment needs (Fay et al. 2017).

Stabilizing short-term macroeconomic fluctuations. Temporary debt accumulation can also play an important role in helping to minimize and reverse short-term economic downturns. During recessions, borrowing-financed government spending or tax cuts can provide stimulus to support demand and activity (World Bank 2015; Yared 2019; figure 2.1).

A large literature provides estimates of the output effects (fiscal multipliers) of additional government spending or tax cuts (Huidrom et al. 2016, 2019; Ramey 2019). The estimates vary widely—from a 1.1-dollar output decline to a 3.8-dollar output increase for every dollar of additional government spending or reduced revenues—depending on the cyclical position of the economy; structural country characteristics, including the coherence of fiscal frameworks; and the fiscal instrument employed. Broadly speaking, output effects tend to be larger during recessions than during expansions; larger for advanced economies than for EMDEs; larger for expenditure increases than for tax cuts; and larger when accompanied by more accommodative monetary policy.[7]

In EMDEs, lack of fiscal space has often constrained fiscal policy during recessions, although there is some evidence that fiscal policy may have become less procyclical during the 2000s.[8] The correlation between cyclical swings in output and government consumption, for example, has turned from positive (procyclical) before the global financial crisis to negative (countercyclical) after the crisis. In advanced economies, proactive fiscal policy has gained in importance in the past decade, at least potentially, as monetary policy interest rates have approached or breached the zero lower bound (Battistini, Callegari, and Zavalloni 2019).

Providing safe assets. Sovereign debt constitutes a relatively safe asset for investors, as an alternative to private debt whose issuers are more likely to default (Azzimonti and Yared 2019). When risk aversion rises, demand for safe assets increases while borrowing constraints on private borrowers tighten. In these circumstances, government borrowing to finance income

---

[7] For details, see Alichi, Shibata, and Tanyeri (2019); Auerbach and Gorodnichenko (2013); Bachmann and Sims (2012); Candelon and Lieb (2013); Kraay (2012, 2014); and Leeper, Traum, and Walker (2017).

[8] For a discussion of these developments, see Frankel, Vegh, and Vuletin (2013); Huidrom, Kose, and Ohnsorge (2018); and Vegh, Lederman, and Bennett (2017).

support for private households or corporations can ease financing constraints (Yared 2019). Because the safe asset benchmarks private borrowing and can be used for collateral, government debt can play an important role in financial deepening (Hauner 2009; World Bank and IMF 2001). The availability of government debt instruments is also the prerequisite for monetary policy operations that rely on repurchase agreements of safe assets or open-market operations (Kumhof and Tanner 2005).

Costs of debt

The most basic cost of public debt is the servicing cost—the interest to be paid to creditors—which may be compared with the rate of return on the spending financed by debt to provide the simplest guide to whether public borrowing is worthwhile. An important argument against heavy borrowing, which may outweigh the benefits of borrowing in some cases, is the risk that rollover costs—the costs of refinancing when debt matures—can increase sharply during periods of financial stress and perhaps even trigger a financial crisis. High debt can also limit the feasible size and effectiveness of fiscal stimulus during downturns. Finally, high debt can constrain growth over the long term by crowding out productivity-enhancing private investment.

Deteriorating debt sustainability. During the postcrisis period, the cost of government borrowing has been historically low, for both advanced economies and EMDEs. As discussed in chapter 6, demographic shifts and slowing productivity growth are expected to contribute to a further secular decline in real interest rates in advanced economies, continuing a multiyear trend (Holston, Laubach, and Williams 2017). Nevertheless, a sudden increase in global borrowing costs could occur and test the sustainability of high debt in some countries (Henderson 2019; Rogoff 2019a, 2019b).

The recent discussion of debt has focused on the differential between nominal interest rates and nominal GDP growth, which has generally become markedly negative in advanced economies. If nominal interest rates (the cost of capital) are below nominal output growth (the presumed rate of return on capital), then the real burden of a given debt will decline over time because the rate of return on debt-financed spending will outweigh debt service. However, the interest rate-growth rate differential has to be weighed against the accumulation of new debt—the primary fiscal deficit. If, every year, the primary deficit adds more to the debt than is repaid on past debt (even if high rates of return are more than sufficient to service the debt), the debt stock will be on a rising trajectory. This rise is captured in the sustainability gap as a summary indicator of the debt trajectory (Buckle and Cruickshank 2013; Escolano 2010; Kose et al. 2017; figure 2.2). Such

FIGURE 2.2 **Debt sustainability**

Whereas debt levels in advanced economies are on a sustainable path, debt levels in almost half of EMDEs are on a rising path.

A. Sustainability gaps

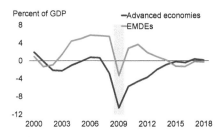

B. Share of economies with negative sustainability gaps

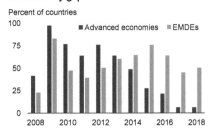

Sources: Huidrom et al. (2019); Kose et al. (2017); World Bank.
Note: A sustainability gap is defined as the difference between the actual primary balance and the debt-stabilizing balance. Averages computed with current U.S. dollar GDP as weights, based on at most 34 advanced economies and 83 emerging market and developing economies (EMDEs).
B. Share of economies in which sustainability gaps are negative (for example, debt is on a rising trajectory, or fiscal positions are debt-increasing).

calculations have to take into account the tendency for borrowing costs to rise as debt rises, in some cases abruptly (Gruber and Kamin 2012; Mauro and Zhou 2019).[9]

Debt sustainability has deteriorated since the global financial crisis both in advanced economies and in EMDEs (Aizenman et al. 2019). In advanced economies, debt-reducing fiscal positions (that is, positive sustainability gaps) in 2007 turned into debt-increasing fiscal positions (that is, negative sustainability gaps) from 2008. Subsequently, sustainability gaps narrowed and, in 2017, returned to debt-reducing positions.

In EMDEs, debt-reducing positions in 2007 turned into debt-increasing positions in 2015. In commodity-exporting EMDEs, this deterioration partly reflected the sharp growth slowdown that came in the wake of the steep slide in commodity prices. Subsequent recoveries in commodity prices and economic activity helped improve debt sustainability in these economies and, by 2018, fiscal positions in commodity exporters had become debt-reducing. In commodity-importing EMDEs, fiscal positions have remained

---

[9] The sustainability gap is defined as the difference between the primary balance and the debt stabilizing primary balance under specific assumptions about the target stock of debt, the interest rate, and the growth rates (Kose et al. 2017). For the purposes here, the target debt ratio, d*, is defined as the historical median in advanced economies or EMDEs. The target (and median) debt ratios for advanced economies and EMDEs are, respectively, 54 percent of GDP and 46 percent of GDP.

weak as a result of fiscal stimulus implemented during the global financial crisis, chronic primary deficits, and, in some cases, anemic postcrisis growth, leading to debt-increasing fiscal positions in 2018.

Increasing vulnerability to financial crises. A growing debt-to-GDP ratio could erode investor confidence, requiring the government to pay a rising risk premium on its debt. These pressures could culminate in a debt crisis if investors fear that the accumulation of government debt is no longer sustainable (Blanchard 2019; Henderson 2019; Rogoff 2019a, 2019b). Rapid debt accumulation can also lead to a currency crisis if investor concerns about the ability to repay foreign-currency-denominated debt induce a speculative attack on a fixed or pegged currency (Krugman 1979; Obstfeld and Rogoff 1986), or a banking crisis if private sector balance sheet vulnerabilities trigger banking panics (Chang and Velasco 2000; Krugman 1999).[10]

For reserve currency-issuing advanced economies, like the United States, it has been argued that such a spike in risk premiums is unlikely because these countries are often viewed as safe havens during periods of market turbulence (Furman and Summers 2019; Krugman 2014). Indeed, government debt in some advanced economies has reached very high levels with interest rates remaining low. The extreme case is Japan, where the 10-year government bond yield has been below 0.1 percent for most of the time since mid-2015 even while gross government debt has exceeded 230 percent of GDP.

For EMDEs, however, this risk is more acute. As documented in the next three chapters, EMDE borrowing costs have tended to rise sharply during episodes of financial stress, and higher debt servicing costs can cause debt dynamics to deteriorate and rollover risk to rise (Arellano and Ramanarayanan 2012).[11] A recent example is Argentina, where five-year U.S.

---

[10] Models of currency crises have evolved with their history (Burnside, Eichenbaum, and Rebelo 2008). In the 1970s and 80s, the focus of theoretical models was on understanding how pegs were abandoned as a consequence of the collapse of gold prices and the Bretton Woods system of exchange rates, and later pegs to the U.S. dollar. This began with the seminal work of Krugman (1979) and Flood and Garber (1984) in which excessive debt accumulation can be the trigger of a currency crisis. Following these "first generation models" were models that highlighted the existence of multiple equilibria (Obstfeld 1986). When the nature of currency crises changed in the 1998 Asian financial crisis, models evolved to include other theoretical links, including balance sheet mismatches (Chang and Velasco 2000; Krugman 1999).

[11] The incentive to avoid excessive depreciation is especially strong if there are large foreign currency debt exposures in one or more sectors of the economy (the concept of "original sin" described by Eichengreen, Hausmann, and Panizza 2006; and Jeanne 2003). Once a government starts using large amounts of reserves to defend an exchange rate peg, market participants (such as speculators or wage setters) start anticipating a depreciation. This triggers a self-reinforcing cycle of further reserve losses and depreciation expectations (see Flood and Garber 1984; Flood and Marion 2000; Krugman 1979; and Obstfeld 1986).

dollar-denominated sovereign bond yields more than doubled during 2018, to over 11 percent by early September. Indeed, as discussed in the next three chapters, every decade since the 1970s has witnessed debt crises in EMDEs, often combined with banking or currency crises (figure 2.3).[12]

Financial crises tend to result in large economic costs. In many cases, recessions associated with financial crises have tended to be more severe than others. For example, the average duration of recessions associated with financial crises is some six quarters, two quarters longer than other recessions. There has also typically been a larger output decline in recessions associated with financial crises than in other recessions (Claessens and Kose 2014).[13]

Constraining government action during downturns. High debt constrains governments' ability to respond to downturns with countercyclical fiscal policy (Obstfeld 2013; Reinhart and Rogoff 2010; Romer and Romer 2018). This was the case during the global financial crisis: fiscal stimulus during 2008-09 was considerably smaller in countries with high government debt than in those with low debt (Huidrom, Kose, and Ohnsorge 2018; figure 2.4). This is one of the reasons why weak fiscal positions tend to be associated with deeper and longer recessions, a situation that worsens if the private sector also falls into distress and its debt migrates to government balance sheets as the government attempts to rescue private enterprises.

Reducing the effectiveness of fiscal policy. High government debt tends to render expansionary fiscal policy less effective (Adam and Bevan 2005; Debrun and Kinda 2016). Specifically, high government debt can reduce the size of fiscal multipliers through two channels.

- *Ricardian channel.* When a government with high debt implements fiscal stimulus, consumers will be more likely to expect that tax increases will soon follow than when debt is low. This expectation will lead consumers to cut consumption and save more (the "Ricardian" reaction to government dis-saving). The Ricardian channel is consistent with empirical studies showing that the effect of government spending shocks on private consumption has often depended on government debt.[14]

---

[12] For a discussion of these episodes see Kose and Terrones (2015) and Laeven and Valencia (2018).

[13] For example, the cumulative cost of banking crises has been estimated, on average, at about 23 percent of GDP during the first four years (Claessens and Kose 2014). Eight years after a debt crisis, output is, on average, 10 percent lower (Furceri and Zdzienicka 2012).

[14] For theoretical studies discussing the Ricardian channel see Blanchard (1990a, 1990b) and Sutherland (1997). For empirical studies, see Giavazzi and Pagano (1990, 1995) and Perotti (1999). Distortionary taxation and frictions at the financial markets may, however, result in departures from Ricardian equivalence (Heathcote 2005).

FIGURE 2.3 Potential cost of debt: Financial crises

Financial crises have become less frequent over the 2000s. Banking crises have tended to impose high fiscal cost as governments have supported economic activity and assumed private debt. During financial crises, government debt has often risen whereas private debt has tended to remain stable, ratings have fallen, and negative sustainability gaps widened.

A. Financial crisis frequency

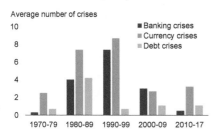

B. Government debt around banking crises

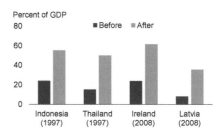

C. Government debt around financial crises

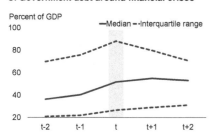

D. Sovereign ratings around financial crises

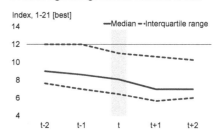

E. Sustainability gaps around financial crises

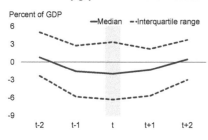

F. Private debt around financial crises

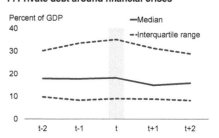

Sources: International Monetary Fund; Kose et al. (2017); Laeven and Valencia (2018); World Bank.

A. The figure shows the average number of financial crises in each decade.

B. "Before" and "after" denote, respectively, one year before and after the onset of each banking crisis, dated as shown. Government debt refers to general government debt in all cases except for Indonesia, where data are for central government only.

C.-F. Year "t" refers to the year of onset of financial crises in emerging market and developing economies. Medians, as well as interquartile ranges, based on balanced samples. Crises considers banking, currency, and debt crises, as defined in Laeven and Valencia (2018). When there are multiple crises identified within five years, the one with the lowest real GDP growth is counted as an event.

Sample comprises 80 crisis episodes (panel C), 56 episodes (panel D), 35 episodes (panel E), and 127 episodes (panel F).

FIGURE 2.4 **Cost of debt: Less effective fiscal policy**

High debt limits the ability of governments to support economic activity during recessions and blunts the effectiveness of fiscal stimulus. Higher debt is associated with higher interest payments but not with higher public investment.

A. Cyclically adjusted fiscal balance in EMDEs around the global financial crisis

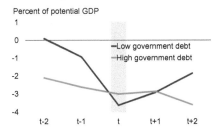

B. Fiscal multipliers after two years

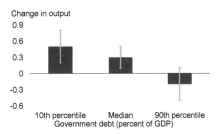

C. Public investment and debt in EMDEs, 2017

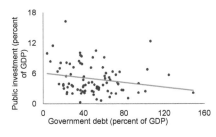

D. Government debt and interest payments in EMDEs, 2018

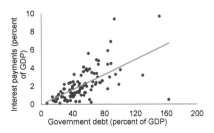

Sources: International Monetary Fund; World Bank.
Note: EMDEs = emerging market and developing economies.
A. Year "t" is the year of trough of business cycle in 2008 or 2009. Median of balanced samples over t-2 to t+2, based on 23 EMDEs where troughs are identified. Small states, as defined by the World Bank, are excluded. Troughs are defined as the years of negative GDP growth that is one standard deviation below average growth over 1960-2018 per economy. When there are multiple troughs identified within six years, the one with deeper contraction is counted as an event. "Low government debt" indicates economies with below-median debt-to-GDP ratio (33 percent of GDP) in 2007 in the sample economies; "high government debt" indicates economies with above-median ratio in 2007.
B. Bars show the conditional fiscal multipliers for different levels of government debt after two years. Fiscal multipliers are defined as cumulative change in output relative to cumulative change in government consumption in response to a 1-unit government consumption shock. They are based on estimates from the interacted panel vector autoregression model, where model coefficients are conditioned only on government debt. X-axis values correspond to the 10th to 90th percentiles in the sample. Bars represent the median, and vertical lines are the 16-84 percent confidence bands.
C. Public investment refers to a sum of net investment in nonfinancial assets and consumption of fixed capital, in general or central government (depending upon data availability). Sample includes 85 EMDEs.
D. Total (external and domestic) government debt versus total (external and domestic) government interest payments (both in percent of GDP).

- *Investor sentiment channel.* Countries with high sovereign debt are more likely to have to pay a risk premium to borrow (Alcidi and Gros 2019). When debt is higher, fiscal stimulus can increase creditors' concerns about sovereign credit risk, raising sovereign bond yields and, hence, borrowing costs across the whole economy. Higher risk premiums, especially during times of sovereign financial stress, have been shown to feed into lower corporate borrowing (Bocola 2016). This, in turn, will crowd out private investment and consumption, reducing the fiscal multiplier.

Empirical evidence suggests that, regardless of the time horizon considered, fiscal multipliers are smaller when government debt is higher. Similarly, evidence points to less effective monetary policy in the presence of high government debt because of poorly anchored inflation expectations.[15]

Slowing investment and growth. With higher debt typically comes higher debt service. Spending on higher debt service needs to be financed through some combination of increased borrowing, increased taxes, and reduced government spending. Spending cuts may even include spending on critical government functions such as social safety nets or growth-enhancing public investment (Debrun and Kinda 2016; Obstfeld 2013; Reinhart and Rogoff 2010). Separately, high and rising government debt may raise long-term interest rates and yield spreads.[16] High debt could also create uncertainty about macroeconomic and policy prospects, including risks that the government may need to resort to distortionary taxation to rein in debt and deficits (IMF 2018; Kumar and Woo 2010). Higher interest rates and uncertainty would tend to crowd out productivity-enhancing private investment and weigh on output growth.[17] While there is empirical evidence for a negative association between debt and growth, evidence on the direction of causality is mixed (Panizza and Presbitero 2014).

Debt: How much is too much?

Weighing these benefits and costs of debt, the literature has attempted to identify how much debt is "too much"—a threshold level of debt below which it is sustainable and not harmful to economic growth. A rich theoretical literature has focused on the interactions between governments, monetary authorities, and private agents in response to numerous shocks. The empirical literature has estimated a wide range of threshold values that appear to be tipping points for adverse effects of debt.

---

[15] For details, see Auerbach and Gorodnichenko (2012, 2013); Huidrom et al. (2016, 2019); Ilzetzki, Mendoza, and Vegh (2013); and Nickel and Tudyka (2014).

[16] See, for example, Ardagna, Caselli, and Lane (2007); Codogno, Favero, and Missale (2003); Laubach (2009); and Rubin, Orszag, and Sinai (2004).

[17] For in-depth discussions of these issues, see Auerbach, Gale, and Krupkin (2019); Croce et al. (2018); Gale and Orszag (2003); Huang, Pagano, and Panizza (2017); and Panizza, Huang, and Varghese (2018). Earlier literature on the impact of debt overhang on investment includes Krugman (1988) and Cohen (1993).

Theoretical considerations

Government debt. Government debt differs from private debt in the more limited ability of creditors to enforce debt service (Weidemaier and Gelpern 2014). Theoretical frameworks often model government debt as the outcome of the government's maximizing the social welfare of domestic agents, including the beneficiaries of government spending, taxpayers, and debtholders, subject to an intertemporal budget constraint that captures debt sustainability. The literature has taken two paths, one which takes the government's willingness to honor its debt as given, and the other modeling the government's willingness to service debt as a strategic decision.

- *Honoring debt obligations.* Assuming a government's willingness to service debt, the optimal level of debt depends on the nature of adverse shocks and the responses of economic agents to "unsustainable debt dynamics" (Guimaraes 2011). Early models, still widely used by policy makers, assess debt sustainability using the accounting identity of the intertemporal budget constraint, as defined in Blanchard (1990b), for scenario analysis. Debt sustainability can deteriorate rapidly in the presence of adverse shocks. Models that incorporate stochastic shocks to growth, revenues, expenditures, or borrowing cost offer a range of possible debt paths (Bohn 1998; Ghosh et al. 2013; Mendoza and Oviedo 2006, 2009). Debt sustainability also depends on the response of governments, monetary authorities, and private agents, captured in general equilibrium models (D'Erasmo, Mendoza, and Zhang 2016).

  Several models allow government debt to serve additional functions by introducing incomplete markets, spillovers from public investment, or interactions with monetary policy. In models with incomplete markets, government debt is a financial instrument that provides liquidity to the private sector and helps households smooth consumption.[18] If public investment offers spillovers that raise private productivity, the optimal level of debt is higher (Chatterjee, Gibson, and Rioja 2017). Finally, the optimal stock of government debt can also depend on interactions between fiscal and monetary policy (Leeper and Leith 2016), between lenders' and borrowers' financial health (Kashyap and Lorenzoni 2019), and income inequality.[19]

---

[18] For these models, see Aiyagari and McGrattan (1998); Canzoneri, Cumby, and Diba (2016); Flodén (2001); Harding and Klein (2019); Peterman and Sager (2018); and Röhrs and Winter (2017).

[19] For these interactions in different model environments, see Andreasen, Sandleris, and Van der Ghote (2019); Dovis, Golosov, and Shourideh (2016); and Jeon and Kabukcuoglu (2018).

- *Making a strategic decision to honor debt obligations.* Several studies model a government's strategic decision to default on external debt (D'Erasmo and Mendoza 2019). In contrast with corporate debt, creditors to sovereigns typically have few mechanisms to enforce debt obligations, although over time some mechanisms have evolved to strengthen enforcement (Panizza, Sturzenegger, and Zettelmeyer 2009). Creditors can, however, retaliate against defaulting governments by excluding them from financial markets for future access to credit (Eaton and Gersovitz 1981), imposing sanctions (Bulow and Rogoff 1989), or demanding default on other creditors.[20] Default risk also introduces monetary frictions that can discourage debt accumulation (Arellano, Bai and Mihalache 2019). Thus, a government's decision to default is modeled as a trade-off between short-term savings on debt service and longer-term costs, including output losses and loss of market access as a result of default, as discussed in chapter 5.

Private debt. A large literature has examined the optimal capital structure of corporate borrowers, starting with Modigliani and Miller (1958) who showed that in the absence of frictions the choice between debt and equity finance is irrelevant to firm value (see Claessens and Kose 2018 for a survey). Subsequent studies introduced frictions that helped identify an optimal composition for capital structure including the share of debt finance.[21]

- *Tax advantages versus debt distress cost.* More advantageous tax treatment of debt than equity can tilt decisions about optimal capital structure toward debt (DeAngelo and Masulis 1980). However, any tax advantage of debt has to be weighed against the cost of potential debt distress, including the cost of renegotiating debt contracts and suffering production disruptions, the cost of bankruptcy, and the economy-wide cost of weaker competition from risk-averse highly leveraged firms.[22]

---

[20] For these models, see Aguiar et al. (2016); Catão, Fostel, and Kapur (2009); Catão and Kapur (2006); Cole and Kehoe (1998); and Sandleris (2008). Some of these models also consider multiple equilibria because of self-reinforcing cycles: in one equilibrium, insolvency or illiquidity results in default, whereas in another, the government manages to roll over its debt (Calvo 1988; Cole and Kehoe 2000; Mendoza and Yue 2012). The decision to default also depends on the availability of financial assistance (Corsetti, Erce, and Uy 2019).

[21] For reviews of these, see Myers (2001, 2003). Some studies also look at the composition of debt, for example, share of foreign-currency denominated debt at the firm level (Eren and Malamud 2019; Kalemli-Ozcan, Liu, and Shim 2019; Salomao and Varela 2019).

[22] See Jensen and Meckling (1976); Leland and Toft (1996); and Myers (1977) for discussions of tax advantage; see Bradley, Jarrell, and Kim (1984); Kim (1982); Leland (1994); and Titman (1984) for discussions of the costs associated with bankruptcy. See Chevalier (1995) for discussion of the cost of less vigorous competition from risk-averse highly leveraged firms.

- *Pecking order.* When equity investors do not have complete information, they cannot distinguish between issuance of overvalued equity and equity issuance to finance growth and profit opportunities. To offset the cost of this information asymmetry, firm management that maximizes existing shareholder value can develop a pecking order of financing options, starting with internal finance, followed by debt and eventually equity (Myers 1984; Myers and Majluf 1984).

- *Agency considerations.* Views on what constitutes an optimal capital structure may differ between firm management and shareholders, especially in an environment of incomplete outside information. The chosen capital structure will then depend on the design of compensation for firm management (Dybvig and Zender 1991; Ross 1977). Debt can serve as a disciplining device to reduce how much a management with the objective of expanding operations may wish to invest in projects with negative net present value (Stulz 1990).

Empirical evidence

The empirical literature has looked for tipping points at which debt triggers financial crises or becomes otherwise economically costly. One strand of the literature has estimated sustainable levels of debt in advanced economies if fiscal deficits remain consistent with past performance or if movements in sovereign bond yields are consistent with the past. Other studies have identified debt thresholds above which the likelihood of a financial crisis increases. A third strand of the literature has explored the debt levels above which debt burdens become detrimental to long-term growth.

Sustainable debt. One strand of the literature has estimated the sustainable levels of government and private debt that do not culminate in debt distress.[23] Using data for 23 advanced economies, studies have estimated debt limits for governments borrowing at the risk-free rate to be 150-250 percent of GDP depending on country characteristics (Ghosh et al. 2013).[24] Advanced economies with government debt above 80 percent of GDP and persistent current account deficits have been shown to be vulnerable to sudden fiscal deteriorations (Greenlaw et al. 2013). Prudent debt management can help ensure a sustainable fiscal position that provides insurance against macroeconomic shocks (Missale 2012). For private sector debt, studies have focused on the link between financial system credit to the

---

[23] See Debrun et al. (2019) for a survey on the practical aspects of debt sustainability assessments.

[24] One commonly used "golden rule" is that borrowing should match growth-enhancing investment (Ostry, Ghosh, and Espinoza 2015).

private sector, as a proxy for private debt, and on nonperforming loans. A typical credit boom has been estimated to more than double nonperforming loans (Mendoza and Terrones 2008).

Early warning indicators. Another strand of the literature has identified government or private debt, especially external debt, among several early warning indicators of financial crises, as discussed in chapter 5. Government debt thresholds have been defined relative to government revenues (Manasse and Roubini 2009) or exports (Kraay and Nehru 2006) and as depending on the magnitude of other early warning indicators. "Safe" levels of external debt in EMDEs have been shown to be low and to depend heavily on a country's record of macroeconomic management (Reinhart, Rogoff, and Savastano 2003).[25] Correlates of private debt or private debt accumulation—credit-to-GDP ratios or their change over time—have also been identified as early warning indicators.[26]

Long-term growth effects. A third strand of the literature has estimated the debt levels above which debt burdens became detrimental to investment and long-term output growth. One study found that growth has tended to be lower in both advanced economies and EMDEs with government debt above 90 percent of GDP (Reinhart and Rogoff 2010), whereas another found, for 18 OECD countries, a threshold of 85 percent of GDP (Cecchetti, Mohanty, and Zampolli 2011). The thresholds for adverse short-term output effects may be lower, at 67 percent of GDP for advanced economies (Baum, Checherita-Westphal, and Rother 2013). Some studies, however, find no such threshold effects between debt and growth outcomes (Chudik et al. 2017; Panizza and Presbitero 2014; Pescatori, Sandri, and Simon 2014).

In EMDEs, the impact of external debt on per capita growth has been estimated to be negative at debt levels above 35-40 percent of GDP (Patillo, Poirson, and Ricci 2002). In low-income countries, the threshold has been shown to be even lower, at 20-25 percent of GDP (Clements, Bhattacharya, and Nguyen 2003).

For the private sector, high corporate leverage has been associated with weaker investment, because the benefits of productive investment for owners

---

[25] A separate literature examines the incentives of borrowers to accept or reject debt restructuring ("hold-out problem"; Fang, Schumacher, and Trebesch 2019).

[26] For discussions of these topics, see Claessens, Kose, and Terrones (2009, 2012), Dell'Ariccia et al. (2016); Eichengreen and Arteta (2002); Gourinchas and Obstfeld (2012); Rodrik and Velasco (2000); and Schularick and Taylor (2012).

are diluted by obligations to creditors.[27] Although some of these studies find a more negative association between leverage and investment for higher levels of debt, however, none provides estimates of specific thresholds of corporate leverage beyond which it detracts from investment. Higher household debt has been associated with lower output growth (Kim and Zhang 2019).

The elusive optimal level of debt. In a nutshell, the empirical evidence suggests that the optimal level of debt depends on a wide range of trade-offs and borrower characteristics (Ostry, Ghosh, and Espinoza 2015), which in part reflects a broader theoretical challenge in the literature. A basic insight from theory is that an increase in government debt tends to increase output in the short run, but to reduce it in the long run (Elmendorf and Mankiw 1999). Debt-financed fiscal expansion can be beneficial in the short run to limit economic downturns and smooth macroeconomic fluctuations; and borrowing can be beneficial also in the long run, when used to finance investments that yield a higher rate of return than the cost of debt. Elevated debt levels, however, can lead to sustainability challenges, increase vulnerability to crises, erode the size and effectiveness of fiscal expansion, and weigh on investment and growth.

Political economy considerations

When weighing benefits against costs of debt, "political-economy" forces may tilt the scale toward underestimating the cost of borrowing while overestimating its benefits. There are two strands of literature in analyzing the interactions between political-economy forces and debt accumulation.

- *Lack of consensus, short tenures.* Disagreements over spending priorities or short-lived government tenures may cause incentives to expand government spending envelopes, financed by debt (Aguiar and Amador 2011, 2013; Alesina and Tabellini 1990; Drazen 2001).

- *Incomplete information.* Voters do not have complete information about election candidates, which may create incentives to generate short-lived, debt-fueled growth spurts before elections (Dubois 2016; Nordhaus 1975). Especially ahead of elections, the absence of full information may create incentives that encourage political incumbents to employ debt-financed fiscal stimulus to improve short-term growth prospects (Aidt, Veiga, and Veiga 2011; Rogoff and Sibert 1988; Shi and Svensson 2006).

---

[27] For details of these arguments, see Borensztein and Ye (2018); Chen and Lu (2016); Das and Tulin (2017); IMF (2018); Kalemli-Ozcan, Laeven, and Moreno (2018); and Magud and Sosa (2015).

As a result, government expenditures, public debt, and deficits have tended to increase statistically significantly, albeit modestly, around elections (Brender and Drazen 2005; Klomp and De Haan 2011; Philips 2016). Such political cycles in budget pressures tend to be stronger in countries with weaker fiscal transparency, without balanced-budget requirements, and with compromised governance.[28]

Conclusion

The literature on debt has extensively documented the potential benefits and costs of debt accumulation. It has also concluded that no generally applicable level of debt exists but depends on a wide range of factors. The basic implication of this brief literature review is that striking the right balance between taking advantage of the present low interest rate environment and avoiding the risks posed by excessive debt accumulation remains a major challenge for EMDEs.

In light of the insights from the literature review here, the next four chapters explore the global and national debt accumulation episodes in EMDEs.

References

Adam, C. S., and D. L. Bevan. 2005. "Fiscal Deficits and Growth in Developing Countries." *Journal of Public Economics* 4 (April): 571-97.

African Development Bank. 2010. *African Development Report 2010: Ports, Logistics, and Trade in Africa.* Oxford, U.K.: Oxford University Press.

Aguiar, M., and M. Amador. 2011. "Growth in the Shadow of Expropriation." *Quarterly Journal of Economics* 126 (2): 651-97.

Aguiar, M., and M. Amador. 2013. "Sovereign Debt: A Review." NBER Working Paper 19388, National Bureau of Economic Research, Cambridge, MA.

Aguiar, M., S. Chatterjee, H. Cole, and Z. Stangebye. 2016. "Quantitative Models of Sovereign Debt Crises." In *Handbook of Macroeconomics* Vol. 2: 1697-755. Amsterdam: Elsevier.

Aidt, T. S., F. J. Veiga, and L. G. Veiga. 2011. "Election Results and Opportunistic Policies: A New Test of the Rational Political Business Cycle Model." *Public Choice* 148 (1-2): 21-44.

---

[28] For discussions of political budget cycles, see Alt and Lassen (2006a, 2006b); Alt and Rose (2009); Cioffi, Messina, and Tommasino (2012); Klomp and De Haan (2011); Shi and Svensson (2006); and Streb, Lema, and Torrens (2009).

Aiyagari, S. R., and E. R. McGrattan. 1998. "The Optimum Quantity of Debt." *Journal of Monetary Economics* 42 (3): 447-69.

Aizenman, J., Y. Jinjarak, H. T. K. Nguyen, and D. Park. 2019. "Fiscal Space and Government-Spending and Tax-Rate Cyclicality Patterns: A Cross-Country Comparison, 1960-2016." *Journal of Macroeconomics* 60 (June): 229-52.

Alcidi, C., and D. Gros. 2019. "Public Debt and the Risk Premium: A Dangerous Doom Loop." VoxEU.org, May 22, 2019. https://voxeu.org/article/public-debt-and-risk-premium.

Alesina, A., and G. Tabellini. 1990. "A Positive Theory of Fiscal Deficits and Government Debt." *Review of Economic Studies* 57 (3): 403-14.

Alichi, A., I. Shibata, and K. Tanyeri. 2019. "Fiscal Policy Multipliers in Small States." IMF Working Paper 19/72, International Monetary Fund, Washington, DC.

Alt, J. E., and D. Lassen. 2006a. "Transparency, Political Polarization, and Political Budget Cycles in OECD Countries." *American Journal of Political Science* 50 (3): 530-50.

Alt, J. E., and D. Lassen. 2006b. "Fiscal Transparency, Political Parties, and Debt in OECD Countries." *European Economic Review* 50 (6): 1403-39.

Alt, J. E., and S. Rose. 2009. "Context-Conditional Political Budget Cycles." In *The Oxford Handbook of Comparative Politics*, edited by C. Boix and S. C. Stokes. Oxford: Oxford University Press.

Andreasen, E., G. Sandleris, and A. Van der Ghote. 2019. "The Political Economy of Sovereign Defaults." *Journal of Monetary Economics* 104 (June): 23-36.

Ardagna, S., F. Caselli, and T. Lane. 2007. "Fiscal Discipline and the Cost of Public Debt Service: Some Estimates for OECD Countries." *The B.E. Journal of Macroeconomics* 7 (1): 1-35.

Arellano, C., Y. Bai, and G. Mihalache. 2019. Monetary Policy and Sovereign Risk in Emerging Economies." Prepared for the Twentieth Jacques Polak Annual Research Conference, Washington, DC, November 7-8.

Arellano, C., and A. Ramanarayanan. 2012. "Default and the Maturity Structure in Sovereign Bonds." *Journal of Political Economy* 120 (2): 187-232.

Auerbach, A. J., W. G. Gale, and A. Krupkin. 2019. "If Not Now, When? New Estimates of the Federal Budget Outlook." Brookings Report, February 11, Brookings Institution, Washington, DC.

Auerbach, A. J., and Y. Gorodnichenko. 2012. "Measuring the Output Responses to Fiscal Policy." *American Economic Journal: Economic Policy* 4 (2): 1-27.

Auerbach, A. J., and Y. Gorodnichenko. 2013. "Fiscal Multipliers in Recession and Expansion." In *Fiscal Policy after the Financial Crisis*, edited by A. Alesina and F. Giavazzi, 63-98. Chicago: University of Chicago Press.

Azzimonti, M., and P. Yared. 2019. "The Optimal Public and Private Provision of Safe Assets." *Journal of Monetary Economics* 102 (April): 126-44.

Bachmann, R., and E. R. Sims. 2012. "Confidence and the Transmission of Government Spending Shocks." *Journal of Monetary Economics* 59 (3): 235-49.

Battistini, N., G. Callegari, and L. Zavalloni. 2019. "Dynamic Fiscal Limits and Monetary-Fiscal Policy Interactions." ECB Working Paper 2268, European Central Bank, Frankfurt.

Baum, A., C. Checherita-Westphal, and P. Rother. 2013. "Debt and Growth: New Evidence for the Euro Area." *Journal of International Money and Finance* 32 (1): 809-21.

Blanchard, O. J. 1990a. "Comment: Can Severe Fiscal Contractions Be Expansionary? Tales of Two Small European Countries." In *NBER Macroeconomics Annual 1990*, Volume 5, edited by O. J. Blanchard and S. Fischer, 111-16. Cambridge: MIT Press.

Blanchard, O. J. 1990b. "Suggestions for a New Set of Fiscal Indicators." OECD Economics Department Working Paper 79, Organisation for Economic Co-operation and Development, Paris.

Blanchard, O. J. 2019. "Public Debt and Low Interest Rates." *American Economic Review* 109 (4): 1197-229.

Blanchard, O. J., and L. H. Summers. 2019. *Evolution or Revolution? Rethinking Macroeconomic Policy After the Great Recession.* Cambridge: MIT Press.

Blanchard, O. J., and T. Tashiro. 2019. "Fiscal Policy Options for Japan." PIIE Policy Brief 19-7, Peterson Institute for International Economics, Washington, DC.

Blanchard, O. J., and A. Ubide. 2019. "Why Critics of a More Relaxed Attitude on Public Debt Are Wrong." PIIE Realtime Economic Issues Watch, July 15, PIIE Realtime Economic Issues Watch (blog), July 15, 2019. https://www.piie.com/blogs/realtime -economic-issues-watch/why-critics-more-relaxed-attitude-public-debt-are-wrong.

Blimpo, M. P., and M. Cosgrove-Davies. 2019. *Electricity Access in Sub-Saharan Africa: Uptake, Reliability, and Complementary Factors for Economic Impact.* Washington, DC: World Bank.

Bocola, L. 2016. "The Pass-Through of Sovereign Risk." *Journal of Political Economy* 124 (4): 879-926.

Bohn, H. 1998. "The Behavior of U.S. Public Debt and Deficits." *Quarterly Journal of Economics* 113 (3): 949-63.

Borensztein, E., M. Chamon, O. Jeanne, P. Mauro, and J. Zettelmeyer. 2004. "Sovereign Debt Structure for Crisis Prevention." IMF Occasional Paper 237, International Monetary Fund, Washington, DC.

Bradley, M., G. E. Jarrell, and E. H. Kim. 1984. "On the Existence of an Optimal Capital Structure: Theory and Evidence." *Journal of Finance* 39(3): 857-78.

Brender, A., and A. Drazen. 2005. "Political Budget Cycles in New versus Established Democracies." *Journal of Monetary Economics* 52 (7): 1271-95.

Buckle, R. A., and A. A. Cruickshank. 2013. "The Requirements for Long-Run Fiscal Sustainability." Treasury Working Paper 13/20, New Zealand Treasury, Wellington.

Bulow, J., and K. Rogoff. 1989. "A Constant Recontracting Model of Sovereign Debt." *Journal of Political Economy* 97 (1): 155-78.

Burnside, C., M. Eichenbaum, and S. Rebelo. 2004. "Government Guarantees and Self-Fulfilling Speculative Attacks." *Journal of Economic Theory* 119 (1): 31-63.

Calderón, C., C. Cantu, and P. Chuhan-Pole. 2018. *Infrastructure Development in Sub-Saharan Africa: A Scorecard.* Washington, DC: World Bank.

Calderón, C., and L. Servén. 2010. "Infrastructure and Economic Development in Sub-Saharan Africa." *Journal of African Economies* 19 (suppl_1): i13-i87.

Calvo, G. A. 1998. "Capital Flows and Capital-Market Crises: The Simple Economics of Sudden Stops." *Journal of Applied Economics* 1(1): 35-54.

Candelon, B., and L. Lieb. 2013. "Fiscal Policy in Good and Bad Times." *Journal of Economic Dynamics and Control* 37 (12): 2679-94.

Canzoneri, M., R. Cumby, and B. Diba. 2016. "Optimal Money and Debt Management: Liquidity Provision vs Tax Smoothing." *Journal of Monetary Economics* 83 (August): 39-53.

Catão, L., A. Fostel, and S. Kapur. 2009. "Persistent Gaps and Default Traps" *Journal of Development Economics* 89 (2): 271-84.

Catão, L., and S. Kapur. 2006. "Volatility and the Debt-Intolerance Paradox." *IMF Staff Papers* 53 (2): 195-218.

Cecchetti, S., M. Mohanty, and F. Zampolli. 2011. "The Real Effects of Debt." BIS Working Paper 352, Bank for International Settlements, Basel.

Chang, R., and A. Velasco. 2000. "Financial Fragility and the Exchange Rate Regime." *Journal of Economic Theory* 92 (1): 1-34.

Chatterjee, S., J. Gibson, and F. Rioja. 2017. "Optimal Public Debt Redux." *Journal of Economic Dynamics and Control* 83: 162-74.

Chen, S., and Y. Lu. 2016. "Does Balance Sheet Strength Drive the Investment Cycle? Evidence from Pre- and Post-Crisis Cyprus." IMF Working Paper 16/248, International Monetary Fund, Washington, DC.

Chevalier, J. A. 1995. "Do LBO Supermarkets Charge More? An Empirical Analysis of the Effects of LBOs on Supermarket Pricing." *Journal of Finance* 50 (4): 1095-112.

Chudik, A., K. Mohaddes, M. Hashem, and M. Raissi. 2017. "Is There a Debt-Threshold Effect on Output Growth?" *The Review of Economics and Statistics* 99 (1): 135-50.

Cioffi, M., G. Messina, and P. Tommasino. 2012. "Parties, Institutions and Political Budget Cycles at the Municipal Level." Bank of Italy Working Paper 885, Bank of Italy, Rome.

Claessens, S., and M. A. Kose. 2014. "Financial Crises Explanations, Types, and Implications." In *Financial Crises: Causes, Consequences, and Policy Responses*, edited by S. Claessens, M. A. Kose, L. Laeven, and F. Valencia, 3-59. Washington, DC: International Monetary Fund.

Claessens, S., and M. A. Kose. 2018. "Frontiers of Macrofinancial Linkages." BIS Papers 95, Bank for International Settlements, Basel.

Claessens, S., M. A. Kose, and M. Terrones. 2009. "What Happens During Recessions, Crunches, and Busts?" *Economic Policy* 24 (60): 653-700.

Claessens, S., M. A. Kose, and M. Terrones. 2010. "The Global Financial Crisis: How Similar? How Different? How Costly?" *Journal of Asian Economics* 21(3): 247-64.

Clements, B., R. Bhattacharya, and T. Q. Nguyen. 2003. "External Debt, Public Investment, and Growth in Low-Income Countries." IMF Working Paper 03/249, International Monetary Fund, Washington, DC.

Codogno, L., C. Favero, and A. Missale. 2003. "Yield Spreads on EMU Government Bonds." *Economic Policy* 18 (37): 505-32.

Cohen, D. 1993. "Low Investment and Large LDC Debt in the 1980s."*American Economic Review* 83 (3): 437-49.

Cole, H. L., and T. J. Kehoe. 1998. "Models of Sovereign Debt: Partial Versus General Reputations." *International Economic Review* 39 (1): 55-70.

Cole, H. L., and T. J. Kehoe. 2000. "Self-Fulfilling Debt Crises." *The Review of Economic Studies* 67 (1): 91-116.

Corsetti, G., A. Erce, and T. Uy. 2019. "Debt Sustainability and the Terms of Official Support." Prepared for the Twentieth Jacques Polak Annual Research Conference, Washington, DC, November 7-8.

CRFB (Committee for a Responsible Federal Budget). 2019. "Why Should We Worry About the National Debt?" Budgets & Projections paper, April 16, Committee for a Responsible Federal Budget, Washington, DC.

Croce, M. M., T. T. Nguyen, S. Raymond, and L. Schmid. 2018. "Government Debt and the Returns to Innovation." *Journal of Financial Economics*. Advance online publication.

D'Erasmo, P., and E. Mendoza. 2019. "History Remembered: Optimal Sovereign Default on Domestic and External Debt." Working Paper 19-31, Federal Reserve Bank of Philadelphia.

D'Erasmo, P., E. G. Mendoza, and J. Zhang. 2016. "What Is a Sustainable Public Debt?" In *Handbook of Macroeconomics, Volume 2*, edited by J. B. Taylor and H. Uhlig, 2493-597. Amsterdam: Elsevier.

Das, S., and V. Tulin. 2017. "Financial Frictions, Underinvestment, and Investment Composition: Evidence from Indian Corporates." IMF Working Paper 17/134, International Monetary Fund, Washington, DC.

DeAngelo, H., and R. W. Masulis. 1980. "Optimal Capital Structure under Corporate and Personal Taxation." *Journal of Financial Economics* 8 (1): 3-29.

Debrun, X., and T. Kinda. 2016. "That Squeezing Feeling: The Interest Burden and Public Debt Stabilization." *International Finance* 19 (2): 147-78.

Debrun, X., J. D. Ostry, T. Willems, and C. Wyplosz. 2019. "Public Debt Sustainability." CEPR Discussion Paper 14010, Centre for Economic Policy Research, London.

Dell'Ariccia, G, D. Igan, L. Laeven, and H. Tong. 2016. "Credit Booms and Macrofinancial Stability." *Economic Policy* 31 (86): 299-355.

Dincer, N., and B. Eichengreen. 2014. "Central Bank Transparency and Independ-ence: Updates and New Measures." *International Journal of Central Banking* 10 (1): 189-259.

Dovis, A., M. Golosov, and A. Shourideh. 2016. "Political Economy of Sovereign Debt: A Theory of Cycles of Populism and Austerity." NBER Working Paper 21948, National Bureau of Economic Research, Cambridge, MA.

Drazen, A. 2001. "The Political Business Cycle after 25 Years." In *NBER Macroeconomics Annual 2000, Volume 15*, edited by B. S. Bernanke and K. Rogoff, 75-117. Cambridge: MIT Press.

Dubois, E. 2016. "Political Business Cycles 40 Years after Nordhaus." *Public Choice* 166 (1-2): 235-59.

Dybvig, P. H., and J. F. Zender. 1991. "Capital Structure and Dividend Irrelevance with Asymmetric Information." *Review of Financial Studies* 4 (1): 201-19.

Eaton, J., and M. Gersovitz. 1981. "Debt with Potential Repudiation: Theoretical and Empirical Analysis." *Review of Economic Studies* 48 (2): 289-309.

Égert, B., T. J. Kozluk, and D. Sutherland. 2009. "Infrastructure and Growth: Empirical Evidence." CESifo Working Paper 2700, CESifo, Munich.

Eichengreen, B. 2019. "The Return of Fiscal Policy." *Project Syndicate*, May 13, 2019. https://www.project-syndicate.org/commentary/return-of-fiscal-policy-by-barry-eichengreen-2019-05.

Eichengreen, B., and C. Arteta. 2002. "Banking Crises in Emerging Markets: Presumptions and Evidence." In *Financial Policies in Emerging Markets*, edited by M. I. Blejer and M. Skreb. Cambridge: MIT Press.

Eichengreen, B., A. El-Ganainy, R. Esteves, and K. J. Mitchener. 2019. "Public Debt through the Ages." NBER Working Paper 25494, National Bureau of Economic Research, Cambridge, MA.

Eichengreen, B., R. Hausmann, and U. Panizza. 2006. "The Pain of Original Sin." In *Other People's Money*, edited by B. Eichengreen and R. Hausmann. Chicago: University of Chicago Press.

Elmendorf, D. W., and N. G. Mankiw. 1999. "Government Debt." In *Handbook of Macroeconomics, Volume 1*, edited by J. B. Taylor and M. Woodford, 1615-69. Amsterdam: North Holland.

Eren, E., and S. Malamud. 2019. "Dominant Currency Debt." Prepared for the Twentieth Jacques Polak Annual Research Conference, Washington, DC, November 7-8.

Escolano, J. 2010. "A Practical Guide to Public Debt Dynamics, Fiscal Sustainability, and Cyclical Adjustment of Budgetary Aggregates." IMF Technical Notes and Manuals 10/02, International Monetary Fund, Washington, DC.

Fang, C., J. Schumacher, and C. Trebesch. 2019. "Restructuring Sovereign Bonds: Holdouts, Haircuts and the Effectiveness of CACs." Prepared for the Twentieth Jacques Polak Annual Research Conference, Washington, DC, November 7-8.

Fatás, A., A. Ghosh, U. Panizza, and A. Presbitero. 2019. "The Motives to Borrow." CEPR Discussion Paper 13735, Centre for Economic Policy Research, Washington, DC.

Fay, M., L. Andres, C. Fox, U. G. Narloch, S. Straub, and M. A. Slawson. 2017. *Rethinking Infrastructure in Latin America and the Caribbean: Spending Better to Achieve More*. Washington, DC: World Bank.

Flodén, M. 2001. "The Effectiveness of Government Debt and Transfers as Insurance." *Journal of Monetary Economics* 48 (1): 81-108.

Flood, R. P., and P. M. Garber. 1984. "Collapsing Exchange Rate Regimes: Some Linear Examples." *Journal of international Economics* 17 (1-2): 1-13.

Flood, R. P., and N. P. Marion. 2000. "Self-Fulfilling Risk Predictions:: An Application to Speculative Attacks." *Journal of International Economics* 50 (1): 245-68.

Foster, V., and M. C. Briceño-Garmendia. 2010. *Africa's Infrastructure: A Time for Transformation*. Washington, DC: World Bank.

Frankel, J. A., C. A. Vegh, and G. Vuletin. 2013. "On Graduation from Fiscal Procyclicality." *Journal of Development Economics* 100 (1): 32-47.

Furceri, D., and A. Zdzienicka. 2012. "How Costly Are Debt Crises?" *Journal of International Money and Finance* 31 (4): 726-42.

Furman, J., and L. H. Summers. 2019. "Who's Afraid of Budget Deficits? How Washington Should End Its Debt Obsession." *Foreign Affairs* 98: 82-94.

Gale, W. G., and P. R. Orszag. 2003. "Economic Effects of Sustained Budget Deficits." *National Tax Journal* 56 (3): 463-85.

Ghosh, A. R., J. I. Kim, E. G. Mendoza, J. D. Ostry, and M. S. Qureshi. 2013. "Fiscal Fatigue, Fiscal Space and Debt Sustainability in Advanced Economies." *Economic Journal* 123 (566): F4-F30.

Giavazzi, F., and M. Pagano. 1990. "Can Severe Fiscal Contractions Be Expansionary? Tales of Two Small European Countries." In *NBER Macroeconomics Annual 1990, Volume 5*, edited by O. J. Blanchard and S. Fischer, 75-122. Cambridge: MIT Press.

Giavazzi, F., and M. Pagano. 1995. "Non-Keynesian Effects of Fiscal Policy Changes: International Evidence and the Swedish Experience." NBER Working Paper 5332, National Bureau of Economic Research, Cambridge, MA.

Gourinchas, P.-O., and M. Obstfeld. 2012. "Stories of the Twentieth Century for the Twenty-first," *American Economic Journal: Macroeconomics* 4 (1): 226-65.

Greenlaw, D., J. D. Hamilton, P. Hooper, and F. S. Mishkin. 2013. "Crunch Time: Fiscal Crises and the Role of Monetary Policy." NBER Working Paper 19297, National Bureau of Economic Research, Cambridge, MA.

Gruber, J. W., and S. B. Kamin. 2012. "Fiscal Positions and Government Bond Yields in OECD Countries." *Journal of Money, Credit and Banking* 44(8): 1563-87.

Guimaraes, B. 2011. "Sovereign Default: Which Shocks Matter?" *Review of Economic Dynamics* 14 (4): 553-76.

Harding, D., and A. Pagan. 2002. "Dissecting the Cycle: A Methodological Investigation." *Journal of Monetary Economics* 49 (2): 365-81.

Harding, M., and M. Klein. 2019. "Monetary Policy and Household Net Worth." Prepared for the Twentieth Jacques Polak Annual Research Conference, Washington, DC: November 7-8.

Hauner, D. 2009. "Public Debt and Financial Development." *Journal of Development Economics* 88 (1): 171-83.

Heathcote, J. 2005. "Fiscal Policy with Heterogeneous Agents and Incomplete Markets." *The Review of Economic Studies* 72 (1): 161-88.

Henderson, D. R. 2019. "Who's Afraid of Budget Deficits? I Am." *Defining Ideas*, February 20, 2019. https://www.hoover.org/research/whos-afraid-budget-deficits-i-am.

Holston, K., T. Laubach, and J. C. Williams. 2017. "Measuring the Natural Rate of Interest: International Trends and Determinants." *Journal of International Economics* 108 (Supplement 1): S59-S75.

Huang, Y., M. Pagano, and U. Panizza. 2017. "Local Crowding Out in China." EIEF Working Paper 17/07, Einaudi Institute for Economics and Finance, Rome.

Huidrom, R., M. A. Kose, J. J. Lim, and F. Ohnsorge. 2016. "Do Fiscal Multipliers Depend on Fiscal Positions?" Policy Research Working Paper 7724, World Bank, Washington, DC.

Huidrom, R., M. A. Kose, J. J. Lim, and F. Ohnsorge. 2019. "Why Do Fiscal Multipliers Depend on Fiscal Positions?" *Journal of Monetary Economics.* Advance online publication. https://doi.org/10.1016/.

Huidrom, R., M. A. Kose, and F. Ohnsorge. 2018. "Challenges of Fiscal Policy in Emerging and Developing Economies." *Emerging Markets Finance and Trade* 54 (9): 1927-45.

Ilzetzki, E, E. G. Mendoza, and C. A. Végh. 2013. "How Big (Small?) Are Fiscal Multipliers?" *Journal of Monetary Economics* 60 (2): 239-54.

IMF (International Monetary Fund). 2018. *Fiscal Monitor: Capitalizing on Good Times.* April. Washington, DC: International Monetary Fund.

Jeanne, M. O. 2003. "Why Do Emerging Economies Borrow in Foreign Currency?" IMF Working Paper 03/77, International Monetary Fund, Washington, DC.

Jeon, K., and Z. Kabukcuoglu. 2018. "Income Inequality and Sovereign Default." *Journal of Economic Dynamics and Control* 95 (October): 211-32.

Jensen, M. C., and W. H. Meckling. 1976. "Theory of the Firm: Managerial Behavior, Agency Costs and Ownership Structure." *Journal of Financial Economics* 3 (4): 305-60.

Kalemli-Ozcan, S., L. Laeven, and D. Moreno. 2018. "Debt Overhang, Rollover Risk, and Corporate Investment: Evidence from the European Crisis." NBER Working Paper 24555, National Bureau of Economic Research, Cambridge, MA.

Kalemli-Ozcan, S., X. Liu, and I. Shim. 2019. "Exchange Rate Fluctuations and Firm Leverage." Prepared for the Twentieth Jacques Polak Annual Research Conference, Washington, DC, November 7-8.

Kashyap, A., and G. Lorenzoni. 2019. "Borrower and Lender Resilience." Prepared for the Twentieth Jacques Polak Annual Research Conference, Washington, DC, November 7-8.

Kim, E. H. 1982. "Miller's Equilibrium, Shareholder Leverage Clienteles, and Optimal Capital Structure." *Journal of Finance* 37 (2): 301-19.

Kim, Y. J., and J. Zhang. 2019. "Debt and Growth." Prepared for the Twentieth Jacques Polak Annual Research Conference, Washington, DC, November 7-8.

Klomp, J., and J. De Haan. 2011. "Do Political Budget Cycles Really Exist?" *Applied Economics* 45 (3): 329-41.

Kose, M. A., S. Kurlat, F. Ohnsorge, and N. Sugawara. 2017. "A Cross-Country Database of Fiscal Space." Policy Research Working Paper 8157, World Bank, Washington, DC.

Kose, M. A., and M. E. Terrones. 2015. *Collapse and Revival: Understanding Global Recessions and Recoveries.* Washington, DC: International Monetary Fund.

Kraay, A. 2012. "How Large Is the Government Spending Multiplier? Evidence from World Bank Lending." *Quarterly Journal of Economics* 127 (2): 829-87.

Kraay, A. 2014. "Government Spending Multipliers in Developing Countries: Evidence from Lending by Official Creditors." *American Economic Journal: Macroeconomics* 6 (4): 170-208.

Kraay, A., and V. Nehru. 2006. "When Is External Debt Sustainable?" *World Bank Economic Review* 20 (3): 341-65.

Krugman, P. 1979. "A Model of Balance of Payments Crises." *Journal of Money, Credit, and Banking* 11 (3): 311-25.

Krugman, P. 1988. "Financing vs. Forgiving a Debt Overhang." *Journal of Development Economics* 29 (3): 253-68.

Krugman, P. 1999. "Balance Sheets, the Transfer Problem, and Financial Crises." *International Tax and Public Finance* 6 (4): 459-72.

Krugman, P. 2014. "Currency Regimes, Capital Flows, and Crises." *IMF Economic Review* 62 (4): 470-93.

Krugman, P. 2019. "Perspectives on Debt and Deficits." *Business Economics* 54 (3): 157-59.

Kumar, M., and J. Woo. 2010. "Public Debt and Growth." IMF Working Paper 174, International Monetary Fund, Washington, DC.

Kumhof, M., and E. Tanner. 2005. "Government Debt: A Key Role in Financial Intermediation," IMF Working Paper 05/57, International Monetary Fund, Washington, DC.

Laeven, L., and F. Valencia. 2018. "Systemic Banking Crises Revisited." IMF Working Paper 18/206, International Monetary Fund, Washington, DC.

Laubach, T. 2009. "New Evidence on the Interest Rate Effects of Budget Deficits and Debt." *Journal of the European Economic Association* 7 (4) 858-85.

Leeper, E. M., and C. Leith. 2016. "Understanding Inflation as a Joint Monetary-Fiscal Phenomenon." In *Handbook of Macroeconomics 2,* edited by J. B. Taylor and H. Uhlig, 2305-2415. Amsterdam: Elsevier.

Leeper, E. M., N. Traum, and T. B. Walker. 2017. "Clearing up the Fiscal Multiplier Morass." *American Economic Review* 107 (8): 2409-54.

Leland, H. E. 1994. "Corporate Debt Value, Bond Covenants, and Optimal Capital Structure." *Journal of Finance* 49 (4): 1213-52.

Leland, H. E., and K. B. Toft. 1996. "Optimal Capital Structure, Endogenous Bankruptcy, and the Term Structure of Credit Spreads." *Journal of Finance* 51 (3): 987-1019.

Magud, N., and S. Sosa. 2015. "Investment in Emerging Markets: We Are Not in Kansas Anymore...Or Are We?" IMF Working Paper 15/77, International Monetary Fund, Washington, DC.

Manasse, P., and N. Roubini. 2009. "'Rules of Thumb' for Sovereign Debt Crises." *Journal of International Economics* 78 (2): 192-205.

Mauro, P., and J. Zhou. 2019. "Can We Sleep More Soundly?" Prepared for the Twentieth Jacques Polak Annual Research Conference, Washington, DC, November 7-8.

Mazza, J. 2019. "Is Public Debt a Cheap Lunch?" *Bruegel* (blog), January 21, 2019. https://bruegel.org/2019/01/is-public-debt-a-cheap-lunch/.

Mendoza, E. G., and P. M. Oviedo. 2006. "Fiscal Policy and Macroeconomic Uncertainty in Developing Countries: The Tale of the Tormented Insurer." NBER Working Paper 12586, National Bureau of Economic Research, Cambridge, MA.

Mendoza, E. G., and P. M. Oviedo. 2009. "Public Debt, Fiscal Solvency and Macroeconomic Uncertainty in Latin America: The Cases of Brazil, Colombia, Costa Rica and Mexico." *Economía Mexicana: Nueva Época* XVIII (2):133-73.

Mendoza, E. G., and M. E. Terrones. 2008. "An Anatomy of Credit Booms: Evidence from Macro Aggregates and Micro Data." NBER Working Paper 14049, National Bureau of Economic Research, Cambridge, MA.

Mendoza, E. G., and V. Z. Yue. 2012. "A General Equilibrium Model of Sovereign Default and Business Cycles." *The Quarterly Journal of Economics* 127 (2): 889-946.

Missale, A. 2012. "Sovereign Debt Management and Fiscal Vulnerabilities." BIS Papers 65, Bank for International Settlements, Basel.

Modigliani, F., and M. H. Miller. 1958. "The Cost of Capital, Corporate Finance, and the Theory of Investment." *American Economic Review* 48 (4): 261-97.

Myers, S. C. 1977. "Determinants of Corporate Borrowing." *Journal of Financial Economics* 5 (2): 147-75.

Myers, S. C. 1984. "The Capital Structure Puzzle." *Journal of Finance* 39 (3): 575-92.

Myers, S. C. 2001. "Capital Structure." *Journal of Economic Perspectives* 15 (2): 81-102.

Myers, S. C. 2003. "Financing of Corporations." In *Handbook of the Economics of Finance 1A*, edited by G. M. Constantinides, M. Harris, and R. M. Stulz, 215-53. Amsterdam: Elsevier.

Myers, S. C., and N. S. Majluf. 1984. "Corporate Financing and Investment Decisions When Firms Have Information That Investors Do Not Have." *Journal of Financial Economics* 13 (2): 187-221.

Nickel, C., and A. Tudyka. 2014. "Fiscal Stimulus in Times of High Debt: Reconsidering Multipliers and Twin Deficits." *Journal of Money, Credit and Banking* 46 (7): 1313-44.

Nordhaus, W. D. 1975. "The Political Business Cycle." *Review of Economic Studies* 42 (2): 169-90.

Obstfeld, M. 1986. "Rational and Self-Fulfilling Balance of Payments Crises." *American Economic Review* 76 (1): 72-81.

Obstfeld, M. 2013. "On Keeping Your Powder Dry: Fiscal Foundations of Financial and Price Stability." *Monetary and Economic Studies* 31 (November): 25-37.

Obstfeld, M., and Rogoff, K. 1986. "Ruling Out Divergent Speculative Bubbles." *Journal of Monetary Economics* 17 (3): 349-62.

Ostry, J. D., A. R. Ghosh, and R. A. Espinoza. 2015. "When Should Public Debt Be Reduced?" IMF Staff Discussion Note 15-10, International Monetary Fund, Washington, DC.

Panizza, U., Y. Huang, and R. Varghese. 2018. "Does Public Debt Crowd Out Corporate Investment? International Evidence." CEPR Discussion Paper 12931, Centre for Economic Policy Research, London.

Panizza, U., and A. F. Presbitero. 2014. "Public Debt and Economic Growth: Is There a Causal Effect?" *Journal of Macroeconomics* 41 (September): 21-41.

Panizza, U., F. Sturzenegger, and J. Zettelmeyer. 2009. "The Economics and Law of Sovereign Debt and Default." *Journal of Economic Literature* 47 (3): 651-98.

Patillo, C., H. Poirson, and L. Ricci. 2002. "External Debt and Growth." IMF Working Paper 02/69, International Monetary Fund, Washington, DC.

Perotti, R. 1999. "Fiscal Policy in Good Times and Bad." *Quarterly Journal of Economics* 114 (4): 1399-436.

Pescatori, A., D. Sandri, and J. Simon. 2014. "Debt and Growth: Is There a Magic Threshold?" IMF Working Paper 14/34, International Monetary Fund, Washington, DC.

Peterman, W. B., and E. Sager. 2018. "Optimal Public Debt with Life Cycle Motives." Finance and Economics Discussion Series Working Paper 2018-028, Board of Governors of the Federal Reserve System, Washington, DC.

Philips, A. 2016. "Seeing the Forest through the Trees: A Meta-Analysis of Political Budget Cycles." *Public Choice* 168 (3): 313-41.

Rachel, L., and L. H. Summers. 2019. "On Falling Neutral Real Rates, Fiscal Policy, and the Risk of Secular Stagnation." BPEA Conference Draft, March 7-8, Brookings Institution, Washington, DC.

Ramey, V. A. 2019. "Ten Years After the Financial Crisis: What Have We Learned from the Renaissance in Fiscal Research?" *Journal of Economic Perspectives* 33 (2): 89-114.

Reinhart, C. M., and K. S. Rogoff. 2010. "Growth in a Time of Debt." *American Economic Review* 100 (2): 573-78.

Reinhart, C., K. Rogoff, and M. Savastano. 2003. "Debt Intolerance." *Brookings Papers on Economic Activity* 34 (1): 1-74.

Riedl, B. 2019. "Yes, We Should Fear Budget Deficits." *Economics 21* (blog), February 8, 2019. https://economics21.org/yes-we-should-fear-budget-deficits.

Rodrik, D., and A. Velasco. 2000. "Short-Term Capital Flows," In *Annual World Bank Conference on Development Economics, 1999*, 59-90. Washington, DC: World Bank.

Rogoff, K. 2019a. "Risks to the Global Economy in 2019." *Project Syndicate*, January 11. https://www.project-syndicate.org/commentary/global-economy-main-risks-in-2019-by-kenneth-rogoff-2019-01.

Rogoff, K. 2019b. "Government Debt Is Not a Free Lunch." *Project Syndicate*, December 6, 2019. https://www.project-syndicate.org/commentary/government-debt-low-interest-rates-no-free-lunch-by-kenneth-rogoff-2019-11.

Rogoff, K., and A. Sibert. 1988. "Elections and Macroeconomic Policy Cycles." *Review of Economic Studies* 55 (1): 1-16.

Röhrs, S., and C. Winter. 2017. "Reducing Government Debt in the Presence of Inequality." *Journal of Economic Dynamics and Control* 82 (September): 1-20.

Romer, C. D., and D. H. Romer. 2018. "Phillips Lecture—Why Some Times Are Different: Macroeconomic Policy and the Aftermath of Financial Crises." *Economica* 85 (337): 1-40.

Ross, S. A. 1977. "The Determination of Financial Structure: the Incentive-Signalling Approach." *Bell Journal of Economics* 8 (1): 23-40.

Rozenberg, J., and M. Fay. 2019. *Beyond the Gap: How Countries Can Afford the Infrastructure They Need While Protecting the Planet.* Washington, DC: World Bank.

Rubin, R. E., P. R. Orszag, and A. Sinai. 2004. "Sustained Budget Deficits: Longer-Run U.S. Economic Performance and the Risk of Financial and Fiscal Disarray." Paper presented at the AEA-NAEFA Joint Session, "National Economic and Financial Policies for Growth and Stability," San Diego, CA, January 4.

Salomao, J., and L. Varela. 2019. "Exchange Rate Exposure and Firm Dynamics." Prepared for the Twentieth Jacques Polak Annual Research Conference, Washington, DC, November 7-8.

Sandleris, G. 2008. "Sovereign Defaults: Information, Investment and Credit." *Journal of International Economics* 76 (2): 267-75.

Schularick, M., and A. M. Taylor. 2012. "Credit Booms Gone Bust: Monetary Policy, Leverage Cycles, and Financial Crises, 1870-2008." *American Economic Review* 102 (2): 1029-61.

Shi, M., and J. Svensson. 2006. "Political Budget Cycles: Do They Differ across Countries and Why?" *Journal of Public Economics* 90 (8-9): 1367-89.

Stenberg, K., O. N. Hanssen, T. T.-T. Edejer, M. Bertram, C. Brindley, A. Meshreky, J. E. Rosen, et al. 2017. "Financing Transformative Health Systems Towards Achievement of the Health Sustainable Development Goals: A Model for Projected Resource Needs in 67 Low-Income and Middle-Income Countries." *Lancet Global Health* 5 (9): e875-e887.

Streb, J., D. Lema, and G. Torrens. 2009. "Checks and Balances on Political Budget Cycles: Cross-Country Evidence." *Kyklos* 62 (3): 425-46.

Stulz, R. 1990. "Managerial Discretion and Optimal Financing Policies." *Journal of Financial Economics* 26 (1): 3-27.

Sutherland, A. 1997. "Fiscal Crises and Aggregate Demand: Can High Public Debt Reverse the Effects of Fiscal Policy?" *Journal of Public Economics* 65 (2): 147-62.

Titman, S. 1984. "The Effect of Capital Structure on a Firm's Liquidation Decision." *Journal of Financial Economics* 13 (1): 137-51.

UNCTAD (United Nations Conference on Trade and Development). 2014. *World Investment Report 2014—Investing in the SDGs: An Action Plan.* Geneva: United Nations.

Vegh, C. A., D. Lederman, F. Bennett. 2017. *Leaning Against the Wind: Fiscal Policy in Latin America and the Caribbean in a Historical Perspective.* Washington, DC: World Bank.

Vorisek, D., and S. Yu. 2020. "Understanding the Cost of Achieving the Sustainable Development Goals." Policy Research Working Paper 9164, World Bank, Washington, DC.

Weidemaier, W. M. C., and A. Gelpern. 2014. "Injunctions in Sovereign Debt Litigation." *Yale Journal on Regulation* 31 (1): 189-218.

World Bank. 2015. *Global Economic Prospects Report: Having Fiscal Space and Using It.* January. Washington, DC: World Bank.

World Bank. 2018. *Global Economic Prospects: Broad-Based Upturn, but for How Long?* January. Washington, DC: World Bank.

World Bank and IMF (International Monetary Fund). 2001. *Developing Government Bond Markets: A Handbook.* Washington, DC: World Bank.

Wyplosz, C. 2019. "Olivier in Wonderland." Vox CEPR Policy Portal, June 17, 2019. https://voxeu.org/content/olivier-wonderland.

Yared, P. 2019. "Rising Government Debt: Causes and Solutions for a Decades-Old Trend." *Journal of Economic Perspectives* 33 (2): 115-40.

PART II

Waves of Debt

For the countries, it should be obvious that they are not now shielded from the effects of their bad decisions. They may receive temporary financial assistance, but they also inevitably go through a very difficult economic period before recovery takes hold. No country would opt to go through what Mexico went through, or what various Asian countries are going through now.

Robert Rubin (1998)
Former U.S. Secretary of the Treasury

CHAPTER 3
Global Waves of Debt: What Goes Up Must Come Down?

The buildup of debt in emerging market and developing economies since 1970 has not followed a linear path. In the past 50 years different countries and regions have experienced surges in debt, often followed by steep declines. Before the current wave of debt that began in 2010, emerging and developing economies experienced three waves of debt accumulation: 1970-89, 1990-2001, and 2002-09. Although each of these waves of debt had some unique features, they all shared the same fate: they ended with financial crises and major output losses.

Introduction

Total (domestic and external) debt of public and private nonfinancial sectors in emerging market and developing economies (EMDEs) has increased dramatically over the past half-century, rising from 47 percent of gross domestic product (GDP) in 1970 to about 170 percent in 2018. Government debt has risen from 26 percent to 50 percent, while private debt has increased sixfold (from 20 percent to roughly 120 percent) during this period. The trajectory of debt accumulation has not, however, been smooth. As documented in detail in chapter 5, individual countries have frequently undergone episodes of rapid debt accumulation by the public sector, the private sector, or both. These episodes sometimes ended in financial crises, which were followed by prolonged periods of deleveraging. Similarly, the characteristics of debt have changed over time, with the importance of external debt waxing and waning and the types of debt instruments used evolving.

Different EMDE regions and sectors have experienced diverse debt developments since 1970. In some regions, there have been waves of debt buildups during which many countries simultaneously saw sharp increases in debt, often followed by crises and steep declines in debt ratios. For example, government debt increased sharply in Latin America and the Caribbean (LAC) and Sub-Saharan Africa (SSA) in the 1970s and 1980s, peaked in the late 1980s in LAC and in the late 1990s in SSA, and subsequently fell. The East Asia and Pacific (EAP) region (excluding China) saw a buildup in private debt in the 1990s, which unwound from 1997 onward. Since the global financial crisis, the EAP region (this time mainly driven by China) has once again seen a rapid accumulation of private debt.

This chapter examines the evolution of debt in EMDEs and identifies "waves" of rising debt—periods in which the increase in debt has been substantial and broad-based across many countries in one or more regions. The construct of waves puts national and regional episodes of rapid debt buildup into a common context that takes into account global developments, provides a comparative perspective across waves, and facilitates a unified analysis of these episodes that takes into account the interaction of global drivers, such as global growth and financial market developments, with country-specific conditions.

The waves of rising debt in EMDEs identified by this study occurred in the periods 1970-89, 1990-2001, 2002-09, and the current period, beginning in 2010. The analysis begins in 1970 because of data limitations for earlier years. The dating of the waves is identified using basic criteria. The end of a wave is broadly defined as the year when the total debt-to-GDP ratio in the region or country group concerned peaks and is followed by two consecutive years of decline. The dating of the end of the waves is also approximately consistent with the timing of policies to resolve the financial crises that the waves engendered. In 1989, for example, Mexico issued the first Brady bonds, marking the beginning of the resolution of the Latin American debt crisis. In 1998-2001, a series of policy programs supported by the International Monetary Fund (IMF) led to debt resolution after the financial crises in East Asia and the Russian Federation. In 2009, many governments implemented large-scale, internationally coordinated policies of fiscal stimulus to combat the adverse effects of the global financial crisis.

In principle, waves could be overlapping (indeed, developments in low-income country [LIC] debt reached across all three historical waves). There are, however, visible surges followed by plateaus or declines in regional EMDE debt. The identification of the waves takes these turning points as convenient start and end points for the episodes.

Using the framework of waves of debt, this chapter answers the following questions in the context of the first three waves of debt buildup since 1970:

- How did the three historical waves of debt evolve?

- What were the similarities between the waves?

- How did the waves differ?

Contributions to the literature. This chapter provides the first in-depth analysis of the similarities and differences among the three historical waves of broad-based debt accumulation in EMDEs since 1970. Each wave contains episodes that have been widely examined in the literature but never put into a common framework (for example, the Latin American debt crisis and the East Asia debt crisis). Earlier work that has taken a long historical perspective has focused mainly on debt developments in advanced economies, typically based on case studies. As reviewed in chapter 2, for EMDEs, previous studies have often focused on certain periods of debt distress, crises in individual countries, or repeated occurrence of specific types of crises.[1] Other studies have analyzed the evolution of debt instruments over time.[2]

Main findings. First, the chapter examines the three waves of broad-based and substantial debt buildup by EMDEs before the current wave.

- The *first wave* spanned the 1970s and 1980s, with borrowing primarily accounted for by governments in LAC and LICs, especially LICs in SSA. The combination of low real interest rates in much of the 1970s and a rapidly growing syndicated loan market encouraged EMDE governments to borrow heavily. This debt buildup culminated in a series of crises in the early 1980s. Debt relief and restructuring were prolonged in this wave, ending with the introduction of the Brady plan in the late 1980s mostly for LAC countries, and debt relief in the form of the Heavily Indebted Poor Countries (HIPC) initiative and the Multilateral Debt Relief Initiative (MDRI) in the mid-1990s and early 2000s for LICs, chiefly in SSA.

- The *second wave* ran from 1990 until the early 2000s as financial and capital market liberalization enabled banks and corporations in EAP and governments in Europe and Central Asia (ECA) to borrow heavily; it ended with a series of crises in these regions in 1997-2001.

- The *third wave* was a runup in private sector borrowing in ECA from U.S.- and European Union-headquartered "mega-banks" after regulatory easing. This wave ended when the global financial crisis disrupted bank financing in 2008-09 and tipped several ECA economies into deep (albeit short-lived) recessions.

---

[1] For example, contagion from the Asian crisis has been examined by Baig and Goldfajn (1999); Chiodo and Owyang (2002); Claessens and Forbes (2013); Glick and Rose (1999); Kaminsky and Reinhart (2000, 2001); Kawai, Newfarmer, and Schmukler (2005); Moreno, Pasadilla, and Remolona (1998); and Sachs, Cooper, and Bosworth (1998). De Gregorio and Lee (2004) and Feldstein (2003) compare the crises in Latin America in the 1980s with those of East Asia in the 1990s. For specific types of crises, currency crises have been discussed in Dooley and Frankel (2003) and Edwards and Frankel (2002); Dalio (2018) considers sovereign debt crises.

[2] Some studies have discussed the evolution of financial instruments, for example, Altunbaş, Gadanecz, and Kara (2006) and Borensztein et al. (2004), or specific debt instruments, for example, Arnone and Presbitero (2010) for domestic debt in EMDEs; Cline (1995) for LAC's experience with syndicated loans and Brady bonds; and Eichengreen et al. (2019) for two millennia of government debt instruments.

Second, the chapter distills similarities among these three waves. They began during prolonged periods of low real interest rates and were facilitated by financial innovations and changes in financial markets that encouraged borrowing. The waves ended with widespread financial crises and coincided with global recessions (1982, 1991, and 2009) or downturns (1998 and 2001). These crises were typically triggered by shocks that resulted in sharp increases in investor risk aversion, risk premiums, or borrowing costs, followed by sudden stops of capital inflows. These financial crises were generally costly and were usually followed by reforms designed to lower financial vulnerabilities and strengthen policy frameworks. In some EMDEs, various combinations of inflation targeting, greater exchange rate flexibility, and fiscal rules were introduced, and financial sector supervision was strengthened.

Third, the chapter points to important differences among the three completed waves. The financial instruments used for borrowing have evolved as new instruments or financial actors have emerged. The nature of EMDE borrowers in international financial markets has changed, with the private sector accounting for a growing share of debt accumulation through the three waves. The severity of the economic damage done by the financial crises that ended the waves varied among them, and across regions. Output losses were particularly large in the wake of the first wave, when most debt accumulation had been by government sectors.

This chapter proceeds as follows: The first three sections examine the three historical waves in detail, following a consistent framework—each section begins with a discussion of the financial market changes that facilitated borrowing and continues with a deep dive into the features of each wave, such as macroeconomic and debt developments, the financial crises, and subsequent debt restructuring. Each section then examines reforms to regulatory policies and macroeconomic policy frameworks in response to the crises in each wave. The subsequent two sections compare the three waves and identify commonalities and differences among them. The chapter concludes with a brief summary.

The first wave, 1970-89: Crises in Latin America and low-income countries

The first wave spanned the 1970s and 1980s as EMDE governments in LAC and LICs, predominantly LICs in SSA, borrowed heavily from commercial banks in syndicated loan markets. In LAC, the debt buildup resulted in a crisis that coincided with the global recession of 1982 and was marked by widespread debt distress among borrowers in the region. Attempts at resolving the debt crisis were, at first, ineffective. The Brady plan, and issuance of Brady bonds in 1989-90, eventually began the process of effective resolutions.

In LICs, especially in SSA, levels of debt were much lower in nominal terms than in LAC, although they became very high relative to GDP over the same period. Many of these countries also experienced financial difficulty and faced sovereign debt crises in the 1980s; however, debt relief was provided only in the late 1990s to early 2000s under the HIPC initiative and the MDRI, with debt-to-GDP ratios peaking in the mid-1990s at more than 100 percent.

Financial market developments: Rise of the syndicated loan market

Limited availability of debt financing before 1970. In the aftermath of World War II, EMDEs (many of which had only recently gained independence from colonial governments) generally did not have access to foreign private sector creditors. Debt flows were largely accounted for by intergovernmental loans and multilateral institutions (Eichengreen et al. 2019).[3] Total debt levels were relatively low, with borrowing mainly by the public sector. The World Bank began lending to non-European countries in the late 1940s, starting with a $13.5 million loan to Chile in 1948 for a hydroelectric power generation project (World Bank 2016). This period also saw the creation of the International Finance Corporation in 1956 to stimulate private sector lending to EMDEs and of the International Development Association in 1960 to provide concessional lending to lower-income countries unable to access finance because of their high credit risk, although total amounts were relatively modest.[4]

Rise of syndicated loans. The structure and size of EMDE debt markets changed dramatically in the 1970s with the development of the syndicated loan market. Under a syndicated loan, a group of banks would lend to a single borrower, sharing the associated risk (Gadanecz 2004). Although initially developed in Europe to help fund corporations, syndicated loans

---

[3] Access to debt markets for EMDEs had largely ended with the Latin American debt crises of the 1930s (Eichengreen et al. 2019).

[4] By early 1960, most advanced economies had established their own development agencies—for example, the U.S. Agency for International Development in the United States—partly to counterbalance the influence of the Soviet Union in newly independent states in Africa and Asia (Lancaster 2007).

proved to be an effective way to lend to large borrowers, including sovereigns.[5] The syndicated loan market for sovereign borrowers was dominated by U.S. banks, which saw the market as an opportunity to offset declining domestic loan demand in the 1970s—lending to large U.S. corporates had fallen as they increasingly accessed the commercial paper market (FDIC 1997). The syndicated loan market expanded dramatically, with new issuance rising from $7 billion in 1972 to $133 billion in 1981. Loans were typically offered at variable interest rates pegged to the three- or six-month London Interbank Offered Rate, which proved to be a critical vulnerability when global interest rates increased sharply in the late 1970s (Bertola and Ocampo 2012).

Recycling petrodollars. The syndicated loan market was also boosted by the oil price shocks of the 1970s, which led to large global current account imbalances, with substantial surpluses in oil-exporting countries and corresponding deficits in importers, including EMDEs. Syndicated loans provided a way for the oil exporters' surpluses to be "recycled" to finance the importers' deficits (Altunbaş, Gadanecz, and Kara 2006). The growth in lending was also spurred by real low interest rates. Nominal U.S. policy rates averaged about 7 percent between 1970-79, but real rates were much lower, and even negative in several years, as a result of high inflation.

The combination of low interest rates and substantial liquidity provided strong incentives for EMDEs to borrow heavily (Devlin 1990). Although many EMDEs borrowed externally in the 1970s, the buildup in debt was greatest in LAC, which accounted for over half of all debt flows to EMDEs in 1973-81 and formed the center of the subsequent debt crises (Bertola and Ocampo 2012). Some SSA countries were also affected by these developments, with countries including Liberia, Nigeria, Senegal, and Zambia also making use of the syndicated loan market (Krumm 1985). External debt-to-GDP ratios in LICs rose, on average, from 13 percent in 1970 to 46 percent in 1982.

The Latin American debt crisis

Precrisis developments. In the aftermath of the Second World War, most LAC economies adopted industrialization policies based on import

---

[5] Syndicated lending initially arose in Europe with the development of the Eurobond market, which allowed investors to access dollar bonds outside the United States and issuers to avoid U.S. listing and disclosure requirements. Eurodollar bonds were initially designed for corporates to fund subsidiaries (Chester 1991).

substitution (Bruton 1998).[6] This development strategy encouraged the domestic production of goods that were previously imported. In addition to protectionist policies, such as tariffs and exchange rate controls, many governments used external borrowing to finance projects, including infrastructure designed to support specific domestic industries and direct investment in heavy industries (Baer 1972; Bruton 1998; Diaz-Alejandro, Krugman, and Sachs 1984).

As discussed in chapter 2, debt accumulation raises fewer concerns if it is used to finance investment that increases a country's potential output, and therefore its ability to repay loans in the future (World Bank 2017a). The import substitution strategy in LAC, however, focused on establishing domestic manufacturing industries to meet domestic demand, with little consideration for comparative advantage. There was little focus on promoting exports, with protectionist measures acting as a constraint on export growth—in sharp contrast with other EMDEs, notably in EAP, which employed active export promotion policies (Balassa 1982; Sachs 1985). Despite a large increase in the share of manufacturing in GDP among LAC countries, they had only a modest increase in the share of manufactures in total exports, with primary commodities continuing to account for the bulk of exports.

Import protection and the lack of access to external markets meant that domestic industries were not exposed to international competition and were also unable to benefit from economies of scale, which was a particular issue for industries with high fixed costs, such as steel, which typically suffered from underutilization (Scitovsky 1969). Together, these factors meant that rising investment (and debt) did not translate into higher potential growth and, crucially, higher exports. As such, external debt became increasingly unsustainable in LAC (Catão 2002).

Growing debt, robust growth. In the 1970s, borrowing from abroad started to pick up in several LAC countries as the syndicated loan market increased the availability of lending at low rates of interest.[7] GDP in LAC grew rapidly

---

[6] The import substitution strategy was a response to the Prebisch-Singer hypothesis that primary resource-exporting countries would face a terminal decline in their terms of trade against advanced economies exporting manufactures (Prebisch 1950; Singer 1950). For an early review of industrialization policies involving import substitution in LAC, see Baer (1972). Rodrik (2000) presents an alternative perspective that emphasizes the role of macroeconomic mismanagement (rather than import substitution) in financial crises in LAC.

[7] Advanced economies experienced negative real interest rates for most of the 1970s. The sharp increase in world oil prices triggered a global recession in 1975 with a substantial pickup in inflation and a significant weakening of growth in a number of countries. This recession marked the beginning of a half-decade of stagflation in many advanced economies (Kose, Sugawara, and Terrones 2020).

in the decade, by 6 percent per year on average, and the level of GDP per capita rose by 50 percent between 1970 and 1980 (figure 3.1). In some LAC countries, governments borrowed to fund public investment, which was reflected in both growing fiscal deficits and a rising share of public investment in GDP. As indicated previously, much of the borrowing financed less productive uses; some was also used to finance government current spending, such as higher public sector wages.

External borrowing, particularly by the public sector, accelerated after the first oil price shock of 1973. Fiscal deficits steadily deteriorated over the next few years, particularly in Mexico. Current account deficits also widened in several countries, partly as a result of higher oil prices, with the median deficit increasing from 1.9 percent of GDP in 1970 to 7.0 percent of GDP in 1981. External debt-to-GDP ratios rose from 23 to 43 percent of GDP between 1975 and 1982, and the share of external debt accounted for by short-term debt rose to about one-fifth (figure 3.2). The rise in external debt varied among LAC countries, with the largest increases in Argentina, Mexico, and República Bolivariana de Venezuela. The increase in external debt was primarily accounted for by the public sector, with its share rising to almost 80 percent of total debt by the early 1980s, from 60 percent in 1970. The importance of the syndicated loan market in funding this increase in sovereign borrowing was reflected in the composition of creditors to LAC: the share of external debt owed to private sector banks increased from 42 percent in 1970 to 75 percent in 1982, with a commensurate fall in funding from the official sector.

Deteriorating debt dynamics. In 1979, a second spike in oil prices followed the Iranian revolution, with prices more than doubling from $17 per barrel at the start of the year to $40 per barrel by the end. The rise in prices resulted in weaker growth and a spike in inflation in oil-importing economies. In response to rising domestic inflation, the U.S. Federal Reserve under chairman Paul Volcker raised the federal funds rate from 11 percent in 1979 to a high of 20 percent in June 1980. The associated sharp jump in global interest rates was rapidly transmitted to the cost of borrowing for LAC countries, given their reliance on variable-rate debt, which accounted for more than half of total debt in 1982.

Interest payments on external debt by LAC countries rose sharply, from an average of 1.6 percent of GDP in 1975-79 to 5 percent of GDP by 1982, and interest payments jumped from 15 percent of exports to 33 percent of exports during the same period. The difficulty of LAC countries in servicing their debt was exacerbated by the subsequent slowdown in global growth, because it led to falling commodity prices and weaker demand for exports,

FIGURE 3.1 **The first wave: Crisis in Latin America and the Caribbean**

The 1970s represented a period of rapid growth for many LAC countries, but vulnerabilities were increasing, with large current account and fiscal deficits. Toward the end of the decade, a spike in oil prices and, especially, a rise in global interest rates resulted in substantial pressure on LAC economies. Many economies experienced currency crises and were forced to repeatedly devalue their currencies, with some seeing episodes of hyperinflation in later years.

A. LAC: Growth

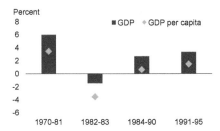

B. LAC: Current account balance

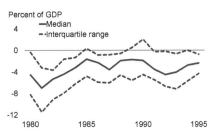

C. Central government fiscal balance in selected countries

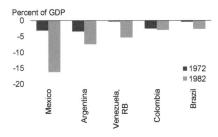

D. Commodity prices

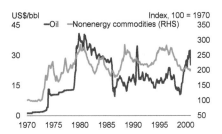

E. Exchange rates

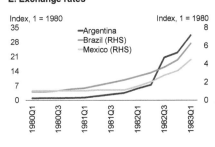

F. Inflation rates

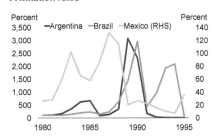

Sources: Haver Analytics; International Monetary Fund; World Bank.
Note: bbl = barrel; LAC = Latin America and the Caribbean.
A. GDP weighted average across 32 LAC countries.
B. Dashed blue lines denote the interquartile range; solid blue line is the median. Sample includes 31 LAC economies.
D. Nominal U.S. dollar prices.
E. Defined as local currency per U.S. dollar. An increase is consistent with a depreciation in the currency.
F. Annual average inflation.

FIGURE 3.2 **The first wave: Debt developments in LAC**

Debt levels in LAC rose during the 1970s, driven by external debt. The growing popularity of syndicated loans resulted in a sharp rise in borrowing from overseas private sector banks. Interest payments relative to GDP and to exports rose rapidly in the buildup to the crisis, whereas international reserve levels fell sharply in several economies amid sustained currency pressures.

A. LAC: Total external debt

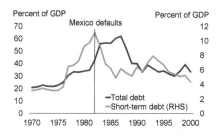

B. LAC: Long-term external debt, by sector

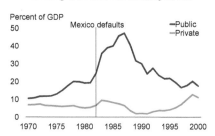

C. External debt in selected countries

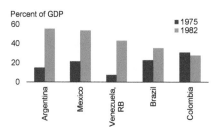

D. LAC: External debt, by creditor

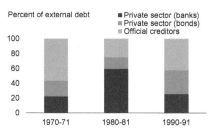

E. LAC: Interest payments on external debt

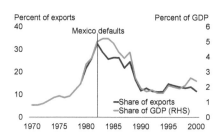

F. Foreign exchange reserves in selected economies

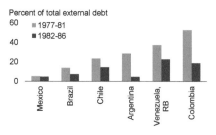

Source: World Bank.
Note: LAC = Latin America and the Caribbean.
A.B.D.E. Sample includes 24 economies.
A. External debt classed as "short-term" when maturities are less than 12 months.
B. "Long-term" external debt has maturity of more than 12 months.
D. Long-term debt only. Private sector (bonds) includes "other" private sector lending.

which resulted in deteriorating terms of trade for LAC countries. Most advanced economies experienced a recession in the early 1980s, with the United States experiencing a double-dip recession in 1980 and 1982.[8]

In addition, interest payments became increasingly difficult to service given the large share of short-term debt that needed to be rolled over at rising interest rates. Debt service payments averaged about 150 percent of exports in 1980-83, ranging from 118 percent in Peru to 215 percent in Argentina (Sachs 1985). As debt levels became increasingly unsustainable, the availability of credit began to dry up, and countries found it more difficult to roll over debt.

Crisis in Latin America. The Latin American debt crisis began in 1982 when Mexico announced that it would not be able to service its debts. The crisis spread rapidly to other LAC countries, and also to EMDEs outside the region, including Algeria, Niger, and Nigeria. In total, 40 countries fell into arrears on their debt payments, and of the 27 that had to restructure their debts, 16 were in LAC (FDIC 1997).

The crisis was compounded by exchange rate arrangements in LAC, with most countries' currencies pegged to a generally appreciating U.S. dollar. Currencies became significantly overvalued as countries maintained their pegs in attempt to control inflation (Diaz-Alejandro, Krugman, and Sachs 1984). Such overvaluation contributed to large-scale capital flight, with Argentina, Mexico, and República Bolivariana de Venezuela collectively experiencing capital flight of $60 billion, equivalent to 67 percent of their gross capital inflows (World Bank 1985). Most countries in LAC experienced downward pressure on their currencies and were forced to defend their currency pegs with currency reserves. Reserve levels proved insufficient, however, and many countries had to sharply devalue their currencies. Between 1981 and 1983, Argentina devalued its currency by two-fifths, Brazil by one-fifth, and Mexico by one-third against the U.S. dollar.

Debt resolution

Baker plan and rescheduling. The Paris Club group of economies initially viewed the debt distress in Latin America as a liquidity problem, rather than

---

[8] The global economy experienced a recession in 1982 that was triggered by several developments, including the second oil price shock, the tightening of monetary policies in advanced economies, and the Latin American debt crisis (Kose and Terrones 2015). The sharp rise in oil prices helped push inflation to new highs in several advanced economies, and in response, monetary policies were tightened significantly, causing sharp declines in activity and significant increases in unemployment in many advanced economies in the early 1980s.

a solvency issue.[9] They therefore responded by rescheduling debt payments (conditional on an IMF-supported policy program) and by attempting to encourage new loans from commercial banks. When this approach proved unsuccessful, it was followed in 1985 by the Baker plan, which again emphasized new lending, conditional on market-oriented reforms designed to return countries to growth. The Baker plan also failed, in part because it was unable to encourage additional lending from the private sector (the share of private lenders in total external financing fell sharply, from 78 percent in 1980-81 to 56 percent in 1990-91) but also because it did not recognize that countries were, in fact, insolvent.

The counterpart to a falling share of private lenders was a rising share of debt owed to the official sector, with new loans often being used to clear arrears on private sector debt (Sachs 1989). The increase in debt owed to the official sector was accounted for largely by the Paris Club group of creditor countries, and, to a lesser extent, by multilateral institutions (Dicks 1991).[10] The prolonged period of debt rescheduling in part reflected an aversion by advanced economies, particularly the United States, to accept outright debt defaults (Dooley 1994). Policy makers in the United States were worried about the solvency of U.S. banks, given their large exposure to LAC: the nine largest money-center banks in the United States held LAC debt equal to 176 percent of their capital (Sachs 1988; Sachs and Huizinga 1987).[11] An official debt restructuring, with its associated haircuts, would have forced banks to realize losses on their investments, which could have resulted in a wave of insolvencies among U.S. banks.

Brady bonds and debt forgiveness. In 1989, the U.S. administration launched the Brady plan as a way of finally resolving the Latin American debt crisis by providing debt relief via the securitization and restructuring of existing loans into bonds. The plan reflected a shift from the previously prevailing view that debtors should pay what they owed, to an acceptance that debtors should pay what they could afford. In part, this shift reflected the problem that a "debt overhang"—high levels of unserviceable debt—would discourage investment and constrain economic growth. Thus, debt

---

[9] The Paris Club is an informal group of creditor governments originally set up by governments belonging to the Development Assistance Committee of the Organisation for Economic Co-operation and Development, with the purpose of finding solutions for countries facing debt difficulties, typically lower-income countries.

[10] The multilateral institutions had preferred creditor status and did not allow rescheduling or debt relief on their loans.

[11] Money-center banks typically rely on nondeposit funding and lend to sovereigns, corporates, and other banks, as opposed to households.

relief could be beneficial for creditors as well as debtors, because it could boost growth prospects and reduce the ultimate loss for investors (Goldberg and Spiegel 1992). In addition, the seven years that had elapsed since the start of the crisis had provided time for U.S. banks to build up capital and loan-loss provisions, reducing solvency concerns (FDIC 1997).

Mexico was the first country to agree to a Brady plan, in 1989. The scheme was voluntary and gave creditors three options: existing loans could be swapped for 30-year "debt reduction bonds," with a 35 percent haircut and an interest rate slightly above the London Interbank Offered Rate; loans could be swapped for 30-year bonds at full value, but with a substantially below-market interest rate; or banks could provide new loans equal to 25 percent of their existing exposure over three years (Cline 1995).

The three options allowed creditor banks to set their exposure to Mexico at anywhere between 65 and 125 percent of their pre-Brady level (Unal, Demirgüç-Kunt, and Leung 1993). In exchange for receiving debt relief, Mexico was to purchase U.S. Treasury securities, with substantial financial assistance from international financial institutions including the IMF and World Bank, in order to collateralize both the principal and interest of the new bonds. These bonds became known as "Brady bonds." Of the about 500 creditor banks to Mexico, 49 percent took the first option of outright debt relief, 41 percent took the second option with full value but lower interest rates, and 10 percent chose the third option of new lending (Vasquez 1996). Of Mexico's $47 billion of eligible debt, just over $14 billion was forgiven, providing debt relief of about 30 percent.

The Mexico debt restructuring set the stage for other countries to negotiate Brady plans, with the largest for Brazil ($50 billion of eligible debt), Argentina ($29 billion), and República Bolivariana de Venezuela ($19 billion). By 1994, 18 countries had agreed to their own (similar) versions of Brady plans, which represented about $190 billion in debt and resulted in debt forgiveness of $60 billion—a reduction in face value of just over one-third.[12] The market-oriented nature of the Brady plan helped boost confidence among international creditors and facilitated a rapid return to capital markets by the affected countries (Cline 1995; Dooley, Fernandez-Arias, and Kletzer 1996).

---

[12] Although economies in LAC accounted for the majority of Brady plan participants, other countries,, such as Nigeria, the Philippines, and Poland, also issued Brady bonds—these countries had also experienced sovereign debt crises during the early 1980s (World Bank 2004).

Macroeconomic implications of the LAC crisis: A lost decade. The debt crisis had severe economic consequences for LAC, resulting in a "lost decade" of growth, after which GDP per capita recovered to its precrisis level only in 1993. During the crisis years of 1982-83, per capita GDP in LAC fell by an average of 3.1 percent per year. The crisis resulted in sharp currency depreciations, which exacerbated the deterioration in debt-to-GDP ratios, because most debt was denominated in U.S. dollars. Depreciations also triggered episodes of high or hyperinflation in a number of countries (Sachs 1985). The currency crises and associated reductions in capital inflows required countries to reduce current account deficits, and the median deficit narrowed from 7.0 percent of GDP in 1981 to 1.7 of GDP by 1985. These reductions were achieved, however, by import compression resulting from sharp contractions in domestic demand, especially investment, which had major adverse effects on future growth.

In the subsequent period until the granting of debt relief (1984-90), per capita GDP growth recovered, but at a subdued pace of 0.6 percent per year, on average. Growth strengthened further following debt relief but remained well below its precrisis rates. Investment ratios fell in the most affected countries and remained subdued even after the crisis.

An example of resilience: Colombia. Colombia was the least affected Latin American country during the region's crisis, avoiding a sovereign debt crisis and restructuring (Laeven and Valencia 2018). Colombia's resilience was due to stronger macroeconomic fundamentals and better debt dynamics relative to those of its peers (Bagley 1987). In the years before the crisis, Colombia had large fiscal and trade surpluses, reduced its external debt from 31 percent of GDP in 1975 to 22 percent in 1980, and accumulated the largest foreign exchange reserves, relative to debt, among the main LAC countries. These factors allowed Colombia to weather the crisis well, despite contagion in the form of reduced availability of external finance and currency depreciation.

Policy changes

Major shift in economic policy consensus. The crisis in Latin America prompted a shift in economic policy away from import substitution toward programs of adjustment and market-orientated reforms supported by the IMF and World Bank, described by one observer as being in line with a "Washington Consensus" (Williamson 1990). These programs were designed to achieve macroeconomic stability and external viability and to boost output and export growth; they generally included fiscal discipline, competitive exchange rates, privatization of state-owned enterprises, financial liberalization, and economic deregulation, including the liberalization of trade and inward direct investment (Williamson 2000). Generally, a program of adjustment and reform was required to qualify for financial assistance from international financial institutions and debt relief from the Paris Club.

As a result, many LAC countries liberalized current and capital accounts and strengthened their policy frameworks in the mid-1980s and 1990s (Catão 2002). There was also a substantial shift toward central bank independence: Chile was the first country to implement legislation designed to greatly enhance central bank independence in 1989 and was shortly followed by many other LAC countries (Cukierman, Webb, and Neyapti 1992; Jácome and Vázquez 2008). Central bank independence was introduced in part to restrict monetary financing of fiscal deficits (Carrière-Swallow et al. 2016). Central banks initially aimed to reduce inflation by targeting the exchange rate via crawling pegs. Over time, they gradually adopted flexible exchange rates and inflation targeting mandates.

Some countries in LAC made substantial improvements to their external positions, with a doubling in reserves relative to short-term external debt across the region as a whole between 1981 and 1991. External debt stocks fell from a high of 62 percent of GDP in 1986 to 30 percent in 1997. Current account balances also improved—among the 10 largest economies in the region, current account balances improved by 6 percentage points of GDP between 1982 and 1990.

Low-income country debt crisis and relief

Prolonged debt buildup. Many LICs, particularly in SSA, also borrowed heavily in the 1970s and 1980s. External debt rose from 13 percent of GDP in 1970 to 46 percent in 1982, primarily accounted for by the public sector (figure 3.3).[13] LICs generally had limited access to private sector lending and relied instead on direct bilateral loans from other governments and their export credit agencies, or private loans that were backed by an export credit agency (Daseking and Powell 1999). Several countries, however, were able to access the syndicated loan market, which contributed to the share of multilateral and bilateral debt in LIC external debt falling from 82 percent in 1970 to 74 percent in 1979.

---

[13] Throughout this section, "LICs" refers to countries with a GNI per capita of $1,005 or less in 2016. From 1987, the World Bank provides income classifications, including for LICs and lower-middle-income countries (LMICs). For previous years, the term LICs is used as in Daseking and Powell (1999).

FIGURE 3.3 **The first wave: Debt developments in LICs**

The debt-to-GDP ratio in LICs rose steadily from the 1970s to the early 1990s. The share of debt held by the official sector rose, whereas that of the private sector shrank. As debt levels and interest payments became unsustainable, many LICs fell into arrears and requested rescheduling. Per capita growth in LICs was negative for many years before debt relief in the late 1990s.

A. LICs: Total external debt

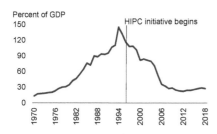

B. LICs: Government debt, by creditor

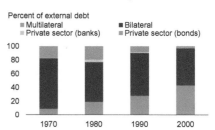

C. LICs: Interest payments on external debt

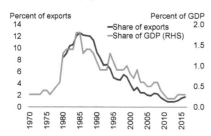

D. Cumulative debt relief in LICs

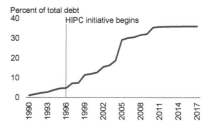

E. LICs: Growth

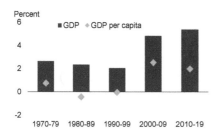

F. LICs: Total investment

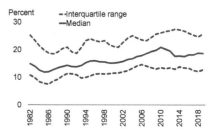

Sources: International Monetary Fund; World Bank
Note: LICs = low-income countries.
A.-C. Sample includes 29 LICs, defined as countries with a gross national income per capita of $1,005 or less in 2016.
B. Long-term debt only. Private sector (bonds) includes "other" private sector lending.
D. Cumulative debt relief since 1990, as a share of total debt in 1996, when the Heavily Indebted Poor Countries (HIPC) initiative began.
E.F. Sample includes 25 countries.

LIC governments initiated externally financed projects in the hope that these would spur growth. But as with LAC countries, debt was often used to finance investment in uncompetitive domestic manufacturing, investment in infrastructure of questionable value, and expansion of current spending, rather than to finance productive expenditures that could boost exports or potential output (Greene 1989). Thus, projects financed by debt were often unproductive or economically unviable (Krumm 1985). Debt burdens in several countries in this period were also exacerbated by conflict and civil strife (Cameroon, Democratic Republic of Congo, and Zambia; IMF 1998).

Unsustainable debt levels. Facing many of the same challenges as LAC countries, including rising interest rates and deteriorating terms of trade, LICs found it increasingly difficult in the 1980s to service their debt obligations, with many falling into arrears. Countries that had borrowed on the syndicated loan market at variable rates were particularly affected (Democratic Republic of Congo, Côte d'Ivoire, Malawi, Niger, Senegal, and Zambia; IMF 1998).

Whereas the Latin American crisis was eventually resolved via debt forgiveness and restructuring, the resolution of debt crises in LICs was even more prolonged, with durations of default averaging 13 years and in several cases significantly longer. Multilateral organizations, including the IMF and World Bank, provided financial support for adjustment and reform programs, while the Paris Club official creditors agreed to "flow rescheduling," under which delays in debt principal and interest payments were allowed during the period of an IMF program.

Despite helping with liquidity issues, these policies resulted in a further steady increase in debt stocks: Average debt of LICs exceeded 100 percent of GDP by 1994 (Daseking and Powell 1999). Many countries had repeated reschedulings in this period, with the average LIC country agreeing to four reschedulings of debt with the Paris Club between 1980 and 1996, highlighting the failure of this approach to provide lasting resolution to the debt issue (Callaghy 2002). New loans from official creditors were often used to pay interest on loans to private creditors, so that by 1996 the share of external LIC debt owed to the private sector had fallen below 10 percent (Easterly 2002; Sachs 1989).

Debt resolution: HIPC initiative and MDRI. In response to the worsening debt crisis in LICs, creditors gradually acknowledged that the debt owed by many of those countries was unlikely to be repaid, and the discussion moved to debt relief (Sachs 1986). Reducing the burden of debt to sustainable levels would free fiscal resources for socially beneficial spending, improve growth and investment prospects, and enable LICs to return to solvency (Sachs 2002). The Paris Club actively shifted from debt rescheduling to partial debt forgiveness with the "Toronto" and "Naples" menus of debt resolution options agreed in 1988 and 1994 (Easterly 2002). A major development was the announcement by the IMF and World Bank, together with other multilateral and bilateral creditors, of the HIPC initiative in 1996, which aimed to provide comprehensive debt relief to LICs by bringing debt down to "sustainable" levels (defined by the IMF and World Bank).

Under the scheme, countries would adhere to a set of economic policies and reforms agreed with the IMF and World Bank for a period of six years, at the end of which countries would be eligible for debt relief from multilateral institutions, official creditors, and commercial creditors. Debt relief by multilaterals represented a significant change from the previous policy that debt owed to these institutions was nonreschedulable given their preferred creditor status (Cosio-Pascal 2008). Progress under the HIPC initiative was very slow, however, and not all highly indebted countries were eligible to join: only 7 of the 39 HIPCs were participating in the program after three years (Callaghy 2002).

In response to these concerns, the enhanced HIPC initiative, launched in 1999, was designed to provide faster access to debt relief for countries. The program also had substantial conditionality, in particular a greater focus on poverty reduction, with countries required to spend fiscal savings from debt relief on increases in poverty-reducing programs, such as health and education. The enhanced HIPC was followed in 2005 by the MDRI, which provided further resources for debt forgiveness, particularly for countries with per capita annual income below $380. Only debt held by the multilateral institutions was reduced under this program, with potential debt relief of up to 100 percent on eligible debt (IMF 2006).

A total of 36 countries were granted debt relief under the HIPC initiative and the MDRI between 1996 and 2015, which helped reduce the median public debt-to-GDP ratio among LICs from close to 100 percent of GDP in the early 2000s to a trough of just over 30 percent of GDP in 2013 (table D.1 in appendix D).[14] The total cost of the HIPC program to date has been $76.9 billion, of which $14.9 was provided by the International Development Association, $4.6 billion by the IMF, $22 billion by Paris

---

[14] Eritrea, Somalia, and Sudan are potentially eligible for debt relief but have not yet started the process.

Club official creditors, and the remainder by other multilateral creditors (World Bank 2017b). Debt relief under the MDRI has totaled $42.4 billion, of which $28.9 billion was provided by the International Development Association.

Macroeconomic developments: Anemic growth, followed by rebound. Although GDP growth was robust in the 1970s, it was persistently weak in the subsequent two decades, averaging just 2.2 percent between 1980 and 1999. GDP per capita fell over this period, by 0.2 percent per year, amid rapid population growth. In addition, the ratio of investment to GDP remained low, despite rising debt, and countries ran persistent fiscal and current account deficits. Weak growth may in part have reflected the fact that high debt "overhangs" inhibited investment and growth (Krugman 1988; Sachs 1988). Moreover, heavy official inflows—direct grants or loans—may have contributed to Dutch disease in LICs, in that these inflows encouraged currency overvaluations and undermined export competitiveness, thus damaging longer-term growth (Nkusu 2004; Rajan and Subramanian 2011).

In the decade after debt relief, growth rebounded, investment and social spending rose, and the number of LICs halved. GDP per capita growth in the LICs of 2001 averaged 2.9 percent a year between 2001 and 2011. Almost half of LICs in 2001 had graduated to middle-income country status by 2017, and about one-third of these had received debt relief (World Bank 2019a). Poverty-related expenditure in the HIPC program countries— primarily spending on health care and education—rose by 1.5 percentage points of GDP (cumulatively) between 2001 and 2015 (World Bank 2017b). Besides debt relief, other factors contributed to these developments, including robust global growth in the period before the global financial crisis, the prolonged commodity price boom over the 2000s, and a reduction in conflict and violence in LICs (Essl et al. 2019).

The second wave, 1990-2001: The East Asian financial crisis and its aftermath

Another wave of debt growth began in the early 1990s. This wave was notably different from the first, with private sector debt accumulation playing a greater role. Policy changes affecting financial markets in the 1990s led to a surge in capital flows to EMDEs. Corporates in the EAP region, and sovereigns in ECA (and, to some extent, in LAC), accumulated substantial amounts of short-term, external debt. A decline in global interest rates after the slowdown in advanced economy growth in 1990-91 also encouraged capital flows to EMDEs.[15] Following a currency crisis in Mexico in 1994, however, contagion spread to some other LAC economies and EMDEs in other regions. In 1997, a sudden stop and reversal of capital flows triggered the East Asian financial crisis, concentrated in the private sector, which ushered in the global downturn of 1998.[16] The crisis also spilled over to other countries, including Argentina, Russia, and Turkey, in the late 1990s and early 2000s (Calvo and Mendoza 2000a, 2000b; Edwards 2000).

Financial market developments: Surging capital inflows

Surging capital inflows. Policies of financial market liberalization and more open capital accounts in several advanced economies in the 1980s and 1990s contributed to a surge in capital flows to EMDEs. Deregulation of banking and securities markets, including in the United Kingdom and the United States, led to substantial consolidation in the banking sector and a shift toward larger banks, with increased international operations, and to an expansion in international finance. These changes, together with financial market and capital account liberalization in EMDEs, particularly the EAP region in the late 1980s and early 1990s, facilitated significant increases in capital flows from advanced economies to EMDEs (Sachs, Cooper, and Bosworth 1998; Schmukler and Kaminsky 2003).

Net capital flows to EMDEs were close to zero in 1989-90 but rose rapidly and averaged 3.3 percent of EMDE GDP between 1991 and 1997. Although about one-third of the capital inflows were foreign direct investment, most were portfolio and other flows, with a large proportion accounted for by debt, often at short maturities. Between 1988 and 1996, the total stock of external debt in EMDEs grew at an average rate of 7 percent per year, while short-term debt grew by 12 percent per year, and the share of short-term debt rose from 12 to 18 percent of total debt.

Emergence of EMDE sovereign bond markets. The 1990s also saw changes in debt markets, with a growing importance of sovereign bonds. The

---

[15] The global economy experienced a recession in 1991 because of a confluence of factors: a sharp increase in oil prices due to the Gulf War; high inflation and output contractions in many transition economies in Central and Eastern Europe; weakness in credit and housing markets in the United States; severe banking crises in Scandinavian countries; recession and a prolonged period of low growth and near-zero inflation in Japan following the bursting of an asset price bubble; and instability in the European Monetary System's exchange rate mechanism in the European Union (Kose and Terrones 2015).

[16] Private sector debt crises relate to the stance of the balance sheet of corporates affected by both the types and quantity of assets and liabilities. Crises can be triggered by changes in the price of assets relative to debt, through asset or credit bubbles, or through balance sheet mismatches in maturity or currency (Calvo, Izquierdo, and Mejía 2004; Claessens et al. 2014).

conversion of syndicated loans into securitized bonds under the Brady plan of the late 1980s put an end to the dominance of foreign banks in external financing of EMDE governments and helped encourage secondary market activity in EMDE debt. When EMDE sovereigns reentered international credit markets in the 1990s, they did so mainly through bond markets. Bond issuance was increasingly used for general budget financing purposes rather than specific projects. New debt issuance gradually extended maturities and moved from floating-rate to fixed-rate instruments (Borensztein et al. 2004). These developments led to a broadening of the investor base in sovereign debt and contributed to a deepening of financial markets in some EMDEs.

Several factors supported a rapid expansion of the international market for EMDE bonds in the 1990s. By the end of the 1980s, the Eurobond market had become well established with an increasing presence of institutional investors and a liquid secondary market (Chester 1991). Most EMDEs found it difficult to return to syndicated bank loans following the Brady restructuring and turned instead to international bond markets instead. Slowing growth and falling interest rates in the United States in the late 1980s and early 1990s provided incentives for investors to search for higher yields, leading to increased demand for EMDE bonds from U.S. investors. Finally, the implementation of macroeconomic adjustment programs in debtor countries and the collateralized nature of Brady bonds helped build confidence in newly issued sovereign bonds (Eichengreen et al. 2019).

Currency crisis in Mexico

Capital flows reversal. Mexico experienced a currency crisis in 1994 and required assistance from the IMF and others, although it avoided a sovereign debt crisis (Laeven and Valencia 2018). Capital inflows soared after the Brady plan in 1989 and capital account liberalization in the following years. Economic growth recovered, and external debt stocks declined as a share of GDP. Interest payments also fell sharply. By early 1994, however, the economy was increasingly vulnerable, with a growing current account deficit (7 percent of GDP in 1994) and weak growth raising concerns about the international competitiveness of the peso and the fiscal outlook amid pro-cyclically increased spending in an election year. As the government sought to defend the peso, reserves dropped rapidly. In December, the central bank announced a devaluation of the peso of 15 percent.[17]

---

[17] For discussions of the evolution of the 1994 crisis in Mexico, see Boughton (2012), Calvo and Mendoza (1996), and Vegh and Vuletin (2014).

Rather than stabilizing the currency, however, the devaluation resulted in further capital flight, as foreign investors anticipated that the currency weakness would deepen. Pressure on the peso intensified, and stock prices plummeted. The government was unable to roll over dollar-denominated debt and was forced to issue peso debt and convert it into dollars, pushing the government close to default (Lustig 1995). Mexico abandoned its peg in late December 1994, allowing the currency to float, which was followed by a further 15 percent depreciation. GDP in Mexico fell by 6.2 percent in 1995, while inflation rose to 35 percent.

Resolution. A bailout package of about $50 billion was coordinated by the United States and the IMF in early 1995. The U.S. administration was concerned about the impact on its economy of the economic crisis in its neighbor, through reduced demand for U.S. products; political turmoil; and a potential rise in illegal immigration (Boughton 2012). The bailout package helped contain the crisis and avoided a sovereign debt crisis, but contagion still spread to other countries, notably elsewhere in Latin America. Brazil also experienced a sharp depreciation of its currency, and Argentina tipped into recession, although the impacts were smaller elsewhere. Mexico's recovery from the crisis was relatively fast, with per capita GDP returning to precrisis levels within three years (Kose, Meredith, and Towe 2004).

Financial crisis in East Asia

Precrisis buildup in debt. Whereas many EMDEs experienced debt buildups in the 1990s, the EAP region experienced some of the largest, with nominal external debt (primarily denominated in U.S. dollars) growing by 14 percent per year, on average, between 1989 and 1996 (figure 3.4). The buildup of debt was particularly large among the five countries that were subsequently at the center of the Asian financial crisis—Indonesia, the Republic of Korea, Malaysia, the Philippines, and Thailand.

Despite the speed of the increase in debt, the debt-to-GDP ratio for the region remained broadly flat as GDP also grew rapidly over this period, by 7.5 percent per year on average (World Bank 1993). The relatively flat total debt ratio also masked a sharp rise in private sector debt; government borrowing was contained by generally disciplined fiscal policies, with government debt typically under 30 percent of GDP.[18] Large inflows of short-term capital fueled domestic credit booms in EAP countries, with

---

[18] A notable exception to low levels of sovereign debt was the Philippines, which had public debt of 60 percent of GDP before the crisis.

FIGURE 3.4 **The second wave: Asian financial crisis**

Total external debt rose rapidly in EAP in the early to mid-1990s, particularly private sector debt, often at short maturities. During the 1997-98 crisis, currencies plummeted, inflation soared, and output collapsed. Economies with larger short-term debt, as well as smaller reserves, were most affected.

A. EAP: Growth in external debt

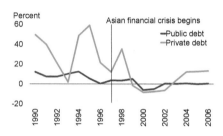

B. EAP: External debt, by sector

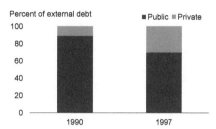

C. EAP: Per capita output growth

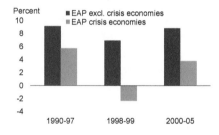

D. Exchange rate in select economies

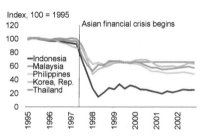

E. Inflation in select economies

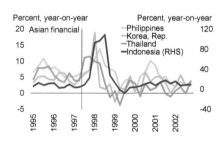

F. Reserves and short-term external debt in selected countries, 1995-96

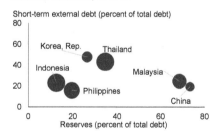

Sources: St Louis Federal Reserve; International Monetary Fund; World Bank.
Note: EAP = East Asia and Pacific.
A.B. Includes long-term external debt only.
C. GDP-weighted average. EAP excl. crisis countries contains 7 countries, EAP crisis countries include Indonesia, the Republic of Korea, Malaysia, the Philippines, and Thailand.
D. Local currency per U.S. dollar. Increase indicates a depreciation relative to the U.S. dollar.
E. Sample based on data availability. Annual average inflation.
F. Size of bubble indicates relative total external debt-to-GDP ratio. Data show average over 1995-96.

rising asset prices and increasing corporate leverage (Kawai, Newfarmer, and Schmukler 2005).

Private debt was primarily financed by commercial banks, with domestic corporations borrowing heavily from abroad, both directly from international lenders and indirectly from domestic financial institutions that in turn accessed international funding. Inadequate bank regulation and supervision, together with implicit government guarantees for banks, encouraged excessive risk taking by the domestic financial sector, allowing already highly leveraged corporates to borrow heavily (Mishkin 1999; Moreno, Pasadilla, and Remolana 1998).[19] The reliance on foreign funding by financial institutions and corporates was exacerbated by exchange rates pegged to the U.S. dollar, which encouraged underestimation of exchange risk.

The counterpart to short-term capital inflows was persistent and widening current account deficits, with the median deficit in EAP averaging about 5 percent of GDP between 1990 and 1996. Whereas capital inflows were used to finance productive investments that might yield export earnings, loans were also invested in nontradable sectors such as commercial real estate (especially in Thailand), and in some cases in inefficient manufacturing enterprises (Krugman 2000; Muchhala 2007). Weak corporate governance, including inadequate oversight of projects and investment decisions and declining profitability, also led to inefficient investment in several EAP countries (Capulong et al. 2000).

The East Asia debt crisis. By 1997, several EAP countries (Indonesia, Korea, Malaysia, the Philippines, and Thailand) had developed excessive reliance on short-term external borrowing and large current account deficits. These vulnerabilities had arisen as a result of several policy failings, including inadequate prudential regulation and supervision, implicit government guarantees for foreign borrowing (including pegged exchange rates), and structural changes in global financial markets. Even though fiscal positions were more soundly based in EAP, these developments made EAP countries increasingly vulnerable to sudden stops—adverse shifts in investor sentiment leading to reversals in capital flows.[20] EAP countries eventually suffered

---

[19] Absent regulation on capital requirements and other restrictions, the amount of risk that a bank undertakes will likely exceed what is socially optimal (Stiglitz 1972).

[20] Sudden stops, or balance of payment crises, closely linked to currency crises, are abrupt disruptions in access to external financing (Claessens et al. 2014). The models of sudden stops are linked to the latter models of currency crises in their focus on the currency and maturity mismatches on balance sheets (Calvo, Izquierdo, and Mejía 2004; Mendoza 2010). Many models of sudden stops link these to both domestic factors (or pull factors), such as mismatches on domestic banks' balance sheets, and international factors (or pull factors), such as global financing conditions (Forbes and Warnock 2012).

banking and currency crises in 1997-98 (Corsetti, Pesenti, and Roubini 1998; World Bank 1998).

Thailand was particularly susceptible, with one of the highest external debt ratios (63 percent of GDP in 1996) and persistently large current account deficits (8 percent of GDP in 1995-96). In late 1996 and early 1997, investor confidence in Thailand began to drop amid concerns over the sustainability of its external position and exchange rate against a backdrop of slowing export growth and a U.S. dollar that was appreciating against other major currencies, and capital inflows tapered off. The Thai baht came under significant pressure in February 1997, requiring government intervention to support the peg. By July 1997, however, the government was no longer able to support the currency and abandoned the peg, triggering the start of the Asian financial crisis.

The financial stress in Thailand quickly spread elsewhere, with large capital outflows leading to substantial currency pressures in Indonesia, Korea, Malaysia, and the Philippines (table D.2 in appendix D).[21] Despite substantial intervention by monetary authorities, these countries all experienced sharp currency depreciations (Kawai, Newfarmer, and Schmukler 2005). Corporates were unable to finance their foreign currency debt payments, resulting in large loan losses for banks and triggering banking crises.

Policy programs to resolve the crises were designed and implemented by the countries involved with the support of the IMF, other multilateral organizations, and partner countries. In the short term, tighter monetary policies with increased interest rates were central to efforts to stem and halt currency depreciations. Governments established frameworks to resolve systemic crises in both financial and corporate sectors, with policies including the creation of bad banks, bank recapitalization, and corporate debt restructuring (Mishkin 1999). Ultimately, 21 commercial banks were nationalized in the five affected countries during the crisis (Claessens, Djankov, and Klingebiel 1999; World Bank 1998). Corporate sector debt resolution was slow, however, and nonperforming loans remained elevated for several years after the crisis (Kawai 2002). EAP countries that were less reliant on short-term debt and had larger foreign exchange reserves—notably China, but also Singapore and Vietnam—were less affected.

---

[21] Contagion also spread, including to LAC and ECA. For discussions of contagion from the 1994 Mexican and 1997-98 Asian financial crises, see Calvo and Mendoza (2000a); Claessens and Forbes (2013); and Kim, Kose, and Plummer (2001).

Although the fiscal positions of the Asian crisis economies were generally sound as they entered the crisis, government debt rose sharply in the ensuing deep recessions as a result of automatic stabilizers and countercyclical support for demand, as well as support of banks and corporates in distress. Government debt rose by more than 30 percentage points of GDP in Indonesia and Thailand during the late 1990s. Although the Asian financial crisis did not lead to widespread sovereign debt crises as in LAC and SSA, several countries required official financial support during and after the crisis. IMF support included $23 billion for Indonesia, $58 billion for Korea, and $20 billion for Thailand (Fischer 1998; IMF 2000).

Macroeconomic developments. The sharp rise in external borrowing by EAP countries before the crisis was matched by rapid GDP growth, which averaged 7.4 percent a year in per capita terms (9 percent a year in aggregate) between 1988 and 1997. This growth was in contrast to the major advanced economies, which experienced growth slowdowns in the early 1990s with recessions in the United Kingdom and United States, among others. Investment-to-GDP ratios in EAP were also very high over this period. In some instances, however, corporates invested in commercial real estate and inefficient manufacturing, suggesting some of the investment went to projects with low rates of return (Krugman 2000). Although countries generally ran fiscal surpluses, current account deficits deteriorated as private sector financial imbalances widened.

During the crisis, GDP growth in EAP plummeted—per capita GDP growth slowed to 1.8 percent a year, on average, in 1998-99—and investment fell. GDP growth declined even more sharply in the five most affected countries. Large currency depreciations led to sharp spikes in inflation in several countries, although these proved short-lived. Growth quickly rebounded, however, and per capita GDP growth in EAP averaged 7.4 percent a year from 2000 to 2005, the same as its precrisis rate. Five years after the crisis, per capita GDP in the five most affected countries had risen 3 percent above precrisis (1996) levels—although this rise was less than half of the GDP per capita gains of the average EMDE over this period.

The plunge in growth in EAP in 1998 contributed to a broader downturn, with global GDP growth slowing from 4 percent in 1997 to 2.6 percent in 1998 (Kose, Sugawara, and Terrones 2020). Growth in advanced economies softened from 3.2 percent to 2.9 percent. The slowdown in global growth was short-lived, with a strong recovery in 1999-2000, although it weakened in the early 2000s as several advanced economies tipped into recession.

Policy changes. In the aftermath of the Asian financial crisis, the affected countries took actions to improve external positions and strengthen policy institutions and frameworks. Over the next decade, foreign exchange reserves as a share of total debt rose sixfold, from 41 percent at the end of 1997 to 253 percent at the end of 2007. Although this increase was largely accounted for by China, reserves also rose substantially in other EAP economies. Total external debt ratios more than halved, from 33 percent of GDP to 15 percent of GDP over the same period. Countries adopted more flexible exchange rate arrangements, and some introduced capital control measures. The EAP region more broadly moved toward independent monetary policy frameworks, and most countries implemented a range of expenditure and revenue management reforms to improve fiscal positions (World Bank 2017c). These reforms included the introduction of fiscal rules and ceilings on fiscal deficits, diversification of the tax base, and reductions in subsidies.

The Asian financial crisis also led to a reevaluation and growing criticism of the "Washington Consensus" (Williamson 2004). Without the necessary regulatory and oversight frameworks in place to assess and mitigate risks, financial market liberalization had allowed the buildup of vulnerabilities, which subsequently turned into crises (Rodrik 1998).[22] There was also increasing discussion after the crisis of the need for bankruptcy reform and bail-in of creditors, as opposed to the bailouts implemented during the crisis. In response, the World Bank, together with other international financial institutions, designed the Insolvency and Creditor Rights Standard to encourage best practices for evaluating and strengthening national insolvency and creditor rights systems (Leroy and Grandolini 2016).

Contagion and crises in other EMDEs

Contagion from the Asian financial crisis contributed to crises in other EMDEs, most notably Russia (1998), Argentina (2001), and Turkey (2001).[23] In contrast to the Asian crisis, these were predominately public debt crises and led to sovereign debt restructuring in Argentina and Russia. Other EMDEs, particularly in LAC, also suffered spillovers from the Asian financial crisis, with currency crises in several cases. However, these countries

---

[22] Some studies examined the implications of financial globalization for growth, volatility and development outcomes in EMDEs (Kose et al. 2009; Kose, Prasad, and Terrones 2003; Obstfeld 2009; Stiglitz 2002). For a discussion of financial crises in EMDEs in the 1990s, see Feldstein (2003).

[23] Shocks that occur elsewhere in the global economy can lead to shifts in access to finance for EMDEs. A globally "anxious" economy, rather than the result of EMDE fundamentals, can result in disruptions to finance for EMDEs (Geanakoplos and Fostel 2008).

(except Argentina) managed to avoid sovereign debt crises, partly reflecting the lessons learned during the earlier Latin American crisis and the protection offered by subsequent policy changes.

Contagion to Russia. Russia experienced a currency, banking, and sovereign debt crisis in 1998, which culminated in sovereign debt restructuring in 2000 (Laeven and Valencia 2018; Pinto and Ulatov 2010). Persistent fiscal deficits in the aftermath of the collapse of the Soviet Union had contributed to a rise in external debt from 18 percent of GDP in 1992 to 33 percent in 1996 (figure 3.5). Contagion from the Asian crisis, together with a sharp fall in commodity prices (in part due to that crisis), led to a deterioration in investor confidence in Russia and capital flight in late 1997 and early 1998. The authorities attempted to defend the currency peg, and reserves fell rapidly, compounded by weaker export receipts as a result of lower oil and metals prices (Chiodo and Owyang 2002). Government bond yields rose sharply, reaching 50 percent in May 1998, while government interest payments rose to 3 percent of GDP (Boughton 2012).

Despite IMF and World Bank assistance, agreed in July 1998, the authorities were unable to maintain the currency peg and were forced to move to a floating exchange rate. By September 1998, the ruble had fallen by two-thirds against the U.S. dollar. The government defaulted on its domestic debt and declared a moratorium on foreign debt payments. Output fell sharply in 1998, by 5.3 percent, but quickly rebounded, with GDP growth reaching 10 percent in 2000. The rebound in growth was aided by a recovery in commodity prices, particularly for oil and gas. Tighter monetary policy helped bring inflation down from almost 100 percent in 1999 to just over 20 percent in 2000 and 2001.

Resilience in LAC despite spillovers. The Russian financial crisis, coming on the heels of the Asian crisis, led to a sharp weakening of risk sentiment in capital markets, which spilled over to many other EMDEs. LAC was particularly affected, with a collapse in capital inflows and a sharp spike in borrowing costs, with interest spreads for the seven largest LAC countries more than tripling from 450 basis points before the Russian crisis to 1,600 basis points within a span of two weeks (Calvo and Talvi 2005; Edwards 2000). Despite the dramatic increase in financing costs and drying up of credit, most LAC countries avoided financial crises, although some, such as Brazil, experienced currency or banking crises. Many countries had taken policy action to build resilience after the previous LAC crisis, including reductions in external debt (particularly short-term debt), increases in

FIGURE 3.5 **The second wave: Crises in Argentina, the Russian Federation, and Turkey**

During the second wave, Argentina, Russia, and Turkey experienced speculative attacks on their currencies. These led to sovereign debt crises, with defaults by Argentina and Russia.

A. Russian Federation: External debt

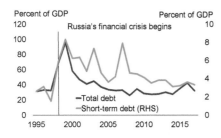

B. Russian Federation: Exchange rate

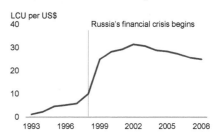

C. Argentina: External debt

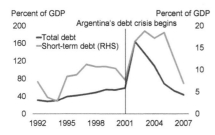

D. Argentina: Growth

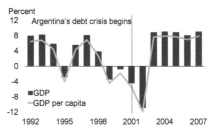

E. Turkey: Growth

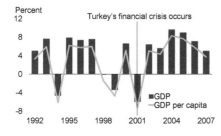

F. Turkey: Inflation

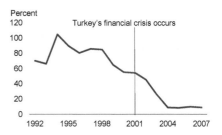

Sources: Haver Analytics; International Monetary Fund; World Bank.
Note: LCU = local currency unit.
A.C. External debt classed as "short-term" when maturities are less than 12 months.
B. Local currency per U.S. dollar. Increase indicates a depreciation relative to the U.S. dollar
F. Annual average inflation.

international reserves, more flexible currency regimes, and increased central bank independence. They had also made substantial progress in boosting exports, such that ratios of debt to exports were much lower.

Vulnerabilities in Argentina. A notable exception in LAC was Argentina, which suffered a banking, currency, and sovereign debt crisis in 2001-02. This collapse was particularly striking because in the early 1990s Argentina had been regarded as a success story, with a robust reform program and with the implementation of a currency board contributing to lower inflation and a strong recovery in growth (IMF 2004).[24] The hyperinflation of the late 1980s had been gradually brought under control, with inflation down to single digits by 1993. Capital inflows had resumed, and GDP per capita grew by 4.6 percent per year, on average, between 1991 and 1998.[25]

Vulnerabilities had been growing, however. GDP growth had slowed in 1998 and turned negative in 1999 and 2000. The current account deficit had widened in the period up to 1998 and remained large even as growth weakened, while the fiscal deficit had also worsened. Exports remained very low as a share of GDP, limiting the country's ability to earn foreign exchange and service external debt. External debt, which had fallen following the Latin American crisis, began to pick up, rising from 28 percent of GDP in 1993 to nearly 50 percent of GDP in 1998, and interest payments increased, as ratios of both GDP and exports.

Argentina's weak external position amid deteriorating economic growth raised questions about its international competitiveness under the fixed exchange rate arrangement of the currency board. But the economy was highly dollarized, with 80 percent of private debt denominated in dollars, considerably higher than in LAC peers: for example, in Chile, only 38 percent of debt was dollar-denominated (Calvo and Talvi 2005). Thus, any currency depreciation would increase the value of liabilities relative to assets and incomes in the economy and would be very costly (Spiegel and Valderrama 2003). Meanwhile, international reserves were very low relative to total debt.

The crisis began with the slowdown in growth in 1998, triggered partly by external shocks, notably the Asian and Russian crises and falling commodity

---

[24] Even after the Asian financial crisis, Argentina was expected to remain resilient and suffer only a small effect from the crisis (Perry and Lederman 1998).

[25] Argentina had fallen into recession in 1995, in part due to spillovers from the Mexico crisis, but swiftly recovered.

prices, and partly by domestic political uncertainty (IMF 2004). Capital inflows came to a sudden stop, and financing costs rose sharply. Argentina had few tools to address the weakness in growth, given its poor fiscal position and the currency board, which ruled out monetary policy actions and currency devaluation (De La Torre, Yeyati, and Schmukler 2003). Exiting the currency board would have triggered a sharp depreciation of the currency, which might have helped with some of Argentina's problems, but it would also have had a major detrimental impact on domestic balance sheets given the currency mismatch arising from the large amount of dollar-denominated debt.

In 2001, Argentina received financial assistance of $14 billion from the IMF, conditional on reforms, including fiscal adjustments. The package proved insufficient, however, to stabilize either the economy or market sentiment, and Argentina experienced further difficulty in rolling over debt (similar to the Latin American crisis in the 1980s). The IMF agreed to provide further financial support of $5 billion toward the end of 2001. This support also proved to be insufficient, and by the end of the year, Argentina announced it would default on its sovereign debt (Mussa 2002).

In early 2002, Argentina announced the end of the currency board, triggering an immediate, steep devaluation in the peso. This devaluation resulted in a sharp increase in debt, given the large amount of dollar-denominated external debt, to a peak of 164 percent of GDP in 2002. Argentina suffered a steep recession, with output dropping by 12 percent in 2002. Positive growth returned in 2003, however, and growth averaged almost 7 percent per year in the period up to the global financial crisis, aided by robust global growth and the commodity price boom.

Prolonged crises in Turkey. Turkey experienced banking, currency, and sovereign debt crises in 2000-01. After implementing an agenda of economic reform in the 1980s, GDP growth averaged about 5 percent per year between 1990 and 1997. Annual growth was nonetheless volatile over this period, fluctuating between -4.6 percent and 7.9 percent. Turkey's macroeconomic policy and regulatory framework also had substantial weaknesses. The fiscal deficit reached 8 percent of GDP in 2000, and inflation remained very high. Banking regulation and supervision were poor, and the domestic banking sector was a key creditor to the public sector, creating a feedback loop between the two (Ozatay and Sak 2002). In contrast to Argentina, Turkey ran a broadly balanced external current account, and total external debt remained relatively unchanged as a ratio to GDP between 1992 and 1998.

In 1994, Turkey experienced a currency crisis, which was the result of weak domestic policies rather than of spillovers from international shocks. Amid high net financing requirements, the government sought to reduce interest payments by lowering rates on Treasury bills, which led to a reduction in appetite for Turkish government debt (Celasun 1998). As a result, the government increasingly turned to monetization to finance the fiscal deficit. These policy decisions, together with a downgrade in Turkey's international credit rating, triggered a loss in market confidence, and the central bank was forced to sell foreign exchange reserves to stabilize the exchange rate (Dufour and Orhangazi 2007; Moghadam 2005).

After recovering from the 1994 crisis, Turkey experienced another weakening of growth in 1998-99, partly as a result of spillovers from the Asian and Russian crises, but also as a result of domestic developments, including an earthquake. The IMF and Turkey agreed on a stabilization program in 1998 designed partly to help control inflation, which remained very high. The program included a reduction in fiscal deficits and the adoption of a crawling exchange rate peg, designed to maintain competitiveness in the context of a declining inflation target (IMF 2000).

The slowdown in growth exacerbated existing vulnerabilities in the banking sector and contributed to rising worries about bank solvency, which resulted in a spike in interbank lending rates. A banking crisis began in late 2000, when a Turkish bank was unable to access financing on the market (OECD 2014).[26] Amid concern about broader contagion, the Turkish central bank provided substantial liquidity to the banking system.

The currency also came under pressure, with uncertainty about the ability of the central bank to maintain the crawling peg. Turkey's current account deficit had increased sharply in 2000. Furthermore, persistently high inflation had resulted in the peg becoming overvalued. Amid capital flight, foreign exchange reserves fell to 78 percent of total short-term debt in 2000. The IMF provided additional financial assistance to Turkey in December 2000 to stave off worries about insufficient reserves. This support proved inadequate, however, and the Turkish lira came under increasing pressure with further capital outflows. In early 2001, the authorities announced they would let the lira float, resulting in an immediate depreciation against the dollar of about one-third.

---

[26] Because banks typically operate with maturity mismatches, a bank run can rapidly spread to other banks amid growing depositor concerns. Bank runs can turn into a self-fulfilling cycle of deposit withdrawals, liquidity shortages, and credit crunches (Bryant 1980; Diamond and Dybvig 1983).

The combination of the fall in the lira with the costs of recapitalizing many of the failing banks led to a sharp increase in the public debt, from 52 percent of GDP in 2000 to 76 percent of GDP in 2001. Amid growing debt sustainability concerns, Turkey announced a new IMF-supported program in May 2001. The program had three pillars: fiscal and monetary discipline, structural reforms, and substantial external financial support (Ozatay and Sak 2003; Moghadam 2005). In particular, it required a public sector primary surplus of 6.5 percent of GDP from 2002 onward. These policies helped alleviate concerns about debt sustainability, and Turkey returned to growth in 2002 (Acemoglu and Ucer 2015).

Changes in debt resolution

Need for a debt restructuring mechanism. The increasingly apparent difficulty of sovereign debt restructuring—and the economic damage done by protracted debt resolutions—highlighted the need for a new approach and framework (Kletzer 2003; Sachs 2002). The problem had increased with the shift away from lending to EMDEs by relatively small groups of commercial banks toward reliance on financing from the sovereign bond market, with creditors more diffuse and harder to coordinate. Most bonds at the time had a unanimous consent clause, that is, any restructuring required the agreement of all bondholders, regardless of how small individual holdings were (Häseler 2009). This requirement was problematic for several reasons, ranging from the practical issue of locating all bondholders to a free-rider problem, because individual creditors had an incentive to hold out in the hope that restructuring by others would allow the debtor to continue to pay the free-riders. Although collective action problems were also an issue for debt held by commercial banks, or bilaterally through government loans, these creditors were typically not nearly as numerous, diverse, or anonymous as bondholders.

Alternative resolution strategies. In 2002, the IMF proposed the creation of a formal resolution framework, the "Sovereign Debt Restructuring Mechanism" (IMF 2002). The framework failed to receive sufficient support from IMF member countries, however, some of which preferred a market-based solution (Bedford, Penalver, and Salmon 2005; Cosio-Pascal 2008). This preference resulted in a growing interest in the introduction of collective action clauses (CACs) in loan contracts to reduce the cost of debt resolution.[27] CACs would enable debt restructuring to take place with the

---

[27] For a discussion of these issues, see Eichengreen, Kletzer, and Mody (2003); Eichengreen and Mody (2000); Haldane and Kruger (2001); and Sturzenegger and Zettelmeyer (2007). The official sector also recommended a shift toward domestic bond markets to lower the exchange rate risks associated with foreign-currency borrowing.

consent of a majority or super-majority of bondholders (typically two-thirds to three-quarters), reducing the likelihood of restructurings being delayed by creditors.

Although CACs had been used in debt contracts agreed under English law for many years, they were rarely used for debt issued under New York law (Drage and Hovaguimian 2004). The broader use of CACs had been promoted in academic circles since 1995, but CACs were unpopular among some creditors, who worried that they would create a bad incentive for debtors by making restructuring easier, thus making defaults more likely (Eichengreen and Portes 1995).[28] As a result, sovereign borrowers did not include CACs in their debt issuance, given fears that they would not be able to find buyers for their bonds (Häseler 2009).

In 2003, Mexico was the first EMDE to issue a bond under New York law containing a CAC, and it was shortly followed by Brazil, Korea, and South Africa. Once issued, it became apparent that markets were not penalizing debt issued with CACs, with little to no premium on CAC bonds compared to other bonds (Richards and Gugiatti 2003). CACs quickly became routine for most sovereign debt issuance, with the share of new issuance covered by CACs rising from less than 10 percent in 2000-02 to more than 90 percent in 2004-06 (Bradley, Fox, and Gulati 2008). Several studies, both theoretical and empirical, have shown that the use of CACs leads to better outcomes for both creditors and debtors.[29] By removing the likelihood of holdout creditors, CACs should accelerate restructuring processes, which in turn could result in faster resolutions of debt, and quicker returns to economic growth, by reducing debt overhangs.

The third wave, 2002-09: The global financial crisis and crisis in the ECA region

The key feature of the third wave of growth in debt, before the global financial crisis, was a sharp increase in borrowing by EMDEs on international debt markets, primarily from banks headquartered in the

---

[28] Early models of sovereign debt default were based on cost-benefit analyses: governments choose to default if the benefits of not servicing their obligations outweigh the costs (for example, reputational loss or a threat of cutoff from international markets; Bulow and Rogoff 1989; Eaton and Gersovitz 1981). The default decision therefore hinges on the willingness—rather than only on the ability—of governments to repay their debt, leading to the concept of "serial default" (Reinhart, Rogoff, and Savastano 2003).

[29] For details, see Eichengreen, Kletzer, and Mody (2003); Ghosal and Thampanishvong (2007); and Weinschelbaum and Wynne (2005).

United States and European Union (EU). Global interest rates were low at the start of this wave, as in the previous two waves. The buildup in debt was greatest in the ECA region and was primarily accounted for by the private sector, particularly households. The subsequent sharp reduction in cross-border lending to EMDEs, in the aftermath of the global financial crisis of 2008 and the global recession of 2009, led to severe credit crunches and economic downturns in the most exposed ECA economies, which relied heavily on cross-border loans from EU banks.

Financial market developments

Global banking. As the economies affected by the Asian financial crisis recovered, global borrowing resumed at a fast pace. This increased borrowing coincided with a period of rapid expansion of U.S.- and EU-headquartered banks following deregulation (Arteta and Kasyanenko 2020). In 1999, the United States repealed the Glass-Steagall Act to remove barriers between commercial and investment banking, opening the way for the formation of "mega-banks" and encouraging the rapid growth of corporate bond markets (Kroszner and Strahan 2014; Sherman 2009).

In the EU the Financial Services Action Plan in 1999 encouraged cross-border connections between banks as well as their rapid expansion (Goddard, Molyneux, and Wilson 2015). For example, in the United Kingdom, bank assets rose from 300 percent of GDP in 2000 to 550 percent of GDP in 2008, and the banking system became highly concentrated, with the three largest U.K. banks each having assets in excess of 100 percent of GDP (Davies et al. 2010). Total assets of the banking systems in Belgium, Denmark, France, Ireland, and the Netherlands all exceeded 200 percent of GDP in 2008 (Demirgüç-Kunt and Huizinga 2013).

The emerging mega-banks fueled a steep increase in direct cross-border lending, lending through subsidiaries, and investment in EMDE debt markets. Between 2000 and 2007, foreign claims by banks reporting to the Bank for International Settlements rose by 220 percent—about three times the pace of global nominal output growth. The ECA region in particular was a major recipient of these bank flows (Balakrishnan et al. 2011; Takáts 2010). Between 2000 and 2007, foreign bank claims on EMDEs in ECA grew by 9 percentage points of GDP to 18 percent of GDP in 2007. Some countries received much larger bank flows: for example, by 2007, foreign bank claims accounted for 70 percent of GDP in Croatia and 66 percent of GDP in Hungary.

Development of domestic bond markets. Low inflation and fiscal stabilization in many EMDEs helped boost the credibility of domestic macroeconomic policies (Kose and Ohnsorge 2020). This, together with growing domestic investor bases and rapidly growing bank balance sheets, supported domestic bond market development (Hawkins 2002; Mihaljek, Scatigna, and Villar 2002; Turner 2002). Whereas sovereign borrowers increasingly turned to domestic bond markets, corporate issuers increasingly accessed international markets. The increase in corporate bond issuance in part reflected strong demand for funds from commodity-producing companies and improving corporate credit ratings. The amount of debt issued in bond markets by EMDEs almost tripled between 1997 and 2007, to $190 billion. Commercial banks, however, remained the most important source of finance for EMDE corporates, accounting for more than 80 percent of total external debt in 2007.

The global financial crisis

Near-collapse of the U.S. financial system. Triggered by defaults in the U.S. subprime mortgage market, the U.S. financial system came under increasingly severe stress in the second half of 2007 and 2008, culminating in a major crisis in late 2008. This crisis exposed the fragility of banks that were dependent on short-term wholesale funding, which had been essential to the rapid growth of securitization, and also reflected inadequate regulatory oversight (Claessens et al. 2014; Duffie 2019). Meanwhile, the buildup of macrofinancial links between countries had resulted in key vulnerabilities in the global economy (Claessens and Kose 2018). These vulnerabilities became apparent to policy makers only when the crisis erupted. Many banks withdrew from cross-border activities, and liquidity and funding dried up.

The initial shock of the global financial crisis was followed by a severe U.S. recession in which U.S. output contracted more than in any other U.S. recession since the Great Depression.[30] Overall, advanced economy GDP growth dropped from 2.6 percent in 2007 to -3.4 percent in 2009 in a broad-based global recession. Global per capita GDP contracted by 3 percent in 2009—more than in any other global recession over the past 70 years.

The shock to U.S.- and EU-headquartered banks also reverberated through EMDE financial systems. Syndicated lending and other cross-border lending

---

[30] Claessens, Kose, and Terrones (2014) discuss the origins and implications of the global financial crisis. For descriptions of the crisis, see Bernanke (2013), Blinder (2013), Gorton and Metrick (2012), Lewis (2010), Paulson (2010), Sorkin (2010), Turner (2012), and Wessel (2010). Lo (2012) presents a review of 21 books on the global financial crisis.

by foreign banks, and domestic lending by foreign-owned banks contracted sharply (Cetorelli and Goldberg 2011; De Haas and van Horen 2012). Both domestically and foreign-owned banks in EMDEs that relied on funding from external capital markets cut back their lending (figure 3.6).[31] EMDE bond markets suffered liquidation sales, and bond and equity flows to EMDEs reversed.

Although most EMDEs proved resilient to the crisis, those that had relied heavily on borrowing from EU and U.S. financial institutions suffered severe recessions (BIS 2009; Frank and Hesse 2009). The deterioration in financial conditions was especially pronounced in the ECA region, as the withdrawal of Western European banks caused a severe credit crunch.[32]

Crisis in the ECA region

Rising external debt, rapid growth. External debt rose sharply in the ECA region between 2000 and 2007. Overall external debt-to-GDP ratios were mostly unchanged, however, with rapid growth in private sector external debt offset by slower growth in public sector external debt. The growth of external debt was particularly large in the household sector: its external debt, relative to GDP, doubled from 10 to 20 percent in the period. Private sector debt rose to 65 percent of total debt in 2007 from 25 percent in 2000. The precrisis buildup of debt in the ECA region was matched by rapid rates of GDP growth, aided by many countries' growing ties with the EU, which a number of countries in the region joined in 2004. GDP per capita grew by 6.7 percent per year, on average, between 2000 and 2007, and investment-to-GDP ratios increased (figure 3.7). Rapid economic growth was accompanied by rising inflation, high wage growth, and large current account deficits, although fiscal balances improved.

When the crisis hit, the deterioration in financial conditions resulted in sharp recessions in ECA. Output contracted by 5.1 percent in 2009 (following a 7.3 percent expansion in 2007) and per capita GDP fell by 6.4 percent. Growth fell most sharply in countries with the weakest macroeconomic fundamentals, fixed exchange rates, and the greatest reliance

---

[31] The financial sector can act as a propagator and amplifier of crises though its impact of other sectors of the economy and the real economy (Claessens and Kose 2018). This can be via the "financial accelerator" effect which propagates and amplifies small shocks as changes to access to finance occur (Bernanke and Gertler 1989). Propagation can also occur through the supply side, including the provision of loans (Adrian and Shin 2008; Brunnermeier and Pedersen 2009).

[32] For details on the evolution of the crisis in the region, see Binici and Yörükoğlu (2011); Ranciere, Tornell, and Vamvakidis (2010); and Tong and Wei (2009).

FIGURE 3.6 **Global financial crisis: Debt developments**

*Benign financing conditions and deregulation of the financial sector in advanced
economies fueled cross-border lending before the crisis, particularly in Europe and Central
Asia. Although total debt was flat, private sector debt grew sharply, and its share of total
external debt rose. During the crisis, economies with smaller international reserves and
greater reliance on short-term borrowing were more affected by the ensuing credit crunch.*

A. Cross-border lending to EMDEs

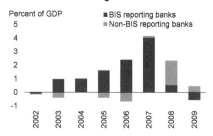

B. Cross-border claims on EMDEs, by region

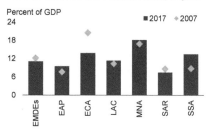

C. ECA: External debt

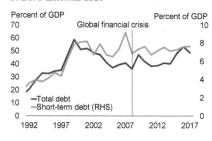

D. ECA: Growth in external debt

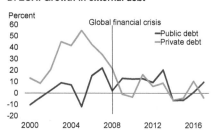

E. ECA: External debt, by sector

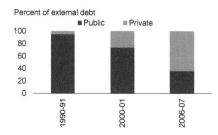

**F. Reserves and short-term external debt in
selected countries, 2006-07**

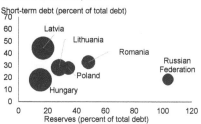

Sources: Bank for International Settlements (BIS); Institute of International Finance; International Monetary Fund (IMF);
World Bank.
Note: EAP = East Asia and Pacific; ECA = Europe and Central Asia; EMDEs = emerging market and developing
economies; LAC = Latin America and the Caribbean; MNA = Middle East and North Africa; SAR = South Asia;
SSA = Sub-Saharan Africa.
A.B. Offshore financial centers are excluded.
A. Based on data for 86 EMDEs excluding China. BIS data are from the BIS locational banking statistics and represents
changes in stock of claims on EMDEs. Lending by non-BIS banks is calculated as total bank loans and deposits from the
IMF Balance of Payment Statistics minus cross-border lending by BIS reporting banks. Cross-border lending flows as a
percentage of GDP are shown as total for all economies in the sample divided by their aggregate nominal GDP.
B. Sample includes 140 EMDEs; ratios are shown as total claims on the region divided by regional nominal GDP
aggregates. Claims include loans and security holds.
D. Annual percent change in nominal level of external debt (in U.S. dollars).
E. Includes long-term debt only (maturity of more than 12 months).
F. Size of bubble indicates relative total external debt-to-GDP ratios. Data are 2006-07 averages.

FIGURE 3.7 Global financial crisis: Macroeconomic developments in ECA

In the 2000s, Europe and Central Asia benefitted from robust economic growth, and investment-to-GDP ratios rose. Most countries had persistent and deteriorating current account deficits, whereas fiscal balances improved. During the crisis, most economies experienced devaluations, which led to some temporary increases in inflation rates.

A. ECA: Growth

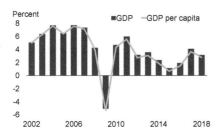

B. Change in investment-to-GDP ratio

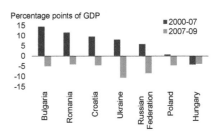

C. ECA: Current account balance

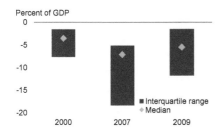

D. ECA: Fiscal balance

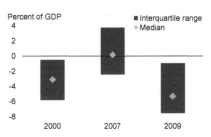

E. Exchange rates in selected countries

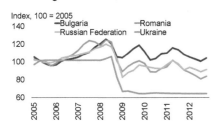

F. Inflation rates in selected countries

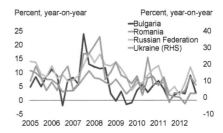

Sources: International Monetary Fund; World Bank.
Note: ECA = Europe and Central Asia.
A.C.D. Based on a sample of 24 ECA economies. U.S. dollar GDP weighted values.
C.D. Diamonds indicate the median value and blue bars denote the interquartile range.
E. U.S. dollars per local currency. An increase denotes an appreciation.
F. Annual average inflation.

on wholesale funding (Frank and Hesse 2009). Some countries in the region experienced large currency depreciations, although pass-throughs to inflation were relatively modest. The deterioration in the real economy resulted in rising nonperforming loans, primarily attributable to households, rather than to corporates as in the Asian crisis.

Economic contractions were particularly severe in Bulgaria, Croatia, Romania, and Ukraine: in each case, output fell by more than 10 percentage points between 2007 and 2009. Ukraine, which registered the largest output decline, of 14.8 percent in 2009, saw a collapse in exports (by 22 percent) and sharp capital flow reversals; cross-border claims on Ukraine fell by 8.7 percentage points of GDP in 2009. Meanwhile, Bulgaria, Croatia, and Romania were exposed to large currency and maturity mismatches in the banking sector (Ranciere, Tornell, and Vamvakidis 2010). The IMF provided support to many countries through flexible credit lines and standby arrangements, and three ECA countries adopted IMF-supported programs in the face of currency or fiscal pressures (Latvia, Hungary, and Romania; Aslund 2010).

Swift crisis resolution. The crisis in ECA was short-lived, partly thanks to the coordinated response by the G20 (Group of Twenty) to the global financial crisis, with the major advanced economies and EMDEs implementing unprecedented monetary and fiscal stimulus in 2009 and 2010. In part because of the European Bank Coordination Initiative ("Vienna Initiative") in 2009, the major foreign banking groups maintained support for their subsidiaries in ECA countries, which also helped to contain the region's financial crisis and to limit the damage caused in the region by the retrenchment of global liquidity and capital flows (Berglof et al. 2009; Pistor 2011).

Aggerate debt levels in general were still modest, despite rapid growth in the run-up to the crisis. Although bank profitability declined, ECA banks were not subject to the concerns about insolvency that afflicted banks in Western Europe, which had weaker capitalization and suffered widespread outright defaults on mortgages (Marer 2010). ECA economies quickly rebounded, such that by 2010 GDP per capita in the region had returned to precrisis (2007) levels. The crisis was primarily a liquidity issue, rather than a solvency problem. During 2010-19, GDP growth averaged 2.6 percent per year.

Impact on other EMDEs and policy responses

Limited contagion to other EMDEs. In contrast to advanced economies and the ECA region, most EMDEs proved remarkably resilient to the global financial crisis (Didier, Hevia, and Schmukler 2012). In part, this was because many had limited vulnerabilities to the shocks of the time (Didier et al. 2015; Kose and Prasad 2010). Furthermore, many countries had implemented fiscal and monetary policy reforms and had accumulated policy buffers during the precrisis period (Koh and Yu 2020). For example, average fiscal balances in EMDEs improved from a deficit of 3 percent of GDP in 2002 to a surplus of 1.4 percent of GDP in 2007, and government debt, on average, declined sharply from 78 percent of GDP in 2002 to 45 percent of GDP in 2007. Foreign exchange reserves rose from 28 percent of external debt in 2000 to 114 percent of external debt in 2008. Many EMDEs had also improved debt management, supporting reductions in currency, interest rate, and maturity risks (Anderson, Silva, and Velandia-Rubiano 2010; Arteta and Kasyanenko 2020).

Robust policy response. Furthermore, as a result of the buildup of policy buffers prior to the crises, many EMDEs were able to implement substantial countercyclical fiscal and monetary policies during the crisis (Koh and Yu 2020). In addition, EMDE central banks used a variety of tools to ease or absorb foreign exchange market pressures. About one-fifth of EMDEs intervened in foreign exchange markets in 2009, on average using 15 percent of their international reserves. Such operations included selling foreign currency in the spot market (for example, Brazil, India, and Mexico) and swap market auctions (Brazil, Hungary, and Poland). Other measures included setting up repo facilities (Argentina, Brazil, and the Philippines), providing guarantees on foreign currency deposits (India, Malaysia, and Turkey), and changing regulations to facilitate foreign borrowing (Chile and India). In the fourth quarter of 2008, the U.S. Federal Reserve extended swap lines to Brazil, Korea, Mexico, and Singapore; and the European Central Bank and the Swiss National Bank provided support to Hungary and Poland through swaps and repurchase agreements (Arteta and Kasyanenko 2020).

EMDEs relied primarily on macroeconomic policies to manage capital flow volatility. Adjustments to external shocks were facilitated by exchange rate flexibility (especially in EMDEs where currencies were initially overvalued, such as Brazil, Indonesia, the Philippines, Russia, South Africa, and Turkey), foreign exchange market interventions, and monetary and fiscal policy adjustments. Several EMDEs tightened capital flow management measures during stress episodes (Belarus, Nigeria, and Ukraine), or when financial stability was threatened by macroeconomic rebalancing (China), global shocks (Russia), significant exposures in foreign currency (Peru), or financial contagion risks (North Macedonia).

As these economies implemented macroeconomic adjustment programs, in some cases involving the resolution of failed financial institutions, some capital flow management measures (CFMs) were subsequently eased or removed. Several EMDEs also used CFMs to reduce the heavy capital inflows in 2009-12 triggered by the unprecedented monetary policy accommodation, including quantitative easing in major advanced economies (Fratzscher, Lo Duca, and Straub 2017). Most of these measures were either removed or eased when the inflow surge abated (IMF 2018).

Policy changes. The global financial crisis led to some major changes in the design and implementation of policies.[33] First, in light of persistent low inflation and weak growth, advanced economy central banks have implemented a range of unconventional monetary policy measures. Second, because powerful adverse feedback loops between the real economy and the financial sector pushed many countries into recessions during 2007-09, strengthened regulation, supervision, and monitoring of financial institutions and markets have become a more integral part of macroeconomic and financial sector surveillance and policy design (Claessens and Kose 2018).

The crisis also vividly illustrated how cycles in housing markets and credit tend to amplify each other. This recognition has translated into stricter rules and standards for mortgage lending as well as larger countercyclical buffers to moderate fluctuations in banks' capital positions (Adrian 2017; Claessens 2015; World Bank 2019b). In addition, there has been broader acceptance of the need to strengthen the global aspects of financial regulation and surveillance policies because domestic financial cycles are often highly synchronized internationally (Kose and Ohnsorge 2020).

Similarities between waves

The three waves of broad-based debt accumulation featured several similarities, including changes in financial markets, their macroeconomic effects, and resulting policy changes. In part as a result of these policy changes, countries weathered subsequent crises better.

Beginning of the waves. The initial debt buildup in each wave was associated with low or falling global interest rates and major changes in financial markets, often in response to deregulation. These changes enabled many previously credit-constrained borrowers to access international

---

[33] Akerlof et al. (2014), Blanchard et al. (2012, 2016), and Blanchard and Summers (2019) discuss changes in economic policies and new approaches since the global financial crisis.

financial markets and accumulate debt. Shortcomings in domestic policy frameworks often contributed to substantial debt buildups and exacerbated the severity of crises.

- *Low or falling global interest rates.* The beginning of each of the three waves was associated with low, or falling, global real interest rates, which encouraged borrowing (figure 3.8). In the first wave, during 1970-79, the U.S. real policy rate averaged about 0.6 percent and was negative for several years. During the second wave, the U.S. real policy rate declined from a high of 5 percent in 1989 to a low of 0.5 percent in 1993 as the Federal Reserve cut policy rates in response to the 1991 global recession. Similarly, the U.S. real policy rate fell into negative territory at the beginning of the third wave, following the 2001 recession in the United States.

- *Financial innovations.* The emergence of the syndicated loan markets in the 1970s set the stage for the first wave. The introduction of Brady bonds in the early 1990s spurred the development of sovereign bond markets that underpinned the rapid growth of sovereign borrowing in the second wave, and capital account liberalization in many EMDEs in the 1990s, especially in EAP, facilitated private sector borrowing. The third wave in the 2000s largely consisted of cross-border flows via international banks in advanced economies after deregulation in the United States allowed deposit banks into investment banking activities and the EU loosened rules on cross-border lending. The latter change helped countries in ECA to borrow extensively.

- *Economic upturns.* The beginning of each debt wave was typically accompanied by an economic upturn. The early stages of the first and second waves coincided with recoveries from global recessions (1975, 1991)—which was also true for the fourth wave, beginning in 2010— and the beginning of the third wave coincided with the recovery from the global downturn of 2001 (Kose and Terrones 2015).

During the waves. Borrower country policies often encouraged debt accumulation or exacerbated the risks associated with it. Fixed exchange rate regimes and weak prudential frameworks encouraged risk taking; weak fiscal frameworks encouraged unfunded government spending; and government spending priorities or weak prudential supervision often directed funding to inefficient uses.

- *Fixed exchange rate regimes.* During the first and second waves, especially, exchange rate pegs in EAP, ECA, and LAC encouraged capital inflows

FIGURE 3.8 **Comparison of the first three waves**

The start of each debt wave generally coincided with a period of low, or falling, interest rates. There has been a secular decline in nominal and real interest rates since the 1970s. Financial crises and their aftermaths were typically associated with a sharp slowdown in capital inflows to EMDEs. Debt episodes that ended in banking crises typically resulted in large increases in government debt. The region and sector accounting for the buildup of debt varied among the waves, but there has been an ongoing shift in the share of debt from the public to the private sector.

A. U.S. policy interest rates

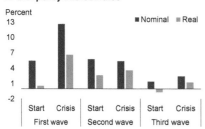

B. Capital flows to EMDEs

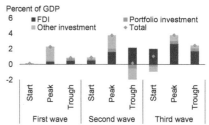

C. Government debt during past banking crises

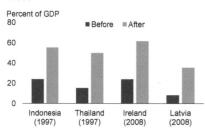

D. Change in government EMDE debt, by region

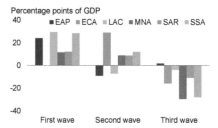

E. Change in private EMDE debt, by region

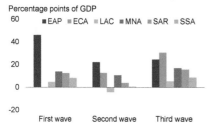

F. Composition of external debt in EMDEs

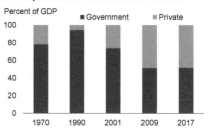

Sources: Haver Analytics; International Monetary Fund; Laeven and Valencia (2018); World Bank.

Note: EAP = East Asia and Pacific; ECA = Europe and Central Asia; EMDEs = emerging market and developing economies; FDI = foreign direct investment; LAC = Latin America and the Caribbean; MNA = Middle East and North Africa; SAR = South Asia; SSA = Sub-Saharan Africa.

A. Start of a wave defined as the first three years of the wave. Crisis defined as the year before, and year of, widespread crises. First wave: 1970-72 and 1981-82; second wave: 1990-92 and 1996-97; third wave: 2002-04, and 2008-09. Real interest rates are deflated by the GDP deflator.

B. Net capital inflows to EMDEs. The start of each wave is the first year, the peak is the year of peak capital inflows before the start of crisis, and the trough is the year of lowest capital inflows after the crisis. First wave: 1970, 1978, and 1988; second wave: 1990, 1995, and 2000; third wave: 2002, 2007, and 2009.

C. "Before" and "after" denote, respectively, one year before and after the onset of banking crisis (defined as in Laeven and Valencia 2018). Indonesia refers to central government debt only.

D.E. Sample of 142 EMDEs.

F. Long-term external debt only.

by leading lenders and borrowers to underestimate exchange rate risks. With interest rates on foreign currency loans below those for domestic currency loans, and the peg interpreted as an implicit exchange rate guarantee, borrowers readily took on foreign currency debt and domestic banks offered dollarized or euro-ized accounts on a large scale to local clients (Impavido, Rudolph, and Ruggerone 2013; Magud, Reinhart, and Rogoff 2011; Spiegel and Valderrama 2003). Reliance on dollar-denominated debt often ended with rising debt-to-GDP ratios when EMDE currencies eventually depreciated against the U.S. dollar.

- *Weak prudential frameworks.* Structural changes in financial markets were typically not accompanied by appropriate reforms to prudential regulatory or supervisory frameworks, which allowed excessive risk taking and often culminated in currency and banking crises. In the second wave, for example, rapid liberalization of capital markets encouraged EAP banks to borrow heavily from international markets (Furman et al. 1998). In the third wave, the risks posed by growing cross-border lending and macrofinancial links were underappreciated by financial supervisors (Claessens and Kose 2018).

- *Weak fiscal frameworks.* In episodes of government debt buildup—in LAC and SSA in the first wave, and in ECA in the second wave—many countries ran persistent fiscal deficits, often financed with external debt.

- *Inefficient use of debt.* Rising external debt is less of a concern if it is used to finance growth-enhancing investments, particularly if they boost exports and therefore the foreign currency revenues to repay loans in the future (World Bank 2017a). Although debt flows were often used to finance productive investment, in some cases debt was used for domestic-facing investments, such as the import-substitution industry-alization that eroded international competitiveness in LAC in the first wave or construction and property booms that did not raise export revenues in EAP and ECA in the second and third waves. Weak corporate governance, including inadequate oversight of projects and investment decisions as well as declining profitability, also led to inefficient investment in several EAP countries.

End of waves. Although debt accumulation tended initially to support growth, it was subsequently associated with financial crises in many cases.

- *Triggers.* Financial crises have often been triggered by shocks that resulted in a sharp increase in investor risk aversion, risk premiums, and borrowing costs, followed by a sudden stop of capital flows.[34] Growth slowdowns have also been important triggers, because they tend to have adverse effects on public finances, the capacity to service debt, and bank profitability (Easterly 2002). In the first wave, around the global recession of 1982, these factors restricted access to new borrowing in LAC and SSA. In the second wave, capital flows to EMDEs stalled or reversed in the global slowdown of 1998 amid a loss of investor confidence following the Asian and Russian crises (Kaminsky 2008; Kaminsky and Reinhart 2001). In the third wave, banking system liquidity dried up during the 2007-09 global financial crisis, interrupting cross-border lending especially to ECA. Domestic political events have also contributed to some crises, for example in Argentina and Turkey in the third wave (IMF 2004; Ozatay and Sak 2002).

- *Types of financial crises.* Many crises began with sharp currency depreciations and capital outflows, which were occasionally the precursor to sovereign debt crises. Large depreciations increased service costs on dollar-denominated debt and led to surges in inflation, requiring monetary policy to be tightened. Sudden stops or reversals in capital flows complicated debt rollovers. In all three waves, countries that slid into crises had sizable vulnerabilities, such as large external, short-term, foreign currency-denominated or variable-rate debt; uncompetitive pegged exchange rates; low international reserves; and weak monetary, fiscal, and prudential policy frameworks.

- *Pockets of resilience.* In the first three waves, there were examples of countries that weathered crises and contagion better than others, for example, Colombia and Indonesia in the first wave, India and Brazil in the second, and Poland and Chile in the third (Blanchard et al. 2010). These countries generally had had more moderate debt increases and enjoyed levels of reserves.

- *Macroeconomic effects.* Debt buildup in the first three waves was associated with crises or stagnation in many cases, especially when the debt buildup consisted predominantly of sovereign debt. Currency depreciations were often large, especially during the first and second waves, triggering sharp spikes in inflation and deteriorating debt-to-GDP ratios when debt was denominated in dollars. That said, there were considerable differences in the severity of macroeconomic outcomes between the waves, as discussed in the next section.

---

[34] For the sources of financial crises, see Claessens and Kose (2014), Frankel and Rose (1996), Kaminsky and Reinhart (2000), and Summers (2001).

- *Fiscal effects.* Financial crises were often fiscally costly. In the first wave, defaulting governments in LAC lost access to international capital markets for many years. In the second and third waves, governments had to support ailing banks in recognition of implicit guarantees for financial systems. Ninety percent of banking crises have required bank restructuring, and roughly 60 percent have led to the nationalization of one or more banks. On average, the fiscal cost of these bailouts during the second and third waves amounted to 12 percent of GDP in affected countries—a multiple of the typical sovereign guarantee.[35] Bank rescue operations can thereby impair the sustainability of public finances in a negative feedback loop (Acharya, Drechsler, and Schnabl 2014).

- *Policy responses.* In all three waves, the countries suffering crises implemented policy responses that were aimed not only at resolving the crises and addressing their repercussions, but also at building resilience to future crises. In the first two waves, LAC and EAP governments took measures to increase reserves and limit future buildups of external debt. Many moved toward inflation targeting and flexible exchange rates. In the second and third waves, EAP and ECA governments eventually strengthened bank supervision, corporate bankruptcy laws, and fiscal frameworks. Progress has varied across countries, however, with some remaining more vulnerable to shocks than others.

Differences across waves

The three waves differed in the most active borrowing sectors and regions, the financial instruments involved, the speed of resolution of crises, and their macroeconomic impact.

Borrowing sectors and regions. In the first wave, the increase in borrowing was primarily accounted for by the public sector in LAC and SSA.[36] In these two regions, governments ran persistent fiscal deficits, which were used to

---

[35] For a global sample, the average cost of government intervention in the financial sector during crises in 1990-2014 amounted to 9.7 percent of GDP, with a maximum of 55 percent of GDP (IMF 2016). The average cost of government intervention in public sector enterprises during 1990-2014 amounted to about 3 percent of GDP, and the average cost of the realization of contingent liabilities from public-private partnerships was 1.2 percent of GDP (Bova et al 2016). Government-guaranteed long-term external debt amounted to less than 1 percent of EMDE GDP at end-2017 (based on data available for 40 EMDEs).

[36] The first and third waves were global in the sense that total EMDE debt rose whereas the second had a narrower regional focus in Asia. During the first wave, EMDE government debt rose sharply; during the third, EMDE private debt rose sharply, in each case driving up EMDE total debt. In contrast, during the second wave, EMDE government debt declined while EMDE private debt rose, resulting in a limited overall increase in total EMDE debt.

fund current expenditures in some cases as well as investment. In the second wave, both the private sector (in EAP) and the public sector (in ECA and LAC) played a role. In the third wave—which had a smaller number of EMDEs with large debt runups than in the previous two waves—the private sector in ECA was the primary borrower. Governments in EAP (second wave) and ECA (third wave) typically had sound fiscal positions in the run-up to their crises. As a result of these shifts, the share of the public sector in external borrowing fell from a high of 95 percent in 1989 to 53 percent in 2018.

Financial instruments. The sources of credit in each wave also evolved. In the first wave, sovereigns were able to borrow from the official sector, bilaterally and multilaterally, as well as from commercial banks via the syndicated loan market: lending from commercial banks accounted for around one-third of total external public debt in EMDEs by 1980-81. The introduction of Brady bonds in the early 1990s spurred the development of sovereign bond markets, and financial market liberalization enabled the private sector to access international borrowing. In the 2000s, local bond markets deepened, allowing governments to obtain long-term finance, including from foreign investors. In the ECA region, borrowing was mainly cross-border lending from banks headquartered in advanced European economies, including through local subsidiaries and branches.

These developments contributed to the gradual shift in the composition of debt from public sector to private sector borrowers over the waves. There has also been a shift from international debt to domestic debt and a move toward debt securities, including local currency bonds. These changes have been driven by policy changes, global macroeconomic trends, and improvements in debt management capacity.

Debt resolution. The speed of resolution has largely depended on whether the debtors were in the public or private sector. The difficulty of debt restructuring led to gradual progress in debt resolution and restructuring mechanisms.

- *Slow sovereign debt restructuring.* In the first wave, the resolution of widespread sovereign debt defaults in LAC and SSA was slow, given Paris Club concerns about advanced economy bank solvency and the lack of a well-defined restructuring mechanism.[37] In the second wave,

---

[37] Borensztein and Panizza (2009) find that the reputational and economic costs of sovereign defaults is significant but short-lived, in part because crises precede defaults and defaults tend to happen at the trough of recessions.

debt resolution was again prolonged for sovereign debt crises in Argentina, which required IMF assistance, and Turkey. Restructuring after Argentina's 2001 debt default was not completed until many years later.[38]

- *Faster private debt resolution.* In the second wave, private sector debt in EAP was resolved quite quickly, with speedy support from the public sector through bank recapitalization and other support schemes, often with IMF assistance. Nonfinancial corporate sector debt resolution, particularly among larger conglomerates, was much slower than for the financial sector, and nonperforming loans remained elevated for several years after the crisis (Kawai 2002). In the third wave, globally accommodative policies, IMF assistance, the European Bank Coordination ("Vienna") Initiative in 2009, and other banking system support together helped stem currency and banking crises.

- *New resolution mechanisms.* At the start of the first wave, the prevailing view was that countries should repay debt, with little consideration for their ability to service their debt. Over time, creditors gradually moved toward acceptance of some debt reduction, which paved the way for the issuance of Brady bonds for commercial debt, and later the HIPC initiative and MDRI for official debt. CACs were introduced to facilitate debt restructuring in situations with multiple bondholders. For private debt, the Insolvency and Creditor Rights Standard developed best practices for national insolvency and creditor rights systems (Leroy and Grandolini 2016). Insolvency protections have improved substantially over the course of the three waves (World Bank 2019c).

Macroeconomic impact. In all three waves, financial crises resulted in substantial economic damage, but the severity varied between the waves and across regions (figure 3.9).

- *Output cost.* In the first wave, LAC suffered a lost decade of no per capita income growth following the 1982 crisis. Per capita income levels in LICs in SSA fared even worse, with GDP per capita declining for many years. Sovereign debt crises in Russia and Turkey during the second wave also generated severe output losses. In contrast, in the second wave, EAP countries with predominantly private debt buildups experienced

---

[38] Argentina arranged a first restructuring of its debt in 2005, which was accepted by about three-quarters of bond holders (Hornbeck 2013). A second restructuring was agreed in 2010, when two-thirds of the remaining bondholders accepted. The remaining 7 percent of bondholders were "holdout" creditors, who eventually reached a settlement in 2016.

FIGURE 3.9 GDP per capita in EMDEs during the first three waves

In the first wave of debt, countries in LAC and SSA saw prolonged stagnation in per capita growth after debt crises erupted. In the second wave, rapid growth in EAP was interrupted by the Asian financial crisis in 1998 but growth soon recovered. In the third wave, growth in ECA was robust throughout the period but fell in the final year when the crisis hit. In the most recent wave, growth has been high in EAP and SAR but flat in LAC and SSA.

A. First wave

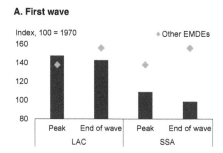

B. Second wave: EAP

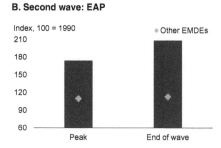

C. Second wave: ECA

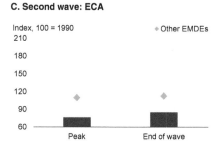

D. Third wave: ECA

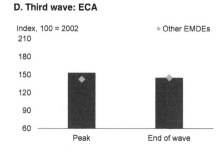

Source: World Bank.
Note: Data are per capita GDP level (at 2010 prices and exchange rates) in each region at the precrisis peak and the end of the wave in each region, indexed to the start of the wave. For LAC and SSA in the first wave, the peak was in 1980; in EAP and ECA in the second wave it was 1997; and in ECA in the third wave it was in 2008. The orange diamonds in panels A-D show the average for all EMDEs excluding the highlighted regions in each chart, for the corresponding years. EAP = East Asia and Pacific; ECA = Europe and Central Asia; EMDEs = emerging market and developing economies; LAC = Latin America and the Caribbean; SSA = Sub-Saharan Africa.

only short-lived slowdowns in the wake of the Asian crisis. In the third wave, ECA countries with largely private debt buildups saw large but short-lived declines in output. In contrast to those economies in the ECA region, most EMDEs weathered the global financial crisis relatively well (Kose and Ohnsorge 2020). They used the ample policy buffers that they had accumulated before the crisis and put their reformed frame-works of monetary, fiscal, and financial policies to good use (Koh and Yu 2020).

- *Currency depreciations.* Depreciations were substantially larger and more common in the first and second waves, when exchange rates had been mostly fixed or attached to crawling pegs and often had to be abandoned in the face of speculative attacks (Bolivia, Brazil, and Mexico in the first wave; Argentina, Indonesia, Russia, and Thailand in the second wave). By the third wave, more countries had flexible exchange rates, reducing the likelihood of currencies becoming substantially overvalued to begin with.

• *Inflation.* Increases in inflation following crises were greatest in the first wave, although they were also substantial in some cases in the second (Indonesia). Inflation outcomes have generally reflected the magnitude of currency depreciations. The smaller rise in inflation in the third wave also reflected improved monetary policy frameworks—the move toward inflation-targeting and independent central banks, which helped anchor inflation expectations (Ha, Kose, and Ohnsorge 2019).

Conclusion

EMDEs experienced three waves of broad-based debt accumulation over the period 1970-2009. During these waves, multiple countries in one or more regions experienced a broad-based buildup of debt. These buildups were often triggered by a combination of financial market deregulation and innovation alongside very low interest rates. Over time—across the waves—borrowing has shifted from the public to the private sector, and the importance of bond issuance has risen, particularly for the public sector.

Each wave ended with widespread financial crises, which had severe macroeconomic repercussions. The crises in LAC and SSA in the first wave were particularly damaging, leading to a lost decade of weak or no growth in LAC and almost two decades of negative per capita income growth in SSA. Debt resolution in the first wave took much longer to implement than in the subsequent waves. Policy reforms implemented in the aftermath of crises have generally led to stronger monetary, fiscal, and prudential policy frameworks, contributing to greater resilience in EMDEs.

EMDEs are currently undergoing the fourth wave of broad-based accumulation of debt. It is critical to understand the sources, evolution, and likely consequences of the current wave to inform policies and enable policy makers to undertake the necessary measures to ensure that the current wave does not follow its predecessors and end in crisis. Chapter 4 presents a detailed discussion of the current wave of debt accumulation in EMDEs.

References

Acemoglu, D., and M. Ucer. 2015. "The Ups and Downs of Turkish Growth, 2002-2015: Political Dynamics, the European Union and the Institutional Slide." NBER Working Paper 21608, National Bureau of Economic Research, Cambridge, MA.

Acharya, V., I. Drechsler, and P. Schnabl. 2014. "A Pyrrhic Victory? Bank Bailouts and Sovereign Credit Risk." *Journal of Finance* 69 (6): 2689-739.

Adrian, T. 2017. "Macroprudential Policy and Financial Vulnerabilities." Speech at the 2017 European Systemic Risk Board Annual Conference, Frankfurt.

Adrian, T., and H. Shin. 2008. "Liquidity and Leverage." Federal Reserve Bank of New York Staff Reports, 328.

Akerlof, G. M., O. J. Blanchard, D. Romer, and J. Stiglitz. 2014. *What Have We Learned?: Macroeconomic Policy after the Crisis.* Cambridge, MA: MIT Press.

Altunbaş, Y., B. Gadanecz, and A. Kara. 2006. "The Evolution of Syndicated Loan Markets." *The Service Industries Journal* 26 (6): 689-707.

Anderson, P. R. D., A. C. Silva, and A. Velandia-Rubiano. 2010. "Public Debt Management in Emerging Market Economies: Has This Time Been Different?" Policy Research Working Paper 5399, World Bank. Washington, DC.

Arnone, M., and F. Presbitero. 2010. *Debt Relief Initiatives: Policy Design and Outcomes.* Surrey, U.K.: Ashgate Publishing Limited.

Arteta, C., and S. Kasyanenko. 2020. "Financial Sector Developments." In *A Decade after the Global Recession: Lessons and Challenges for Emerging and Developing Economies,* edited by M. A. Kose and F. Ohnsorge. Washington, DC: World Bank.

Aslund, A. 2010. *The Last Shall Be the First: The East European Financial Crisis.* Washington, DC: Peterson Institute for International Economics.

Baer, W. 1972. "Import Substitution and Industrialization in Latin America: Experiences and Interpretations." *Latin American Research Review* 7 (1): 95-122.

Bagley, B. M. 1987. "Colombian Politics: Crisis or Continuity?" *Current History* 86 (516): 21.

Baig, T., and I. Goldfajn. 1999. "Financial Market Contagion in the Asian Crisis." *IMF Staff Papers* 46 (2): 167-95.

Balakrishnan, R., S. Danninger, S. Elekdag, and I. Tytell. 2011. "The Transmission of Financial Stress from Advanced to Emerging Economies." *Emerging Markets Finance and Trade* 47 (2): 40-68.

Balassa, B. 1982. *Development Strategies in Semi-Industrial Economies.* Washington, DC: World Bank.

Bedford, P., A. Penalver, and C. Salmon. 2005. "Resolving Sovereign Debt Crises: The Market Based Approach and the Role of the IMF." *Financial Stability Review,* June, Bank of England, London.

Berglöf, E., Y. Korniyenko, A. Plekhanov, and J. Zettelmeyer. 2009. "Understanding the Crisis in Emerging Europe." EBRD Working Paper 109, European Bank for Reconstruction and Development, London.

Bernanke, B. 2013. *The Federal Reserve and the Financial Crisis*. Princeton, NJ: Princeton University Press.

Bernanke, B., and M. Gertler. 1989. "Agency Costs, Net Worth, and Business Fluctuations." *American Economic Review* 79 (1): 14-31.

Bertola, L., and J. A. Ocampo. 2012. *The Economic Development of Latin America since Independence*. Oxford: Oxford University Press.

Binici, M., and M. Yörükoğlu. 2011. "Capital Flows in the Post-Global Financial Crisis Era: Implications for Financial Stability and Monetary Policy." BIS Papers 57, Bank for International Settlements, Basel.

BIS (Bank for International Settlements). 2009. *79th Annual Report, 2008/09*. Basel: Bank for International Settlements.

Blanchard, O. J., H. Faruqee, M. Das, K. Forbes, and L. Tesar. 2010. "The Initial Impact of the Crisis on Emerging Market Countries." *Brookings Papers on Economic Activity* 2010 (Spring): 263–323.

Blanchard, O. J., M. K. Rogoff, R. Rajan, and L. Summers, eds. 2016. *Progress and Confusion: The State of Macroeconomic Policy*. Cambridge, MA: MIT Press.

Blanchard, O. J., D. Romer, A. Spence, and J. Stiglitz, eds. 2012. *In the Wake of the Crisis: Leading Economists Reassess Economic Policy*. Cambridge, MA: MIT Press.

Blanchard, O. J., and L. H. Summers. 2019. *Evolution or Revolution? Rethinking Macroeconomic Policy after the Great Recession*. Cambridge: MIT Press.

Blinder, A. 2013. *After the Music Stopped: The Financial Crisis, the Response, and the Work Ahead*. London: Penguin Books.

Borensztein, E., M. Chamon, O. Jeanne, P. Mauro, and J. Zettelmeyer. 2004. "Sovereign Debt Structure for Crisis Prevention." IMF Occasional Paper 237, International Monetary Fund, Washington, DC.

Borensztein, E., and U. Panizza. 2009. "The Costs of Sovereign Default." *IMF Staff Papers* 56 (4): 683-741.

Boughton, J. 2012. *Tearing Down Walls: The International Monetary Fund 1990-1999*. Washington, DC: International Monetary Fund.

Bova, E., M. Ruiz-Arranz, F. Toscani, and H. E. Ture. 2016. "The Fiscal Costs of Contingent Liabilities; A New Dataset." IMF Working Paper 16/14, International Monetary Fund, Washington, DC.

Bradley, M., J. Fox, and G. Gulati. 2008. "The Market Reaction to Legal Shocks and their Antidotes: Lessons from the Sovereign Debt Market." *Duke Law School Legal Studies Research Paper* 211, Durham, NC.

Brunnermeier, M., and L. Pedersen. 2009. "Market Liquidity and Funding Liquidity." *The Review of Financial Studies*, 22(6): 2201-38.

Bruton, H. 1998. "A Reconsideration of Import Substitution." *Journal of Economic Literature* 36 (2): 903-36.

Bryant, J. 1980. "A Model of Reserves, Bank Runs, and Deposit Insurance." *Journal of Banking and Finance* 4 (4): 335-44.

Bulow, J., and K. Rogoff. 1989. "A Constant Recontracting Model of Sovereign Debt." *Journal of Political Economy* 97 (1): 155-78.

Callaghy, T. 2002. "Innovation in the Sovereign Debt Regime: From the Paris Club to Enhanced HIPC and Beyond." Operations Evaluation Department, World Bank, Washington, DC.

Calvo, G. A., A. Izquierdo, and L. Mejia. 2004. "On the Empirics of Sudden Stops: The Relevance of Balance Sheet Effects." NBER Working Paper 10520, National Bureau of Economic Research, Cambridge, MA.

Calvo, G. A., and E. G. Mendoza. 1996. "Mexico's Balance-of-Payments Crisis: A Chronicle of a Death Foretold." *Journal of International Economics* 41 (3-4): 235-64.

Calvo, G. A., and E. G. Mendoza. 2000a. "Rational Contagion and the Globalization of Securities Markets." *Journal of International Economics* 51(1): 79-113.

Calvo, G. A., and E. G. Mendoza. 2000b. "Capital-Markets Crises and Economic Collapse in Emerging Markets: An Informational-Frictions Approach." *American Economic Review* 90 (2): 59-64.

Calvo, G., and E. Talvi. 2005. "Sudden Stop, Financial Factors and Economic Collapse in Latin America: Learning from Argentina and Chile." NBER Working Paper 11153, National Bureau of Economic Research, Cambridge, MA.

Capulong, M.V., D. Edwards, D. Webb, and J. Zhuang. 2000. *An Analytic Framework of Corporate Governance and Finance. Corporate Governance and Finance in East Asia: A Study of Indonesia, Republic of Korea, Malaysia, Philippines, and Thailand.* Manila: Asian Development Bank.

Carrière-Swallow, Y., L. Jacome, N. Magud, and A. Werner. 2016. "Central Banking in Latin America: The Way Forward." IMF Working Paper 16/197, International Monetary Fund, Washington, DC.

Carstens, A., and H. S. Shin. 2019. "Emerging Markets Aren't Out of the Woods Yet." *Foreign Affairs*, March 15, 2019. https://www.foreignaffairs.com/articles/2019-03-15/emerging-markets-arent-out-woods-yet.

Catão, L. 2002. "Debt Crises: What Is Different about Latin America?" *World Economic Outlook, April 2002*, World Economic and Financial Surveys.

Celasun, O. 1998. "The 1994 Currency Crisis in Turkey." Policy Research Working Paper 1913, World Bank, Washington, DC.

Cetorelli, N., and L. S. Goldberg. 2011. "Global Banks and International Shock Transmission: Evidence from the Crisis." *IMF Economic Review* 59 (1): 41-76.

Chester, A. 1991. "The International Bond Market." *Bank of England Quarterly Bulletin* (Q1): 521-28.

Chiodo, A., and M. Owyang. 2002. "A Case Study of a Currency Crisis: The Russian Default of 1998." *Federal Reserve Bank of St. Louis Review* 84 (6): 7-18.

Claessens, S. 2015. "An Overview of Macroprudential Policy Tools." *Annual Review of Financial Economics* 7 (December): 397-422.

Claessens, S., S. Djankov, and D. Klingebiel. 1999. "Financial Restructuring in East Asia: Halfway There?" Financial Sector Discussion Paper 3, World Bank, Washington, DC.

Claessens, S., and K. Forbes, eds. 2013. *International Financial Contagion.* Berlin: Springer.

Claessens, S., and M. A. Kose. 2014. "Financial Crises Explanations, Types, and Implications." In *Financial Crises: Causes, Consequences, and Policy Responses*, edited by S. Claessens, M. A. Kose, L. Laeven, and F. Valencia, 3-59. Washington, DC: International Monetary Fund.

Claessens, S., and M. A. Kose. 2018. "Frontiers of Macrofinancial Linkages." BIS Papers 95, Bank for International Settlements, Basel.

Claessens, S., M. A. Kose, L. Laeven, and F. Valencia. 2014. *Financial Crises: Causes, Consequences, and Policy Responses.* Washington, DC: International Monetary Fund.

Claessens, S., M. A. Kose, and M. Terrones. 2014. "The Global Financial Crisis: How Similar? How Different? How Costly?" In *Financial Crises: Causes, Consequences, and Policy Responses*, edited by S. Claessens, M. A. Kose, L. Laeven, and F. Valencia. Washington, DC: International Monetary Fund.

Cline, W. 1995. *International Debt Reexamined.* Washington, DC: Institute for International Economics.

Corsetti, G., P. Pesenti, and N. Roubini. 1998. "What Caused the Asian Financial Crisis? Part I: A Macroeconomic Overview." NBER Working Paper 6833, National Bureau of Economic Research, Cambridge, MA.

Cosio-Pascal, E. 2008. "The Emerging of a Multilateral Forum for Debt Restructuring: The Paris Club."UNCTAD Discussion Paper No. 192, United Nations, New York.

Cukierman A., S. Webb, and B. Neyapti. 1992. "Measuring the Independence of Central Banks and its Effect on Policy Outcomes." *World Bank Economic Review* 6 (September): 352-98.

Dalio, R. 2018. *Principles for Navigating Big Debt Crises.* Bridgewater Associates.

Daseking C., and R. Powell. 1999. "From Toronto Terms to the HIPC Initiative: A Brief History of Debt Relief for Low-Income Countries." IMF Working Paper 99/142, International Monetary Fund, Washington, DC.

Davies, R., P. Richardson, V. Katinaite, and M. J. Manning. 2010. "Evolution of the UK Banking System." *Bank of England Quarterly Bulletin* (Q4): 321-32.

De Gregorio, J., and J. Lee. 2004. "Growth and Adjustment in East Asia and Latin America." *Economía* 5 (1): 69-134.

De Haas, R., and N. Van Horen. 2012. "International Shock Transmission after the Lehman Brothers Collapse: Evidence from Syndicated Lending." *American Economic Review* 102 (3): 231-37.

De La Torre, A., E. Yeyati, and S. Schmukler. 2003. "Living and Dying with Hard Pegs: The Rise and Fall of Argentina's Currency Board." *Economia* 5 (2): 43-99.

Demirgüç-Kunt, A., and H. Huizinga. 2013. "Are Banks Too Big to Fail or Too Big to Save? International Evidence from Equity Prices and CDS Spreads." *Journal of Banking and Finance* 37 (3): 875-94.

Devlin, R. 1990. *Debt and Crisis in Latin America: The Supply Side of the Story.* Princeton, NJ: Princeton University Press.

Diamond, D., and P. Dybvig. 1983. "Bank Runs, Deposit Insurance, and Liquidity." *Journal of Political Economy* 91 (3): 401-19.

Diaz-Alejandro, C., P. Krugman, and J. Sachs. 1984. "Latin American Debt: I Don't Think We Are in Kansas Anymore." *Brookings Papers on Economic Activity* 1984 (2): 335-403.

Dicks, M. 1991. "The LDC Debt Crisis." *Bank of England Quarterly Bulletin* (Q4): 498-508.

Didier, T., C. Hevia, and S. Schmukler. 2012. "How Resilient and Countercyclical Were Emerging Economies to the Global Crisis?" *Journal of International Money and Finance* 31 (8): 2052-77.

Didier, T., M. A. Kose, F. Ohnsorge, and L. Ye. 2015. "Slowdown in Emerging Markets: Rough Patch or Prolonged Weakness?" Policy Research Note 4, World Bank, Washington, DC.

Dooley, M. P. 1994. "A Retrospective on the Debt Crisis." NBER Working Paper 4963, National Bureau of Economic Research, Cambridge, MA.

Dooley, M. P., E. Fernandez-Arias, and K. Kletzer. 1996. "Is the Debt Crisis History? Recent Private Capital Inflows to Developing Countries." *The World Bank Economic Review* 10 (1): 27-50.

Dooley, M., and J. Frankel. 2003. *Managing Currency Crises in Emerging Markets.* National Bureau of Economic Research Conference Report. Chicago: University of Chicago Press.

Drage, J., and C. Hovaguimian. 2004. "Collective Action Clauses (CACS): An Analysis of Provisions Included in Recent Sovereign Bond Issues." *Financial Stability Review* 17 (7): 105-6.

Duffie, D. 2019. "Prone to Fail: The Pre-Crisis Financial System." *Journal of Economic Perspectives* 33 (1): 81-106.

Dufour, M., and O. Orhangazi. 2007. "The 2000-2001 Financial Crisis in Turkey: A Crisis for Whom?" MPRA Paper 7837, University Library of Munich, Germany.

Easterly, W. 2002. "How Did the Heavily Indebted Poor Countries Become Heavily Indebted? Reviewing Two Decades of Debt Relief." *World Development* 30 (10): 1677-96.

Eaton, J., and M. Gersovitz. 1981. "Debt with Potential Repudiation: Theoretical and Empirical Analysis." *Review of Economic Studies* 48 (2): 289-309.

Edwards, S., 2000. "Contagion." *World Economy* 23 (7): 873-900.

Edwards, S., and J. Frankel. 2002. *Preventing Currency Crises in Emerging Markets*. Chicago: University of Chicago Press.

Eichengreen, B. 2019. "The Return of Fiscal Policy." *Project Syndicate*, May 13, 2019. https://www.project-syndicate.org/commentary/return-of-fiscal-policy-by-barry-eichengreen-2019-05.

Eichengreen, B., A. El-Ganainy, R. Esteves, and K. J. Mitchener. 2019. "Public Debt through the Ages." NBER Working Paper 25494, National Bureau of Economic Research, Cambridge, MA.

Eichengreen, B., K. Kletzer, and A. Mody. 2003. "Crisis Resolution: Next Steps." In *Brookings Trade Forum 2003*, edited by S. M. Collins and D. Rodrik. Washington, DC: Brookings Institution.

Eichengreen, B., and A. Mody. 2000. "Would Collective Action Clauses Raise Borrowing Costs? An Update and Additional Results." Policy Research Working Paper 2363, World Bank, Washington, DC.

Eichengreen, B., and R. Portes. 1995. *Crisis? What Crisis? Orderly Workouts for Sovereign Debtors*. London: Center for Economic Policy Research.

Essl, S., S. Kilic Celik, P. Kirby, and A. Proite. 2019. "Debt in Low-Income Countries: Evolution, Implications, Remedies." Policy Research Working Paper 8794, World Bank, Washington, DC.

FDIC (Federal Deposit Insurance Corporation). 1997. "History of the Eighties: Lessons for the Future. Vol. 1, An Examination of the Banking Crises of the 1980s and Early 1990s." Federal Deposit Insurance Corporation, Washington, DC.

Feldstein, M. 2003. "Economic and Financial Crises in Emerging Market Economies. An Overview of Prevention and Management." In *Economic and Financial Crises in Emerging Market Economies*, edited by M. Feldstein. Cambridge, MA: National Bureau of Economic Research.

Fischer, S. 1989. "Resolving the International Debt Crisis." In *Developing Country Debt and Economic Performance* 1: *The International Financial System*, 359-86. Chicago: University of Chicago Press.

Forbes, K., and F. Warnock. 2012. "Capital Flow Waves: Surges, Stops, Flight, and Retrenchment." *Journal of International Economics,* 88(2): 235-51.

Frank, N., and H. Hesse. 2009. "Financial Spillovers to Emerging Markets during the Global Financial Crisis." IMF Working Paper 9/104, International Monetary Fund, Washington, DC.

Frankel, J. A., and A. K. Rose. 1996. "Currency Crashes in Emerging Markets: An Empirical Treatment." *Journal of International Economics* 41 (3-4): 351-66.

Fratzscher, M., M. Lo Duca, and R. Straub. 2017. "On the International Spillovers of U.S. Quantitative Easing." *Economic Journal* 128 (608): 330-77.

Furman, J., J. Stiglitz, B. Bosworth, and S. Radelet. 1998. "Economic Crises: Evidence and Insights from East Asia." *Brookings Papers on Economic Activity* 1998 (2): 1-135.

Gadanecz, B. 2004. "The Syndicated Loan Market: Structure, Development and Implications." *BIS Quarterly Review*, December, Bank for International Settlements, Basel.

Geanakoplos, J., and A. Fostel. 2008. "Leverage Cycles and the Anxious Economy." *American Economic Review* 98 (4): 1211-44.

Ghosal, S., and K. Thampanishvong. 2007. "Does Strengthening Collective Action Clauses (CACs) Help?" CDMA Working Paper 7/11, Centre for Dynamic Macroeconomic Analysis, University of St. Andrews, Fife, Scotland.

Glick, R., and A. K. Rose. 1999. "Contagion and Trade: Why Are Currency Crises Regional?" *Journal of International Money and Finance* 18 (4): 603-17.

Goddard, J., P. Molyneux, and J. O. S. Wilson. 2015. "Banking in the European Union: Deregulation, Crisis and Renewal." In *Oxford Handbook of Banking*, edited by A. N. Berger, P. Molyneux, and J. O. S. Wilson. Oxford, U.K.: Oxford University Press.

Goldberg, L., and M. Spiegel. 1992. "Debt Write-Downs and Debt-Equity Swaps in a Two-Sector Model." *Journal of International Economics* 33 (November), 267-83.

Gorton, G. B., and A. Metrick. 2012. "Getting up to Speed on the Financial Crisis: A One-Weekend-Reader's Guide." NBER Working Paper 17778, National Bureau of Economic Research, Cambridge, MA.

Greene, J. 1989. "The External Debt Problem of Sub-Saharan Africa." *IMF Staff Papers* 36 (4): 836-74.

Ha, J., M. A. Kose, and F. Ohnsorge. 2019. *Inflation in Emerging and Developing Economies: Evolution, Drivers and Policies*. Washington, DC: World Bank.

Haldane, A., and M. Kruger. 2001. "The Resolution of International Financial Crises: Private Finance and Public Funds." *Bank of Canada Review* 2001-2002 (Winter): 3-13.

Häseler, S. 2009. "Collective Action Clauses in International Sovereign Bond Contracts—Whence the Opposition?" *Journal of Economic Surveys* 23 (5): 882-923.

Hawkins, J. 2002. "Bond Markets and Banks in Emerging Economies." BIS Papers 11, Bank for International Settlements, Basel.

Hornbeck, J. 2013. "Argentina's Defaulted Sovereign Debt: Dealing with the 'Holdouts.'" CRS Report for Congress, Congressional Research Service, Washington, DC.

IMF (International Monetary Fund). 1998. "External Debt Histories of Ten Low-Income Developing Countries: Lessons From their Experience." IMF Working Paper 72, International Monetary Fund, Washington, DC.

IMF (International Monetary Fund). 2000. *Recovery from the Asian Crisis and the Role of the IMF*. Washington, DC: International Monetary Fund.

IMF (International Monetary Fund). 2002. *A New Approach to Sovereign Debt Restructuring*. Washington, DC: International Monetary Fund.

IMF (International Monetary Fund). 2004. *The IMF and Argentina, 1991-2001.* Washington, DC: International Monetary Fund.

IMF (International Monetary Fund). 2006. "The Multilateral Debt Relief Initiative." Factsheet. International Monetary Fund, Washington, DC.

IMF (International Monetary Fund). 2016. *Analyzing and Managing Fiscal Risks—Best Practices.* Washington, DC: International Monetary Fund.

IMF (International Monetary Fund). 2018. *Global Financial Stability Report. A Decade after the Global Financial Crisis: Are We Safer?* Washington, DC: International Monetary Fund.

Impavido, G., H. Rudolph, and L. Ruggerone. 2013. "Bank Funding in Central, Eastern and South Eastern Europe Post Lehman: A 'New Normal'?" IMF Working Paper 13/148, International Monetary Fund, Washington, DC.

Jácome, L. I., and F. Vázquez, 2008. "Any Link between Legal Central Bank Independence and Inflation? Evidence from Latin America and the Caribbean." *European Journal of Political Economy* 24 (4): 788-801.

Kaminsky, G. L. 2008. "Crises and Sudden Stops: Evidence from International Bond and Syndicated-Loan Markets." *Monetary and Economic Studies* 26: 107-29.

Kaminsky, G. L., and C. M. Reinhart. 2000. "On Crises, Contagion, and Confusion." *Journal of International Economics* 51 (1): 145-68.

Kaminsky, G. L., and C. M. Reinhart. 2001. "Bank Lending and Contagion: Evidence from the Asian Crisis." In *Regional and Global Capital Flows: Macroeconomic Causes and Consequences*, edited by T. Ito and A. O. Krueger, 73-99. Chicago: University of Chicago Press.

Kawai, M. 2002. "Exchange Rate Arrangements in East Asia: Lessons from the 1997-98 Currency Crisis." *Monetary and Economic Studies* 20 (S1): 167-204.

Kawai, M., R. Newfarmer, and S. Schmukler. 2005. "Crisis and Contagion in East Asia: Nine Lessons." *Eastern Economic Journal* 31 (2): 185-207.

Kim, S. H., M. A. Kose, and M. G. Plummer. 2000. "Dynamics of Business Cycles in Asia: Differences and Similarities." Working Paper 2000-15, International Centre for the Study of East Asian Development, Kitakyushu, Japan.

Kletzer, K. 2003. "Sovereign Bond Restructuring; Collective Action Clauses and Official Crisis Intervention." IMF Working Paper 03/134, International Monetary Fund, Washington, DC.

Koh, W. C., and S. Yu. 2020. "Macroeconomic and Financial Policies." In *A Decade after the Global Recession: Lessons and Challenges for Emerging and Developing Economies*, edited by M. A. Kose and F. Ohnsorge. Washington, DC: World Bank.

Kose, M. A., G. Meredith, and C. Towe. 2004. "How Has NAFTA Affected the Mexican Economy? Review and Evidence." IMF Working Paper 04/59, International Monetary Fund, Washington, DC.

Kose, M. A., and F. Ohnsorge, eds. 2020. *A Decade after the Global Recession: Lessons and Challenges for Emerging and Developing Economies.* Washington, DC: World Bank.

Kose, M. A., and E. Prasad. 2010. *Emerging Markets: Resilience and Growth amid Global Turmoil.* Washington, DC: Brookings Institution Press.

Kose, M. A., E. Prasad, K. Rogoff, and S.-J. Wei. 2009. "Financial Globalization: A Reappraisal." *IMF Staff Papers* 56 (1): 8-62.

Kose, M. A., E. Prasad, and M. E. Terrones. 2003. "How Does Globalization Affect the Synchronization of Business Cycles?" *American Economic Review* 93 (2): 57-62.

Kose, M. A., N. Sugawara, and M. E. Terrones. 2020. "What Happens During Global Recessions?" In *A Decade after the Global Recession: Lessons and Challenges for Emerging and Developing Economies,* edited by M. A. Kose and F. Ohnsorge. Washington, DC: World Bank.

Kose, M. A., and M. E. Terrones. 2015. *Collapse and Revival: Understanding Global Recessions and Recoveries.* Washington, DC: International Monetary Fund.

Kroszner, R. S., and P. E. Strahan. 2014. "Regulation and Deregulation of the U.S. Banking Industry: Causes, Consequences, and Implications for the Future." In *Economic Regulation and Its Reform: What Have We Learned?* edited by N. L. Rose. Chicago: University of Chicago Press.

Krugman, P. 1988. "Financing vs. Forgiving a Debt Overhang." *Journal of Development Economics* 29 (3): 253-68.

Krugman, P. 2000. *Currency Crises.* Chicago: University of Chicago Press.

Krumm, K. 1985. "The External Debt of Sub-Saharan Africa: Origins, Magnitude and Implications for Action." Staff Working Paper 741, World Bank, Washington, DC.

Laeven, L., and F. Valencia. 2018. "Systemic Banking Crises Revisited." IMF Working Paper 18/206, International Monetary Fund, Washington, DC.

Lancaster, C. 2007. *Foreign Aid: Diplomacy, Development, Domestic Politics.* Chicago: University of Chicago Press.

Leroy, A., and G. Grandolini. 2016. *Principles for Effective Insolvency and Creditor and Debtor Regimes.* Washington, DC: World Bank.

Lewis, M. 2010. *The Big Short: Inside the Doomsday Machine.* New York and London: Norton.

Lo, A. W. 2012. "Reading about the Financial Crisis: A Twenty-One-Book Review." *Journal of Economic Literature* 50 (1): 151-78.

Lustig, N. 1995. *The Mexican Peso Crisis: The Foreseeable and the Surprise.* Washington, DC: Brookings Institution.

Magud, N. E., C. M. Reinhart, and K. S. Rogoff. 2011. "Capital Controls: Myth and Reality—A Portfolio Balance Approach." NBER Working Paper 16805, National Bureau of Economic Research, Cambridge, MA.

Marer, P. 2010. "The Global Economic Crises: Impacts on Eastern Europe." *Acta Oeconomica* 60 (1): 3-33.

Mendoza, E. 2010. "Sudden Stops, Financial Crises, and Leverage." *American Economic Review,* 100 (5): 1941-66.

Mihaljek, D., M. Scatigna, and A. Villar. 2002. "Recent Trends in Bond Markets." BIS Papers 11, Bank for International Settlements, Basel.

Mishkin, F. 1999. "Global Financial Instability: Framework, Events, Issues." *Journal of Economic Perspectives* 13 (4): 3-20.

Moghadam, M. R. 2005. "Turkey at the Crossroads: From Crisis Resolution to EU Accession." Occasional Paper 242, International Monetary Fund, Washington, DC.

Moreno, R., G. Pasadilla, and E. Remolona. 1998. "Asia's Financial Crisis: Lessons and Policy Responses." Pacific Basin Working Paper Series 98-02, Federal Reserve Bank of San Francisco.

Muchhala, B. 2007. "The Policy Space Debate: Does a Globalized and Multilateral Economy Constrain Development Policies?" Asia Program Special Report 136, Woodrow Wilson International Center for Scholars, Washington, DC.

Mussa, M. 2002. *Argentina and the Fund: From Triumph to Tragedy.* Policy Analyses in International Economics, Washington, DC: Peterson Institute for International Economics.

Nkusu, M. 2004. "Aid and the Dutch Disease in Low-Income Countries: Informed Diagnoses for Prudent Prognoses." IMF Working Paper 04/49, International Monetary Fund, Washington, DC.

Obstfeld, M. 2009. "International Finance and Growth in Developing Countries: What Have We Learned?" *IMF Staff Papers* 56 (1): 63-111.

OECD (Organisation for Economic Co-operation and Development). 2014. *OECD Economic Surveys: Turkey 2014.* Paris: Organisation for Economic Co-operation and Development.

Ozatay, F., and G. Sak. 2002. "Banking Sector Fragility and Turkey's 2000-01 Financial Crisis." In *Brookings Trade Forum 2002*, edited by S. M. Collins and D. Rodrik. Washington, DC: Brookings Institution.

Paulson, H. 2010. *On the Brink: Inside the Race to Stop the Collapse of the Global Financial System.* New York and London: Business Plus.

Perry, G., and D. Lederman. 1998. "Financial Vulnerability, Spillover Effects, and Contagion: Lessons From the Asian Crises for Latin America." Latin American and Caribbean Studies, World Bank, Washington, DC.

Pinto, B., and S. Ulatov. 2010. "Russia 1998 Revisited: Lessons for Financial Globalization." Policy Research Working Paper 5312, World Bank, Washington, DC.

Pistor, K. 2011. "Governing Interdependent Financial Systems: Lessons from the Vienna Initiative." Columbia Law and Economics Working Paper 396, Columbia University, New York.

Prebisch, R. 1950. "The Economic Development of Latin America and Its Principal Problems." Economic Commission for Latin America, United Nations, New York.

Rajan, R., and A. Subramanian. 2011. "Aid, Dutch Disease, and Manufacturing Growth." *Journal of Development Economics* 94 (1): 106-18.

Ranciere, R., A. Tornell, and A. Vamvakidis. 2010. "A New Index of Currency Mismatch and Systemic Risk." IMF Working Paper 10/263, International Monetary Fund, Washington, DC.

Reinhart, C., K. Rogoff, and M. Savastano. 2003. "Debt Intolerance." *Brookings Papers on Economic Activity* 34 (1): 1-74.

Richards, A., and M. Gugiatti. 2003. "Do Collective Action Clauses Influence Bond Yields? New Evidence from Emerging Markets." *International Finance* 6 (3): 415-47.

Rodrik, D. 1998. "Who Needs Capital-Account Convertibility?" Paper for a Princeton International Finance Section symposium. https://drodrik.scholar.harvard.edu/files/dani-rodrik/files/who-needs-capital-account-convertibility.pdf.

Rodrik, D. 2000. "Development Strategies for the Next Century." Working Paper 28160, World Bank, Washington, DC.

Rubin, R. 1998. "Treasury Secretary Robert E. Rubin Address on the Asian Financial Situation to Georgetown University Washington, DC." January 2021. https://www.treasury.gov/press-center/press-releases/Pages/rr2168.aspx.

Sachs, J. 1985. "External Debt and Macroeconomic Performance in Latin America and East Asia." *Brookings Papers on Economic Activity* 1985 (2): 523-73.

Sachs, J. 1986. "Managing the LDC Debt Crisis." *Brookings Papers on Economic Activity* 1986 (2): 397-440.

Sachs, J. 1988. "International Policy Coordination. The Case of the Developing Country Debt Crisis." In *International Economic Cooperation,* edited by Martin Feldstein, 233-78. Chicago: University of Chicago Press.

Sachs, J. 1989. "New Approaches to the Latin American Debt Crisis." In *Essays in International Finance* 174 Princeton, NJ: Princeton University Press.

Sachs, J. 2002. "Resolving the Debt Crisis of Low-Income Countries." *Brookings Papers on Economic Activity* 2002 (1): 257-86.

Sachs, J., R. Cooper, and B. Bosworth. 1998. "The East Asian Financial Crisis: Diagnosis, Remedies, Prospects." *Brookings Papers on Economic Activity* 1998 (1): 1-90.

Sachs, J., and H. Huizinga. 1987. "U.S. Commercial Banks and the Developing-Country Debt Crisis." *Brookings Papers on Economic Activity* 1987 (2): 555-606.

Schmukler, S., and G. Kaminsky. 2003. "Short-Run Pain, Long-Run Gain; The Effects of Financial Liberalization." IMF Working Paper 03/34, International Monetary Fund, Washington, DC.

Scitovsky, T. 1969. "Prospects for Latin American Industrialization within the Framework of Economic Integration: Bases for Analysis." In *The Process of Industrialization in Latin America*. Washington, DC: Inter-American Development Bank.

Sherman, M. 2009. *A Short History of Financial Deregulation in the United States*. Washington, DC: Center for Economic and Policy Research.

Singer, H. W. 1950. "The Distribution of Gains between Investing and Borrowing Countries." *American Economic Review* 40 (2): 473-85.

Sorkin, A. R. 2010. *Too Big to Fail: The Inside Story of How Wall Street and Washington Fought to Save the Financial System—and Themselves.* London: Penguin.

Spiegel, M., and D. Valderrama. 2003. "Currency Boards, Dollarized Liabilities, and Monetary Policy Credibility." *Journal of International Money and Finance* 22 (7): 1065-87.

Stiglitz, J. 1972. "Some Aspects of the Pure Theory of Corporate Finance: Bankruptcies and Take-Overs." *Bell Journal of Economics* 3 (2): 458-82.

Stiglitz, J. 2002. "Development Policies in a World of Globalization." Paper presented at the seminar "New International Trends for Economic Development," Brazilian Economic and Social Development Bank, Rio de Janeiro, September 12-13.

Sturzenegger, F., and J. Zettelmeyer. 2007. "Creditors' Losses versus Debt Relief: Results from a Decade of Sovereign Debt Crises." *Journal of the European Economic Association* 5 (2-3): 343-51.

Summers, L. H. 2001. "An Analysis of Russia's 1998 Meltdown: Fundamentals and Market Signals. Comments and Discussion." *Brookings Papers on Economic Activity* 2001 (1): 51-68.

Takáts, E. 2010. "Cross-Border Bank Lending to Emerging Market Economies." BIS Papers 54, Bank for International Settlements, Basel.

Tong, H., and S.-J. Wei. 2009. "The Composition Matters: Capital Inflows and Liquidity Crunch During a Global Economic Crisis." IMF Working Paper 09/64, International Monetary Fund, Washington, DC.

Turner, A. 2012. *Economics After the Crisis: Objectives and Means.* Cambridge, MA: MIT Press.

Turner, P. 2002. "Bond Markets in Emerging Economies: An Overview of Policy Issues." BIS Papers 11, Bank for International Settlements, Basel.

Unal, H., A. Demirgüç-Kunt, and K. Leung. 1993. "The Brady Plan, 1989 Mexican Debt-Reduction Agreement, and Bank Stock Returns in United States and Japan." *Journal of Money, Credit and Banking* 25 (3): 410-29.

Vasquez, I. 1996. "The Brady Plan and Market-Based Solutions to Debt Crises." *Cato Journal* 16 (2): 233-43.

Vegh, C. A., and G. Vuletin. 2014. "The Road to Redemption: Policy Response to Crises in Latin America." *IMF Economic Review* 62 (4): 526-68.

Weinschelbaum, F., and J. Wynne. 2005. "Renegotiation, Collective Action Clauses and Sovereign Debt Markets." *Journal of International Economics* 67 (1): 47-62.

Wessel, D. 2010. *In FED We Trust: Ben Bernanke's War on the Great Panic.* New York: Random House LLC.

Williamson, J., ed. 1990. *Latin American Adjustment: How Much Has Happened?* Washington, DC: Institute for International Economics.

Williamson, J. 2004. "The Strange History of the Washington Consensus." *Journal of Post Keynesian Economics* 27 (2): 195-206.

Williamson, O. E. 2000. "The New Institutional Economics: Taking Stock, Looking Ahead." *Journal of Economic Literature* 38 (3): 595-613.

World Bank. 1985. *World Development Report.* Washington, DC: World Bank.

World Bank. 1993. *The East Asian Miracle: Economic Growth and Public Policy.* New York, NY: Oxford University Press.

World Bank. 1998. *Global Economic Prospects and the Developing Countries: Beyond Financial Crisis.* Washington, DC: World Bank.

World Bank. 2004. *Global Development Finance: Harnessing Cyclical Gains for Development.* Washington, DC: World Bank.

World Bank. 2016. "World Bank's First Development Loans to Chile, 1948." Archives Exhibit Series 057, World Bank, Washington, DC.

World Bank. 2017a. *Global Economic Prospects: A Fragile Recovery.* June. Washington, DC: World Bank.

World Bank. 2017b. "Heavily Indebted Poor Countries (HIPC) Initiative and Multilateral Debt Relief Initiative (MDRI)—Statistical Update." World Bank, Washington, DC.

World Bank. 2017c. "Turmoil to Transformation, 20 Years after the Asian Financial Crisis." *Malaysia Economic Monitor.* December. Washington, DC: World Bank.

World Bank. 2019a. *Global Economic Prospects: Heightened Tensions, Subdued Investment.* June. Washington, DC: World Bank.

World Bank. 2019b. *Global Financial Development Report 2019/2020: Bank Regulation and Supervision a Decade after the Global Financial Crisis.* Washington, DC: World Bank.

World Bank. 2019c. *Doing Business 2019: Training for Reform.* Washington, DC: World Bank.

Perhaps the most remarkable change since the crises of the 1990s has come in the way emerging-market countries finance their debt. Governments now borrow much more in their own currencies than in foreign ones, making them less vulnerable to runs and currency crises.

Agustín Carstens and Hyun Song Shin (2019)
General Manager of the Bank of International Settlements;
Economic Adviser and Head of Research of the Bank for
International Settlements

CHAPTER 4

The Fourth Wave: Ripple or Tsunami?

Since 2010, another global wave of debt accumulation has been building. This wave has already seen the largest, fastest, and most broad-based increase in debt in emerging market and developing economies (EMDEs) in the past half-century. Even excluding China, where corporate debt has soared since the crisis, debt in EMDEs has risen to record highs. The current wave bears many similarities to the previous episodes: it has been fueled by very low interest rates and major changes in financial markets and accompanied by mounting vulnerabilities in EMDEs. It also differs from the previous waves, however, in some important dimensions: the current wave has been exceptional in its size, speed, and breadth but has also taken place in a more resilient global financial system as a result of post-crisis reforms. In addition, many EMDEs have improved their policy frameworks over the past two decades.

Introduction

The current global wave of debt, which started in 2010, has already seen the largest, fastest, and most broad-based increase in debt in emerging market and developing economies (EMDEs) in the past 50 years. Total EMDE debt (both public and private sectors) rose to almost 170 percent of gross domestic product (GDP) at end- 2018 from 114 percent at end-2010. Even excluding China, where the debt buildup has been particularly pronounced, total debt has risen by 19 percentage points since 2010, to 107 percent of GDP at end-2018.

The magnitude and speed of debt accumulation in the current (fourth) wave have triggered an intense debate about the benefits and risks of more borrowing. As summarized in chapter 2, debt can be beneficial if it is used for productive purposes, but high and rising debt can leave EMDEs vulnerable to economic and financial shocks. Despite the current prolonged period of very low interest rates, there is a risk that the latest wave of debt accumulation may follow the historical pattern of its predecessors (as documented in chapter 3) and result in widespread financial crises.

This chapter examines the current wave and puts it in historical context by considering the following questions:

- How has debt evolved in the fourth wave?

- Which factors have contributed to debt accumulation during the fourth wave?

- What are the similarities and differences between the fourth wave and the previous waves?

Contributions to the literature. In contrast to earlier studies, this chapter puts the current wave of broad-based debt accumulation in EMDEs into historical perspective. Earlier work has recognized the steep post-2009 increase in debt in certain regions or groups of countries. For example, some studies have examined mounting government debt in advanced economies.[1] Studies have shown considerable interest in the post-crisis increase in debt in EMDEs, including low-income and lower-middle-income countries, but again, these studies have documented the post-crisis increase in debt without the historical lens of the global waves framework (Essl et al. 2019; World Bank and IMF 2018a, 2018b).

Main findings. The main findings of this chapter are as follows:

- *Another global wave of rising debt underway.* This latest wave of debt accumulation began in 2010 and has already seen the largest, fastest, and most broad-based increase in debt in EMDEs in the past 50 years. The average annual increase in EMDE debt since 2010 of almost 7 percentage points of GDP has been larger by some margin than in each of the previous three waves. Whereas previous waves were largely regional in nature, the fourth wave has been very widespread with total debt rising in more than three-quarters of EMDEs and rising by at least 20 percentage points of GDP in just over one-third of EMDEs.

- *Multiple similarities with the previous waves.* The current wave of debt accumulation bears many similarities to the previous three waves. Global interest rates have been very low since the global financial crisis, and the search for yield by investors has contributed to narrowing spreads for EMDEs. Some major changes in financial markets have again boosted borrowing, including through a rise of regional banks, growing appetite for local currency bonds, and increased demand for EMDE debt from the expanding shadow banking sector. As in the earlier waves,

---

[1] A number of studies have examined rising debt in advanced economies, including BIS (2015); Cecchetti, Mohanty, and Zampolli (2011); Eberhardt and Presbitero (2018); Eichengreen et al. (2019); Mbaye, Moreno-Badia, and Chae (2018); OECD (2017); Panizza and Presbitero (2014); and Reinhart, Reinhart, and Rogoff (2012).

vulnerabilities have mounted as the current wave has proceeded. Borrowing has shifted to riskier debt instruments, including increasing reliance on non-Paris Club bilateral lenders, particularly in low-income countries (LICs). Fiscal and external deficits have increased in many EMDEs since 2010. GDP growth has also slowed in EMDEs since 2010.

- *Some important differences.* The fourth wave looks more worrisome than the previous episodes in terms of the size, speed, and reach of debt accumulation in EMDEs. It has also seen government debt rising in tandem with private sector debt, in contrast to earlier waves. But important policy improvements may mitigate these concerns. Multiple reforms have increased the resilience of the international financial system, and global financial safety nets have been expanded and strengthened since the global financial crisis. Many EMDEs have improved their macroprudential and regulatory policy frameworks over the past two decades.

The remainder of this chapter proceeds as follows. The first section discusses the evolution of debt in the fourth wave, in terms of the location, scale, and type of debt accumulation. Some factors that have contributed to the increase in debt are discussed next. The subsequent two sections place the fourth wave in the context of the previous waves by examining the similarities and differences among the four waves. The chapter concludes with a summary of findings.

The fourth wave

Largest, fastest, and most broad-based wave yet. Including or excluding China, the average annual increase since 2010 in total EMDE debt has been larger, by some margin, than the first three waves—almost 7 percentage points of GDP (or more than 2 percent excluding China (figure 4.1). Just over one-third of EMDEs have seen an increase in debt equivalent to at least 20 percentage points of GDP. In LICs, total debt increased by 19 percentage points of GDP, to 67 percent of GDP at end-2018.

In contrast to the previous three waves, which were largely regional in nature, the current, fourth wave has been global. Total debt has risen in more than 70 percent of EMDEs in each region—previous waves saw higher rates of increase in individual regions, but not big increases across all regions simultaneously. Total debt-to-GDP ratios have risen in all EMDE regions, except South Asia, where it has been flat, and in more than three-quarters of

FIGURE 4.1 **Change in debt across the four waves**

The fourth wave has seen the largest and fastest increase in debt-to-GDP ratios among EMDEs. It has also been the most broad-based across regions and borrowing sectors.

A. Change in total debt, by wave

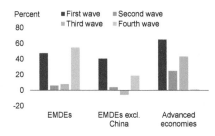

B. Average annual change in total debt, by wave

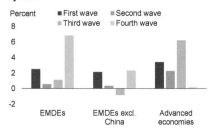

C. Share of economies with increase in government debt, by region

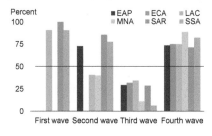

D. Share of economies with increase in private debt, by region

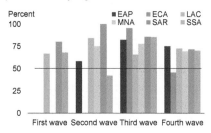

Sources: International Monetary Fund; World Bank.
Note: Sample includes 142 emerging market and developing economies (EMDEs). First wave: 1970-89; second wave 1990-2001; third wave 2002-09, fourth wave 2010+. EAP = East Asia and Pacific; ECA = Europe and Central Asia; LAC = Latin America and the Caribbean; MNA = Middle East and North Africa; SAR = South Asia; SSA = Sub-Saharan Africa.
A. Change in total debt ratio over the course of each wave.
B. Average annual change calculated as total increase in debt-to-GDP ratio over the duration of a wave, divided by the number of years in a wave.
C.D. Data show the share of economies where the debt-to-GDP ratio increased over the duration of the wave. Regions are excluded if country-level data are available for less than one-third of the region.

EMDEs, with over one-third seeing increases of at least 20 percentage points of GDP.[2]

Total debt in EMDEs rose by 54 percentage points of GDP to reach 168 percent of GDP at end-2018—a record high (figure 4.2). China, where corporate debt has soared since the crisis, accounted for the bulk of this debt buildup. Even excluding China, total EMDE debt rose to a near-record 107

---

[2] Total debt has risen particularly rapidly in Argentina, Cambodia, Chile, and China. Turkey stands out as having the third-fastest increase in private sector debt after Cambodia and China. Among LICs, The Gambia, Mozambique, and Togo have seen the largest increases in debt.

FIGURE 4.2 **Debt developments in the fourth wave**

Since the global financial crisis, another wave of EMDE debt accumulation has been underway. The fourth wave has seen a particularly rapid increase in private debt, especially in China. Among EMDEs excluding China, the fourth wave has seen an increase in private debt in 2010-14 and rising government debt in 2014-18. Deteriorating fiscal deficits in the aftermath of the oil price plunge of 2014-16 resulted in increased public sector borrowing. Low-income countries have also seen an increase in debt ratios.

A. Change in debt since 2010

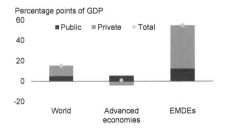

B. Change in debt in EMDEs excluding China

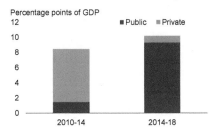

C. Fiscal balances in EMDEs

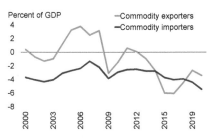

D. Low-income country debt

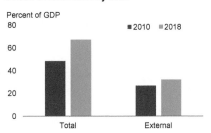

Sources: International Monetary Fund; World Bank.
Note: EMDEs = emerging market and developing economies.
A.-D. U.S. dollar GDP-weighted averages for each group.
A. Change in debt as a share of GDP since 2010.
B. Change in debt ratio over period shown.

percent of GDP at end-2018. Government debt accounted for almost three-fifths and private debt for just over two-fifths of the debt buildup in EMDEs other than China between 2010 and 2018. Debt in EMDEs excluding China has been relatively flat between 2016-18, with a small decrease in private sector debt offsetting a modest increase in government debt. This masks substantial variation between regions, however, with large increases in debt-to-GDP ratios in Latin America and the Caribbean and Sub-Saharan Africa, and declines in Europe and Central Asia and the Middle East and North Africa.

- *Government debt.* Since 2010, EMDE government debt has risen, on average, by 12 percentage points of GDP to 50 percent of GDP at end-

2018. Over this period, government debt relative to GDP has risen in three-quarters of EMDEs and by at least 10 percentage points in almost three-fifths of them. Government debt saw marked increases among commodity-exporting countries in the aftermath of the commodity price plunge of 2011-16, and especially the oil price plunge of 2014-16, as fiscal deficits surged amid declining revenues and fiscal stimulus measures (World Bank 2018a). In LICs, government debt has risen by 13 percentage points of GDP since 2010, to reach 46 percent of GDP at end-2018.

- *Private debt.* The private sector has also accumulated debt rapidly since the global financial crisis, especially in China. In about two-fifths of EMDEs, private sector credit booms occurred in at least one year during 2011-18 (Ohnsorge and Yu 2016; World Bank 2016).[3] The increase in China's private debt accounted for four-fifths of the post-crisis increase in private EMDE debt in 2010-18. It was concentrated in a few sectors, notably real estate, mining, and construction, and among state-owned enterprises. Private debt in EMDEs excluding China has increased by 8 percentage points of GDP since 2010, to reach 57 percent of GDP at end-2018.[4]

Both external and domestic debt. Whereas China's total debt buildup was predominantly with domestic creditors, external and domestic creditors have contributed in almost equal measure to the 19 percentage points of GDP debt buildup in other EMDEs between 2010 and 2018.

- *External debt.* External debt of EMDEs excluding China rose by 9 percentage points of GDP between 2010 and 2019, to 35 percent of GDP at end-2018. The increase in long-term external debt was driven by a rise in public debt (figure 4.3). The pace of China's external debt buildup was considerably slower than that of other EMDEs, so that external debt in EMDEs including China rose by only 4 percentage points of GDP between 2010 and 2018, to 26 percent of GDP at end-

---

[3] About half of all credit booms are followed by at least a mild deleveraging within three years (Ohnsorge and Yu 2016).

[4] Separate data on household and corporate debt are available only for a small sample of countries (27 advanced economies and 16 EMDEs). Among these countries, on average, corporate debt accounted for all (advanced economies) or most (EMDEs) of the post-crisis debt buildup. Whereas household debt-to-GDP ratios declined in 2010-18 in four-fifths of these advanced economies, the ratios rose in almost all of these EMDEs, but on average by only half the corporate debt buildup. Corporate debt-to-GDP ratios fell in two-thirds of these advanced economies but rose in almost all of these EMDEs. In China, household and corporate debt rose rapidly by 25 and 30 percentage points of GDP, respectively (BIS 2019).

FIGURE 4.3 **EMDE external debt and vulnerabilities**

Both government and private debt in EMDEs have shifted toward riskier funding sources. The increase in government debt has been accompanied by a growing share of nonresident investors, whereas corporations increased borrowing in foreign currencies. Borrowing among low-income countries has increasingly shifted toward non-Paris Club bilateral lenders.

A. Long-term external EMDE debt

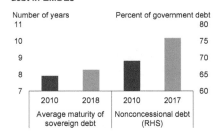

B. Government debt held by nonresidents

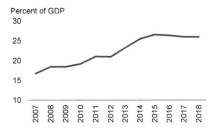

C. Average maturity and nonconcessional debt in EMDEs

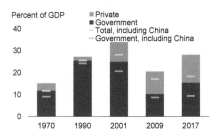

D. Foreign-currency-denominated corporate debt

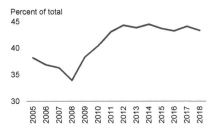

E. Low-income countries' share of nonconcessional debt

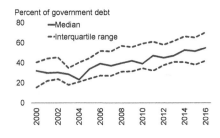

F. Low-income countries' creditor composition of public external debt

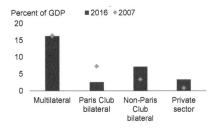

Sources: Bank for International Settlements; Institute of International Finance; International Monetary Fund; World Bank.
Note: EMDEs = emerging market and developing economies.
A. GDP-weighted averages.
B. Average for 45 EMDEs, though the sample size is smaller for earlier years.
C. Median of 35 EMDEs.
D. Average for 21 EMDEs.
E. Includes 30 low-income countries and excludes Somalia, South Sudan, and Syria, because of data restrictions.
F. GDP-weighted average across 32 countries.

2018. In LICs, external debt rose by 5 percentage points of GDP over the same period, to 32 percent of GDP at end-2018.

- *Domestic debt.* Domestic debt in EMDEs excluding China also rose by 9 percentage points of GDP between 2010 and 2018, to 72 percent of GDP at end-2018.[5] China's debt buildup consisted almost entirely of domestic debt. In LICs, domestic debt accounted for more than two-thirds of the post-crisis debt buildup.

Shifts to riskier debt. Both government and private debt have shifted toward riskier funding sources in many EMDEs, making these countries more vulnerable to a sudden deterioration in global investor sentiment or tightening monetary conditions.

- *Government debt.* The increase in government debt has been accompanied by a growing share of debt held by nonresident investors (to 43 percent in 2018) and an increasing reliance on nonconcessional terms. Sovereign ratings have also been downgraded for many EMDEs since 2010 (World Bank 2019b).

- *Private debt.* On average across the 21 EMDEs with available data, foreign-currency-denominated corporate debt rose from 19 percent of GDP in 2010 to 26 percent of GDP in 2018, although its share of total corporate debt remained at about 40 percent over this period (IIF 2019). By end-2018, one-third of the 21 EMDEs had foreign-currency-denominated corporate debt above 20 percent of GDP. In addition, a greater share of corporate debt than before the global financial crisis has been owed by firms with riskier financial profiles, because supportive financing conditions have allowed firms to issue more debt with weaker credit quality (Beltran and Collins 2018; Feyen et al. 2017; IMF 2015a).

- *LIC government debt.* In LICs, debt has also shifted toward nonconcessional, non-Paris Club creditors, notably China, as well as commercial creditors over the past decade (World Bank 2018b; World Bank and IMF 2018a, 2018b). The median share of nonconcessional debt in LIC government debt rose to 55 percent in 2016, an increase of nearly 8 percentage points since 2013, and 15 percentage points higher than a decade earlier. In 2016, non-Paris Club debt accounted for more

---

[5] Domestic debt is estimated as the residual after the reduction from total debt (as reported in Kose et al. 2017) of external debt as reported in the World Development Indicators.

FIGURE 4.4 **Shift toward EMDE-headquartered banks**

As European and U.S.-headquartered banks have downsized their EMDE operations, cross-border bank lending to EMDEs has shifted to EMDE-headquartered banks.

A. Reliance on foreign banks by sector

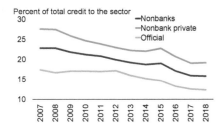

B. Bank credit in total private sector debt

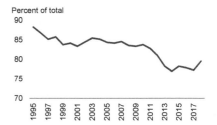

C. Panregional banks

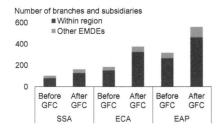

D. Changing sources of cross-border bank loans

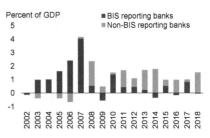

Sources: Bank for International Settlements; International Monetary Fund; World Bank.
Note: BIS = Bank for International Settlements; EAP = East Asia and Pacific; ECA = Europe and Central Asia; EMDEs = emerging market and developing economies; GFC = global financial crisis; SSA = Sub-Saharan Africa.
A. Sample includes Argentina, Brazil, Chile, Colombia, Hungary, India, Indonesia, Mexico, Malaysia, Poland, the Russian Federation, Thailand, Turkey, and South Africa. Claims by foreign banks (on an ultimate risk basis) are a sum of cross-border lending and credit extended by local subsidiaries of foreign banks. Average foreign bank reliance (FBR) is measured across the sample of 15 EMDEs with BIS data on total credit. Sector-specific FBR measure is calculated as a ratio of cross-border lending and local claims by subsidiaries of foreign banks divided by total credit to the sector.
B. Sample includes total debt and bank credit of the nonfinancial private sector in Argentina, Brazil, Chile, China, Colombia, Hungary, India, Indonesia, Malaysia, Mexico, Thailand, Poland, Russia, South Africa, and Turkey.
C. Based on annual bank statements; before the GFC = 2008 or 2009 depending on data availability; after GFC = 2018 or latest data available.
D. Sample includes 115 EMDEs excluding China (data for only 77 EMDEs in 2018). Lending by non-BIS banks is estimated as total bank loans and deposits from the International Monetary Fund's Balance of Payment Statistics (excluding central banks) minus cross-border lending by BIS reporting banks. This difference mostly accounts for the banking flows originating from non-BIS reporting economies.

than 20 percent of the median LIC's external debt, and about 13 percent of its public debt, raising concerns about debt transparency as well as debt collateralization (Essl et al. 2019).

Changes in the composition of creditors. Since the global financial crisis, borrowing by EMDEs has shifted toward capital markets and regional banks, and away from global banks (figure 4.4). Bond issuance has allowed firms to access finance when bank credit supply has tightened or at different terms from bank loans (Becker and Ivashina 2014; Cortina-Lorente, Didier, and Schmukler 2016). The role of regional EMDE banks has also grown as large international banks retrenched from EMDEs in the aftermath of the global financial crisis.[6]

Chinese banks accounted for two-thirds of EMDE-to-EMDE lending between 2013 and 2017 and for most of the doubling in cross-border claims on Sub-Saharan Africa economies in this period, to over 10 percent of GDP on average (Cerutti, Koch, and Pradhan 2018; Dollar 2016). Other EMDE banks have also increased their presence in EMDEs within their respective regions (IMF 2015b). A notable exception has been the Middle East and North Africa, where declining current account surpluses resulting from weaker oil revenues have reduced the region's ability to recirculate savings from high-income oil exporters to lower-income EMDEs with persistent current account deficits (World Bank 2019a).

In Sub-Saharan Africa, banks headquartered in Nigeria, South Africa, and Togo have expanded rapidly to other EMDEs in the region (Arizala et al. 2018). In Europe and Central Asia, Russian Federation banks initially expanded within the region after the crisis, as Western European banks withdrew. Latin America and the Caribbean was an exception, with a growing role of domestic banks, rather than of banks based in other countries in the region, as domestic banks acquired assets from exiting foreign lenders. The regional expansion of EMDE banks has yet to reach the scale of precrisis cross-border activity of advanced economy banks.

Finally, the domestic institutional investor base has continued to grow in EMDEs, offering the prospect of a potentially stabilizing pool of domestic savings. Assets of pension funds and insurance companies were 46 percent of GDP by end-2016, on average, in EMDEs, slightly higher than in 2010. Such assets remain equivalent to only about half of the assets of the bank and nonbank financial system (World Bank 2019b).[7]

---

[6] For details of bank financing in EMDEs after the global financial crisis, see Cerutti and Zhou (2017, 2018); Feyen and Gonzalez de Mazo (2013); IMF (2015a); Milesi-Feretti and Tille (2011); Montoro and Rojas-Suarez (2015); and World Bank (2018c).

[7] Data on assets of pension funds and insurance companies are available only for 22 EMDEs. Foreign institutional investors' role in EMDE financial markets has also grown but in some sectors remains small. For example, in just under 1,000 infrastructure projects since 2011, the share of institutional investors has more than tripled but still accounts for only 0.7 percent of the average project value (World Bank 2018a). Some institutional investors in EMDEs have been shown to behave procyclically, leaving EMDE financial markets during times of stress rather than acting as stabilizing investors with deep pockets (Raddatz and Schmukler 2012).

Similarities with the previous waves

The fourth wave shares a number of common features with the previous three waves. Specifically, the current debt buildup has been associated with very low global interest rates and major changes in financial markets, some of which have facilitated the rapid buildup of debt by previously credit-constrained borrowers. The beginning of the wave coincided with a strong rebound in economic activity in 2010, but EMDE growth subsequently slowed. Vulnerabilities have also risen during the current wave.

Low interest rates. As in the previous three waves, interest rates have been very low, as a result of accommodative monetary policies since the global financial crisis (figure 4.5). In the resulting search for yield environment, spreads on emerging market debt—for both corporate and sovereign bonds—reached all-time lows in 2017, enabling both governments and corporates to borrow at low interest rates. Average spreads on corporate bond issuance have fallen for all EMDEs, including LICs. Spreads have also fallen for lower-rated corporate bonds. The current wave has also seen rising demand for EMDE bonds from international investors such as asset managers (Shin 2014).

Changes in financial markets. As with the previous three waves, the current wave has seen some major changes in financial markets that have facilitated the accumulation of debt in EMDEs. Financial systems in EMDEs have deepened and become more complex (Didier and Schmukler 2014). Domestic debt has become increasingly important, with a rising share of local currency bonds (figure 4.6).[8] The increase in issuance, by both private and government borrowers, has been driven by the largest EMDEs.

Both corporate and sovereign borrowers have increasingly accessed capital markets, in some regions following retrenchment by large international banks. Over the past decade, more than 20 EMDEs have accessed international capital markets for the first time. New frontier market bond indexes, such as J. P. Morgan's NEXGEM (launched in 2011) or Morgan Stanley Capital International's Frontier Market Index (launched in 2007), have facilitated international capital market access and broadened the investor base for countries that previously had only intermittent access or

---

[8] For details, see Arteta and Kasyanenko (2020) and Essl at al. (2019). The growing share of local currency-denominated debt may bring other risks, however, because countries switching from external to domestic debt could be trading a currency mismatch for a maturity mismatch (Broner, Lorenzoni, and Schmukler 2013; Panizza 2008). Nominal interest rates on domestic debt also tend to be higher than on external debt (IMF 2015a).

FIGURE 4.5 **Comparison with previous waves**

As in earlier waves, the start of the fourth wave coincided with a period of low, or falling, interest rates and rising per capita incomes. Whereas earlier waves were concentrated in a few regions, the debt buildup in the fourth wave has been broad-based.

A. U.S. policy interest rates

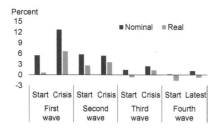

B. Capital flows to EMDEs

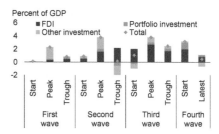

C. Change in EMDE government debt, by region

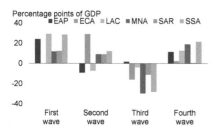

D. Change in EMDE private debt, by region

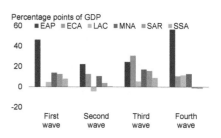

Sources: Haver Analytics; International Monetary Fund; World Bank.
Note: EAP = East Asia and Pacific; ECA = Europe and Central Asia; EMDEs = emerging market and developing economies; FDI = foreign direct investment; LAC = Latin America and the Caribbean; MNA = Middle East and North Africa; SAR = South Asia; SSA = Sub-Saharan Africa.
A. Start of a wave defined as the first three years of the wave. Crisis defined as the year before and year of widespread crises: First wave: 1970-72 and 1981-82; second wave: 1990-92 and 1996-97; third wave: 2002-04, and 2008-09; fourth wave: 2010-12 and 2017-18 (final two years of sample). Real interest rates are deflated by the GDP deflator.
B. Net capital inflows to EMDEs. The start of each wave is the first year, the peak is the year of peak capital inflows before the start of the crisis, and the trough is the year of lowest capital inflows after the crisis. First wave: 1970, 1978, and 1988; second wave: 1990, 1995, and 2000; third wave: 2002, 2007, and 2009; fourth wave: 2010 and 2018 (latest data).

access on less favorable terms. For example, exceptionally long-term (50- and 100-year) international bonds were issued by Mexico in 2010 and Argentina in 2017.

From 2007 to 2017, debt securities issued by EMDE governments increased by 4.4 percentage points of GDP on average, to 22 percent of GDP. In Sub-Saharan Africa, Eurobond issuance has grown, with several countries tapping this market for the first time. Sovereign debt issuance has increased particularly rapidly in certain domestic bond markets, especially in East Asia and Pacific (IMF 2018). Foreign portfolio investors have become more

FIGURE 4.6 **EMDE bond issuance**

Since the global financial crisis, EMDE corporate and sovereign borrowers have turned to capital markets to raise new debt. Domestic debt has become increasingly important, with a rising share of local currency bonds.

A. Change in bond issuance, 2010-16, by issuer

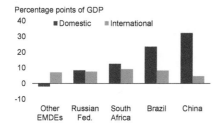

B. Claims on the official sector

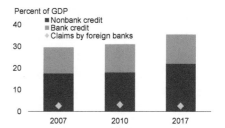

C. Local currency debt

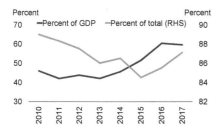

D. Debt securities outstanding

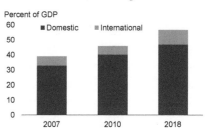

Sources: Bank for International Settlements; Institute of International Finance; International Monetary Fund; World Bank.
Note: EMDEs = emerging market and developing economies.
A. Chart shows the change in debt securities (in percentage points of GDP) between 2010 and 2016 (last observation). Other EMDEs includes eight countries. Data for India are unavailable.
B. Bank for International Settlements estimates of the claims by foreign banks on official sector: sample includes Argentina, Brazil, Chile, Colombia, Hungary, India, Indonesia, Israel, Malaysia, Mexico, Poland, Russian Federation, Thailand, Turkey, Republic of Korea, and South Africa.
C. Local-currency-denominated debt as share of total debt of the general government and nongovernment sectors. Nongovernment sector debt includes debt of financial corporations (including banks) and nonfinancial corporations.
D. Sample includes Argentina, Brazil, Colombia, India, Indonesia, Malaysia, Mexico, Philippines, Russia, South Africa, Thailand, and Turkey.

active in local bond markets, accounting for a growing share of holdings of local-currency-denominated sovereign bonds. In some EMDEs, the share of nonresident investors in local currency sovereign bond holdings has risen above 30 percent, which makes these economies more vulnerable to sudden shifts in investor confidence (IMF 2018).

New financing vehicles such as infrastructure bonds and green finance bonds have stimulated lending to specific EMDE sectors for which banks used to be the primary source of funding (FSB 2018a; McKinsey Global Institute

2018).[9] Infrastructure financing in general, however, has fallen in EMDEs following the sharp decline in cross-border lending amid stricter post-crisis regulations in the financial sector (World Bank 2013, 2019b).[10]

The current wave has also seen a significant increase in shadow banking activities in EMDEs. Shadow banking refers to nonbank financial intermediation that takes place outside of the regulated financial system and may provide credit to riskier borrowers who often lack access to bank credit. Shadow banking systems, which were small before the global recession, have expanded rapidly in a number of EMDEs, particularly in large economies such as China and India (IMF 2014). In these two countries, assets of nonbank financial institutions have recently increased to over a third of total financial system assets. In China alone, this share has more than doubled over the past decade, and the size and complexity of its nonbank financial sector is becoming comparable to those of advanced economies (Ehlers, Kong, and Zhou 2018).

Economic upturn. The beginning of the fourth wave was similar to those of the previous three waves in that it was also marked by a sharp rebound in global economic activity, starting in 2010, and followed an economic downturn—in this case, the deepest global recession of the past 70 years. Global growth has stagnated since then, however, and EMDEs have experienced a sharp slowdown over the course of the fourth wave.

Mounting vulnerabilities. As in previous global waves of debt accumulation, vulnerabilities have once again grown over the course of the fourth wave (Ruch 2020). Since 2010, EMDE total external debt has risen, reflecting sizable and persistent current account deficits. In addition, both government and private debt have shifted toward riskier forms in many EMDEs, as summarized previously. A decade of tightening bank regulation and rapid growth of debt has increased maturity mismatches and credit risk in shadow banking (IMF 2019a, 2019b). Adding to these vulnerabilities are signs that during the current wave, government debt has been used to finance not investment in human or physical capital that could boost potential growth but less efficient and less productive current spending.

---

[9] In advanced economies, some financial instruments that were widely used before the crisis have regained popularity. Especially in the United States, leveraged loan issuances—most of which are now covenant-light with lesser protections for creditors, and which are predominantly held in collateralized loan obligations (CLOs) and loan funds—have risen again above elevated precrisis levels. Concerns have been raised whether CLO prices are fully aligned with risks (Domanski 2018; FSB 2019).

[10] Grants and concessional loans are the primary sources of infrastructure finance in LICs, with bank lending providing complementary funding in only a small number of countries (Gurara et al. 2017).

Differences from the previous waves

Among the four waves of debt, the latest, and current, wave has been exceptional in terms of its greater size, faster speed, and broader country coverage. Some other developments, however, have been more reassuring. During the latest wave, certain reforms have made the international financial system more resilient and enlarged the global financial safety net. Many EMDEs have improved their macroeconomic and prudential policy frameworks over the past two decades. In contrast to previous waves, the current wave has been set against a backdrop of broadly stable advanced economy debt ratios.

Largest wave. The current wave has featured the fastest, largest, and most broad-based accumulation of debt by EMDEs in the past half-century, as documented earlier. In contrast to earlier waves, government debt has risen in tandem with mounting private sector debt.

Better policy frameworks. Many EMDEs learned the lessons from crises in the previous waves and adopted reforms designed to improve their resilience (Ruch 2020). These reforms include greater exchange rate flexibility, more robust monetary policy frameworks with central bank transparency, and the adoption of fiscal rules. More EMDEs now employ macroprudential tools, and many have improved bankruptcy regimes.

Financial regulatory reforms. Implementation of the Group of Twenty (G20) global financial regulatory reform agenda has led to major financial reforms since the global financial crisis (FSB 2018b). These reforms have helped increase the resilience of the international financial system (Arteta and Kasyanenko 2020). Global financial safety nets have also been expanded significantly since the crisis.

Stable debt in advanced economies. In contrast to the first and third waves—when advanced economy debt accumulation outpaced EMDE debt accumulation—the fourth wave has been accompanied by near-stable advanced economy debt-to-GDP ratios. In advanced economies, pronounced private deleveraging has reduced the share of private debt in total debt.

Conclusion

The fourth wave has seen the largest, fastest, and most broad-based increase in debt over the past half-century. As with previous waves, low interest rates and financial market developments have facilitated the buildup of debt. But this wave also has important differences. Policy frameworks are more robust in many EMDEs, with more EMDEs adopting inflation-targeting regimes and fiscal rules. Similarly, global safety nets have been expanded and strengthened. Vulnerabilities have been mounting in EMDEs, however, throughout the current wave.

Key questions confronting policy makers are whether the fourth wave may also end in widespread crises, following its predecessors over the past 50 years, and what needs to be done to prevent such an outcome. Before answering these questions, it is necessary to move beyond the global waves of debt and examine the causes and consequences of national episodes of rapid debt accumulation in EMDEs. That is the topic of the next chapter. Chapter 6 will then revisit the similarities and differences, discussed here, between the current and previous waves, synthesize the main insights from the first five chapters, and offer answers to these key questions.

References

Arizala, F., M. Bellon, M. MacDonald, M. Mlachila, and M. Yenice. 2018. "Regional Spillovers in Sub-Saharan Africa: Exploring Different Channels." *Spillover Notes 18/01*, International Monetary Fund, Washington, DC.

Arteta, C., and S. Kasyanenko. 2020. "Financial Sector Developments." In *A Decade after the Global Recession: Lessons and Challenges for Emerging and Developing Economies*, edited by M. A. Kose and F. Ohnsorge. Washington, DC: World Bank.

Becker, B., and V. Ivashina. 2014. "Cyclicality of Credit Supply: Firm Level Evidence." *Journal of Monetary Economics* 62 (March): 76-93.

Beltran, D.O., and C. G. Collins. 2018. "How Vulnerable Are EME Corporates?" IFDP Notes K.7, Board of Governors of the Federal Reserve System, Washington, DC.

BIS (Bank for International Settlements). 2015. "Debt." BIS Papers 80, Bank for International Settlements, Basel.

BIS (Bank for International Settlements). 2019. *Credit to the Nonfinancial Sector Statistics*. Basel: Bank for International Settlements.

Broner, F., G. Lorenzoni, and S. Schmukler. 2013. "Why Do Emerging Economies Borrow Short Term?" *Journal of the European Economic Association* 11 (1): 67-100.

Cecchetti, S., M. Mohanty, and F. Zampolli. 2011. "The Real Effects of Debt." BIS Working Paper 352, Bank for International Settlements, Basel.

Cerutti, E., C. Koch, and S. Pradhan. 2018. "The Growing Footprint of EME Banks in the International Banking System." *BIS Quarterly Review*. December. Bank for International Settlements, Basel.

Cerutti, E., and H. Zhou. 2017. "The Global Banking Network in the Aftermath of the Crisis: Is There Evidence of De-globalization?" IMF Working Paper 17/232, International Monetary Fund, Washington, DC.

Cerutti, E., and H. Zhou. 2018. "The Global Banking Network: What Is Behind the Increasing Regionalization Trend?" IMF Working Paper 18/46, International Monetary Fund, Washington, DC.

Cortina-Lorente, J. J., T. Didier, and S. L. Schmukler. 2016. "How Long Is the Maturity of Corporate Borrowing? Evidence from Bond and Loan Issuances across Markets." Policy Research Working Paper 7815, World Bank, Washington, DC.

Didier, T., and S. Schmukler. 2014. "Debt Markets in Emerging Economies: Major Trends." *Comparative Economic Studies* 56 (2): 200-28.

Dollar, D. 2016. *China's Engagement with Africa: From Natural Resources to Human Resources.* Washington, DC: Brookings Institution.

Domanski, D. 2018. "Achieving the G20 Goal of Resilient Market-Based Finance." *Banque de France Financial Stability Review* 22 (April): 155-65.

Eberhardt, M., and A. F. Presbitero. 2015. "Public Debt and Growth: Heterogeneity and Non-linearity." *Journal of International Economics* 97 (1): 45-58.

Ehlers, T., S. Kong, and F. Zhu. 2018. "Mapping Shadow Banking in China: Structure and Dynamics." Working Paper 701, Bank for International Settlements, Basel.

Eichengreen, B., A. El-Ganainy, R. Esteves, and K. J. Mitchener. 2019. "Public Debt through the Ages." NBER Working Paper 25494, National Bureau of Economic Research, Cambridge, MA.

Essl, S., S. Kilic Celik, P. Kirby, and A. Proite. 2019. "Debt in Low-Income Countries: Evolution, Implications, Remedies." Policy Research Working Paper 8794, World Bank, Washington, DC.

Feyen, E., N. Fiess, I. Z. Huertas, and L. Lambert. 2017. "Which Emerging Markets and Developing Economies Face Corporate Balance Sheet Vulnerabilities? A Novel Monitoring Framework." Policy Research Working Paper 8198, World Bank, Washington, DC.

Feyen, E., and I. Gonzalez de Mazo. 2013. "European Bank Deleveraging and Global Credit Conditions: Implications of a Multi-Year Process on Long-Term Finance and Beyond." Policy Research Working Paper 6388, World Bank, Washington, DC.

FSB (Financial Stability Board). 2018a. *Evaluation of the Effects of Financial Regulatory Reforms on Infrastructure Finance.* Basel: Financial Stability Board.

FSB (Financial Stability Board). 2018b. *Implementation and Effects of the G20 Financial Regulatory Reforms.* Basel: Financial Stability Board.

FSB (Financial Stability Board). 2019. "FSB Plenary Meets in New York." Press Release. Financial Stability Board, Basel, April 26, 2019.

Gurara, D., V. Klyuev, N. Mwase, A. Presbitero, X. Xu, and G. Bannister. 2017. "Trends and Challenges in Infrastructure Investment in Low-Income Developing Countries." IMF Working Paper 233, International Monetary Fund, Washington, DC.

IIF (Institute of International Finance). 2019. *Global Debt Monitor.* Institute of International Finance, Washington, DC.

IMF (International Monetary Fund). 2014. *Global Financial Stability Report: Risk Taking, Liquidity, and Shadow Banking.* International Monetary Fund, Washington, DC.

IMF (International Monetary Fund). 2015a. *Global Financial Stability Report:, Vulnerabilities, Legacies, and Policy Challenges—Risks Rotating to Emerging Markets.* International Monetary Fund, Washington, DC.

IMF (International Monetary Fund). 2015b. *Pan-African Banks: Opportunities and Challenges for Cross-Border Oversight.* Washington, DC: International Monetary Fund.

IMF (International Monetary Fund). 2018d. "Recent Developments on Local Currency Bond Markets in Emerging Economies." Staff Note for the G20 IFAWG, Seoul, June 15. International Monetary Fund, Washington, DC.

IMF (International Monetary Fund). 2019a. *Global Financial Stability Report. Lower for Longer.* October. Washington, DC: International Monetary Fund.

IMF (International Monetary Fund). 2019b. *Global Financial Stability Report. Vulnerabilities in a Maturing Credit Cycle.* Washington, DC: International Monetary Fund.

Kose, M. A., S. Kurlat, F. Ohnsorge, and N. Sugawara. 2017. "A Cross-Country Database of Fiscal Space." Policy Research Working Paper 8157, World Bank, Washington, DC.

Mbaye, S., M. Moreno-Badia, and K. Chae. 2018. "Bailing Out the People? When Private Debt Becomes Public." IMF Working Paper 18/141, International Monetary Fund, Washington, DC.

McKinsey Global Institute. 2018. "Rising Corporate Debt: Peril or Promise?" Discussion Paper, McKinsey & Company, New York.

Milesi-Ferretti, G. M., and C. Tille. 2011. "The Great Retrenchment: International Capital Flows during the Global Financial Crisis." *Economic Policy* 26 (66): 289-346.

Montoro, C., and L. Rojas-Suarez. 2015. "Credit in Times of Stress: Lessons from Latin America during the Global Financial Crisis." *Review of Development Economics* 19 (2): 309-27.

OECD (Organisation for Economic Co-operation and Development). 2017. *OECD Economic Outlook.* November. Paris: Organisation for Economic Co-operation and Development.

Ohnsorge, F., and S. Yu. 2016. "Recent Credit Surge in Historical Context." Policy Research Working Paper 7704, World Bank, Washington, DC.

Panizza, U. 2008. "Domestic and External Public Debt in Developing Countries." United Nations Conference on Trade and Development Discussion Paper 188, United Nations, New York.

Panizza, U., and A. F. Presbitero. 2014. "Public Debt and Economic Growth: Is There a Causal Effect?" *Journal of Macroeconomics* 41 (September): 21-41.

Raddatz, C., and S. L. Schmukler. 2012. "On the International Transmission of Shocks: Micro-Evidence from Mutual Fund Portfolios." NBER Working Paper 17358, National Bureau of Economic Research, Cambridge, MA.

Reinhart, C., V. Reinhart, and K. Rogoff. 2012. "Public Debt Overhangs: Advanced-Economy Episodes Since 1800." *Journal of Economic Perspectives* 26 (3): 69-86.

Ruch, F. U. 2020. "Prospects, Risks and Vulnerabilities." In *A Decade after the Global Recession: Lessons and Challenges for Emerging and Developing Economies,* edited by M. A. Kose and F. Ohnsorge. Washington, DC: World Bank.

Shin, H. 2014. "The Second Phase of Global Liquidity and Its Impact on Emerging Economies." In *Volatile Capital Flows in Korea: Current Policies and Future Responses,* edited by K. Chung, S. Kim, H. Park, C. Choi, and H. S. Shin, 247-57. London: Palgrave Macmillan.

World Bank. 2013. "Long-Term Investment Financing for Growth and Development: Umbrella Paper." Paper presented to the Meeting of the G20 Ministers of Finance and Central Bank Governors, Moscow, February.

World Bank. 2016. *Global Economic Prospects: Divergences and Risks.* June. Washington, DC: World Bank.

World Bank. 2018a. *Global Economic Prospects: Broad-Based Upturn, but for How Long?* January. Washington, DC: World Bank.

World Bank. 2018b. "Debt Vulnerabilities in IDA Countries." World Bank, Washington, DC.

World Bank. 2018c. "Contribution of Institutional Investors to Private Investment in Infrastructure 2011-H1 2017." World Bank, Washington, DC.

World Bank. 2019a. *MENA Economic Update: Reforms and External Imbalances: The Labor-Productivity Connection in the Middle East and North Africa.* Washington, DC: World Bank.

World Bank. 2019b. *Doing Business 2019: Training for Reform.* Washington, DC: World Bank.

World Bank and IMF (International Monetary Fund). 2018a. "Debt Vulnerabilities in Emerging and Low-Income Economies." October 2018 Meeting of the Development Committee, World Bank, Washington, DC.

World Bank and IMF (International Monetary Fund). 2018b. "G-20 Note: Strengthening Public Debt Transparency: The Role of the IMF and the World Bank." World Bank, Washington, DC.

PART III

Crises and Policies

The sovereign debt restructuring regime looks like it is coming apart. Changing patterns of capital flows, old creditors' weakening commitment to past practices, and other stakeholders' inability to take over, or coalesce behind a viable alternative, have challenged the regime from the moment it took shape in the mid-1990s.

Anna Gelpern (2016)
Professor of Law at Georgetown University

CHAPTER 5

Debt and Financial Crises: From Euphoria to Distress

Emerging market and developing economies have experienced recurrent episodes of rapid debt accumulation over the past 50 years. Half of such episodes were associated with financial crises. Rapid debt buildup, whether public or private, increased the likelihood of a financial crisis, as did a higher share of short-term debt or larger external debt. Countries that experienced financial crises had often employed combinations of unsustainable fiscal, monetary, and financial sector policies and had often suffered from structural and institutional weaknesses.

Introduction

Over the past half-century, emerging market and developing economies (EMDEs) have experienced recurrent episodes of rapid debt accumulation. When they have taken place in many economies, such national episodes together have formed global waves of debt. Whereas the two preceding chapters examined the waves, this chapter turns to the implications of rapid debt accumulation at the country level. Rising or elevated debt increases a country's vulnerability to economic and financial shocks—including increases in the costs of refinancing—which can culminate in financial crises, with large and lasting adverse effects on economic activity.[1]

This chapter provides a more granular perspective on the causes and consequences of debt accumulation by addressing the following questions:

- What were the main features of national episodes of rapid debt accumulation?

- What are the empirical links between debt accumulation and financial crises?

- What major institutional and structural weaknesses were associated with financial crises?

Contributions to the literature. The chapter makes several novel contributions to the already extensive literature on the links between debt and financial crises as reviewed in chapter 2.

---

[1] For a large sample of advanced economies and EMDEs, it has been estimated that output was, on average, 10 percent lower eight years after a debt crisis, and that the fiscal cost of resolving banking crises averaged 13 percent of gross domestic product (Furceri and Zdzienicka 2012; Laeven and Valencia 2018). Recessions associated with financial crises have tended to be worse than other recessions, and recoveries following financial crises have tended to be weaker and slower than other cyclical recoveries (Claessens, Kose, and Terrones 2012).

- *National debt accumulation episodes.* The chapter undertakes the first comprehensive empirical study of the many episodes of government or private debt accumulation since 1970 in a large number of EMDEs. It not only considers what happened during the financial crises associated with rapid debt accumulation but also examines macroeconomic and financial developments during the episodes of debt accumulation. Earlier work has often examined developments in government or private debt markets separately, analyzed these developments over short time intervals around financial crises, or focused on a narrow group of (mostly advanced) economies or regions.[2]

- *Debt and financial crises.* The chapter expands on earlier empirical studies of the correlates of crises by analyzing the links between debt accumulation and financial crises in a single empirical framework and by extending the horizon of analysis to cover the four global waves of debt accumulation since 1970.[3] Whereas some earlier studies examined the roles of different types of debt and a host of potential correlates of crises, most typically examined the links between a composite indicator of vulnerabilities and crises. In contrast, the empirical approach here zooms in on the links between debt and financial crises.

- *Country case studies.* The chapter presents a comprehensive review of country case studies of rapid debt accumulation episodes associated with financial crises. Based on a literature review that extracts common themes from a large set of country case studies, this complementary qualitative approach helps identify the major structural and institutional weaknesses associated with financial crises.

Main findings. The chapter presents the following findings.

- *National debt accumulation episodes.* Since 1970, there have been 519 national episodes of rapid debt accumulation in 100 EMDEs. Such episodes have therefore been common: in the average year, three-quarters of EMDEs were in either a government or a private debt accumulation episode or in both. The duration of a typical debt accumulation episode

---

[2] Government debt crises have been discussed in Abbas, Pienkowski, and Rogoff (2019); Kindleberger and Aliber (2011); Reinhart, Reinhart, and Rogoff (2012); Reinhart and Rogoff (2011); and World Bank (2019). Credit booms have been examined in Dell'Arricia et al. (2014, 2016); Elekdag and Wu (2013); IMF (2004); Jordà, Schularick, and Taylor (2011); Mendoza and Terrones (2008, 2012); Ohnsorge and Yu (2016); Schularick and Taylor 2012; and Tornell and Westermann (2005).

[3] Earlier studies have included either government debt (Manasse, Roubini, and Schimmelpfenning 2003) or private debt (Borio and Lowe 2002; Demirgüç-Kunt and Detragiache 1998; Kaminsky and Reinhart 1999) or both (Dawood, Horsewood, and Strobel 2017; Frankel and Rose 1996; Rose and Spiegel 2012) among a host of potential correlates of crises.

was seven years for government debt episodes and eight years for private debt episodes. The median debt buildup during a government debt accumulation episode (30 percentage points of gross domestic product [GDP]) was double that during a private debt accumulation episode (15 percentage points of GDP).

- *Debt accumulation and financial crises.* About half of the national debt accumulation episodes were accompanied by financial crises. Crises were particularly common in the first and second global waves: of all the national episodes that formed part of these two waves, almost two-thirds were associated with crises. National debt accumulation episodes that coincided with crises were typically associated with larger debt buildups (for government debt), weaker economic outcomes, and larger macroeconomic and financial vulnerabilities than were noncrisis episodes. Crises in rapid *government* debt buildups featured significantly larger output losses than crises in rapid *private* debt buildups: in the case of government (private) debt, after eight years, real GDP in episodes with crises was about 10 (6) percent lower than in episodes without crisis and investment was more than 20 (15) percent lower. Outcomes were particularly weak when crises coincided with combined government and private debt accumulation episodes.

- *Likelihood of financial crises.* An increase in debt, either government or private, was associated with a significantly higher probability of crisis in the following year. In addition, a combined accumulation of both government and private debt resulted in a higher likelihood of a currency crisis than did solely government or solely private debt increases.

- *Debt accumulation as a shock amplifier.* Although financial crises associated with national debt accumulation episodes were typically triggered by external shocks such as sudden increases in global interest rates, domestic vulnerabilities often amplified the adverse impact of these shocks. Crises were more likely, or the economic distress they caused was more severe, in countries with higher external debt—especially short-term—and lower international reserves.

- *Crises associated with inadequate policy frameworks.* Most EMDEs that experienced financial crises during debt accumulation episodes employed various combinations of unsustainable macroeconomic policies, and suffered structural and institutional weaknesses. Many of them had severe fiscal and monetary policy weaknesses, including poor revenue collection, widespread tax evasion, public wage and pension indexing, monetary financing of fiscal deficits, and substantial use of energy and food subsidies. Crisis countries also often borrowed in foreign currency, and employed managed exchange rate regimes, while regulation and supervision of banks and other financial institutions were frequently weak. Debt buildup had often funded import substitution strategies, undiversified economies, or inefficient sectors that did not raise export earnings or had poor corporate governance. Several EMDEs that experienced crises also suffered from protracted political uncertainty.

The rest of the chapter is organized as follows. First, the chapter examines the features of national episodes of rapid private and government debt accumulation. Next, it outlines an empirical framework to analyze how debt accumulation affects the likelihood of financial crises, controlling for other factors. This analysis is followed by a review of selected country case studies to identify the major macroeconomic, structural, and institutional weaknesses in national debt accumulation episodes that were associated with financial crises. The chapter concludes with a summary of findings.

National debt accumulation episodes

Debt accumulation by EMDEs brings benefits, as documented in chapter 2. Some debt accumulation episodes have been particularly rapid, and these episodes are the focus of this section. This section reviews the main features of these national debt accumulation episodes and their links with financial crises in an event study. About half of the national episodes of rapid debt accumulation have begun and ended within the same global wave of debt, among the four discussed in the previous chapters.

Identification of episodes. A national episode of rapid debt accumulation is defined as a period during which the government debt-to-GDP ratio or the private sector debt-to-GDP ratio rises from trough to peak by more than one (country-specific) 10-year rolling standard deviation. This identification approach for rapid debt accumulation episodes closely follows methods used to date the turning points of business cycles.[4] Application of this approach results in 256 episodes of rapid *government debt* accumulation and 263

---

[4] Appendix A describes the methodology used here. For details of similar approaches, see Claessens, Kose, and Terrones (2012); Harding and Pagan (2002); and Mendoza and Terrones (2012). The headline results are robust to using a definition more closely aligned with the literature on credit booms. Episodes are required to have a minimum duration of five years from one peak to the next and two years from trough to peak and peak to trough. Episodes at the beginning and end of the data series are similarly classified, but the beginning and end of episodes are set at the points where the availability for government and private debt data begins and ends.

episodes of rapid *private debt* accumulation in a sample of 100 EMDEs with available data for 1970-2018.[5]

In scaling debt by GDP, this approach implicitly focuses on the concept of the debt burden, which captures the ability of borrowers economy-wide to service their debt. In principle, a sharp increase in the debt burden, as measured by the debt-to-GDP ratio, could mechanically reflect an output collapse, deflation, an exchange rate depreciation that raises the domestic currency value of debt, or a large increase in borrowing. Regardless of the underlying cause, a rise in the debt burden makes it more challenging for the economy to service debt and makes the debt burden more likely to become a source of financial stress.

In practice, output contractions were a source of increased debt-to-GDP ratios in a minority of rapid debt accumulation episodes identified here (one-third of government debt episodes and two-fifths of private debt episodes). Sharp currency depreciations (in currency crises) have been associated with larger debt buildups during debt accumulation episodes, but such depreciations have typically happened before (usually two years before) debt peaks and the increase in debt during the year of the currency crisis has accounted for only between one-tenth (private debt episodes) and one-quarter (government debt episodes) of the total debt buildup during episodes involving currency crises.

Episodes associated with financial crises. Financial crises (banking, sovereign debt, or currency crises) are defined as in Laeven and Valencia (2018).[6] A rapid debt accumulation episode is identified as having been associated with a financial crisis (of any type) if such a crisis occurred at any point between the start of the episode and the year of the episode's peak debt-to-GDP ratio or within two years of the peak debt-to-GDP ratio.[7]

---

[5] Small states, as defined by the World Bank, are excluded. Forty-five government debt and 37 private debt accumulation episodes are still ongoing. Tables A.1 and A.2 in appendix A list completed government and private debt accumulation episodes.

[6] Data for currency crises are extended to 2018 using the same methodology as Laeven and Valencia (2018). Other studies dating crises include, for example, Baldacci et al. (2011), Reinhart and Rogoff (2009), and Romer and Romer (2017).

[7] Table A.3 in appendix A lists financial crises associated with completed rapid debt accumulation episodes. Multiple financial crises occurred in some national debt accumulation episodes. For example, Mexico's government debt accumulation episode of 1980-87 spanned a banking crisis in 1981 and currency and debt crises in 1982. Turkey's government debt accumulation episode of 1998-2001 spanned a banking crisis in 2000 and a currency crisis in 2001. In contrast, El Salvador's government debt accumulation episode of 1977-85 was followed by a currency crisis in 1986.

This identification approach describes an association between rapid debt accumulation and financial crises without necessarily implying any causal link between the two. This approach yields 137 rapid *government* debt accumulation episodes associated with crises and 127 rapid *private* debt accumulation episodes associated with crises between 1970 and 2018 in 100 EMDEs.

Main features

Frequency of episodes. Debt accumulation episodes have been common (figure 5.1). In the average year between 1970 and 2018, three-quarters of EMDEs were in either a government or a private debt accumulation episode or in both. The region with the most episodes was Sub-Saharan Africa (SSA) —where 34 percent of all government and 33 percent of all private debt accumulation episodes occurred—in part reflecting the large number of countries in the region but also its history of debt dependence. The average EMDE in SSA, South Asia, and Latin America and the Caribbean (LAC)— the regions with the most episodes per country—went through three government and three private debt accumulation episodes between 1970 and 2018. Central African Republic, Niger, and Togo had the most (five) *government* debt accumulation episodes, including ongoing ones. Argentina, Burkina Faso, Myanmar, Oman, Pakistan, United Arab Emirates, and Zambia had the most (also five) *private* debt accumulation episodes. Several countries had only one debt accumulation episode (either private or government) in the period (for example, Albania, Côte d'Ivoire, and Serbia).

Duration. The duration of episodes—the number of years from trough to peak debt-to-GDP ratios—varied widely but amounted to about seven and eight years in the median government and private debt accumulation episode, respectively (figure 5.2; tables A.4 and A.5 in appendix A).[8] Most episodes had run their course in less than a decade; however, 21 percent of government debt episodes and 29 percent of private debt episodes lasted for more than a decade. The long duration of some of these episodes suggests that the debt buildup in part reflected healthy financial deepening, which may be especially the case in those countries with exceptionally long accumulation episodes.

Amplitude. Although again with wide heterogeneity among the episodes, the debt buildup in the median episode amounted to 21 percentage points of

---

[8] Most accumulation episodes were short-lived. The shortest episode lasted two years in, for example, Benin (1992-94; government debt), the Lao People's Democratic Republic (1996-98; government debt), and Papua New Guinea (1996-98; private debt).

FIGURE 5.1 **Episodes of rapid debt accumulation**

Episodes of rapid debt accumulation have been common among EMDEs, in both the government and private sectors. In the average year between 1970 and 2018, three-quarters of EMDEs were in either a government or a private debt accumulation episode or in both. Since the early 2000s, the number of combined government and private debt accumulation episodes has increased.

A. Share of EMDEs in rapid debt accumulation episodes

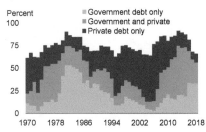

B. Share of EMDEs in rapid debt accumulation episodes

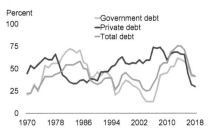

C. Regional distribution of rapid government debt accumulation episodes

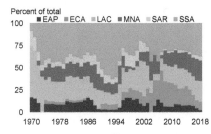

D. Regional distribution of rapid private debt accumulation episodes, by region

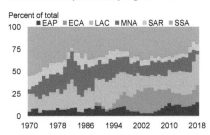

Sources: International Monetary Fund; World Bank.
Note: For definition of episodes and country samples, see appendix A. EAP = East Asia and Pacific; ECA = Europe and Central Asia; EMDEs = emerging market and developing economies; LAC = Latin America and the Caribbean; MNA = Middle East and North Africa; SAR = South Asia; SSA = Sub-Saharan Africa.
A.B. Share of EMDEs in the sample that are in rapid debt accumulation episodes.

GDP. The government debt buildup in the median government debt accumulation episode (30 percentage points of GDP from trough to peak) was double the private debt buildup in the median private debt accumulation episode (15 percentage points of GDP from trough to peak). The largest increases in *government* debt-to-GDP ratios took place in lower-income countries in SSA and LAC over several decades; the largest increases in *private* debt-to-GDP ratios occurred in Europe and Central Asia (ECA), and the smallest in SSA.

Variation in the amplitude of debt accumulation episodes across countries was particularly wide for government debt accumulation episodes. In one-

FIGURE 5.2 **Features of rapid debt accumulation episodes in EMDEs**

During 1970-2018, the median government debt accumulation episode lasted seven years, and the median private debt accumulation episode lasted eight years. During rapid debt accumulation episodes, government debt typically rose (trough to peak) by 30 percentage points of GDP, and private debt by 15 percentage points of GDP.

A. Duration of rapid debt accumulation episodes

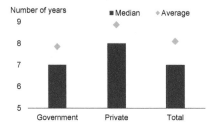

B. Change in debt during rapid debt accumulation episodes

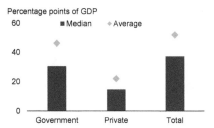

Sources: International Monetary Fund; World Bank.
Note: For definition of episodes and sample, see appendix A. EMDEs = emerging market and developing economies.
A. Median duration of rapid debt accumulation episodes.
B. Median change in debt-to-GDP ratios (trough-to-peak) during a rapid debt accumulation episode.

quarter of such episodes, the government debt buildup amounted to more than 50 percentage points of GDP.[9] Debt accumulation of such a scale was rare for the private sector: in three-quarters of private debt accumulation episodes, private debt rose by less than 30 percentage points of GDP.[10]

Combined episodes. About 70 percent of government and private debt accumulation episodes overlapped. These overlapping, combined government and private episodes were statistically significantly shorter and often more pronounced in amplitude than were solely private or solely government debt accumulation episodes (table A.5 in appendix A).

Episodes with financial crises. Of all the episodes that have concluded in the period 1970-2018, just over half of government debt accumulation episodes and two-fifths of private debt accumulation episodes were associated with financial crises (figure 5.3). Crises were particularly common during the first and second global waves: of all episodes that concluded in either of these two

---

[9] For example, during government debt accumulation episodes, government debt rose by 127 percentage points of GDP in Argentina (1992-2002) and 86 percentage points of GDP in Mozambique (2007-16).

[10] There were some exceptions: private debt rose by 89 percentage points of GDP in China (2008-18), 86 percentage points of GDP in Hungary (1995-2009), and 76 percentage points of GDP in Turkey (2003-18).

FIGURE 5.3 **Crises during rapid debt accumulation episodes in EMDEs**

About half of all episodes of government and private debt accumulation during 1970-2018 were associated with financial crises. Different types of crises often occurred at the same time.

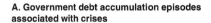

A. Government debt accumulation episodes associated with crises

B. Private debt accumulation episodes associated with crises

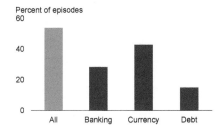
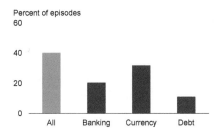

Sources: International Monetary Fund; Laeven and Valencia (2018); World Bank.
Note: Episodes associated with crises are those that experienced financial crises (banking, currency, and debt crises, as in Laeven and Valencia 2018) during or within two years after the end of episodes. For definition of episodes and sample, see appendix A. EMDEs = emerging market and developing economies.

waves, almost two-thirds were associated with crises. Most crises occurred well before the end of the debt accumulation episode (appendix A). Crises were equally common in longer episodes (those lasting a decade or more) and shorter ones (lasting less than a decade). The most common form of crisis in debt accumulation episodes was a currency crisis, often combined with other types of crises.[11] More than three-quarters of debt accumulation episodes associated with crises (either government or private) had currency crises.

Macroeconomic outcomes

The one-half of debt accumulation episodes that were associated with financial crises had considerably weaker macroeconomic outcomes than did those that subsided without crises.

---

[11] Some studies have derived estimates of the incidence of crises around private lending booms. Mendoza and Terrones (2012) find that the peaks of 20-25 percent of credit booms were followed by banking crises or currency crises and that 14 percent were followed by sudden stops in capital flows. Schularick and Taylor (2012) identify credit growth as a significant predictor of financial crises. World Bank (2016c) estimates that about half of credit booms are followed by at least mild deleveraging. See Borio and Lowe (2002); Claessens and Kose (2018); Dell'Ariccia et al. (2016); Enoch and Ötker-Robe (2007); and Gourinchas, Valdes, and Landerretche (2001) for discussions of how lending booms increase vulnerability to financial crisis.

Government debt accumulation episodes. Government debt accumulation episodes that involved crises were typically associated with greater debt buildups, weaker economic outcomes, and higher vulnerabilities than were noncrisis episodes (figure 5.4; tables A.5 and A.6 in appendix A). In the episodes associated with financial crises, the government debt buildup was about 14 percentage points of GDP larger after eight years than in noncrisis episodes. After eight years, GDP and GDP per capita in episodes with crises were about 10 percent lower than in episodes without a crisis, investment was 22 percent lower, and consumption was 6 percent lower. Some external indicators—especially international reserves—deteriorated more in episodes associated with crises than in noncrisis episodes, as governments drew down reserves in an effort to stem currency depreciation. Nevertheless, currencies depreciated, and short-term debt could not be rolled over (see table A.5 in appendix A).

Private debt accumulation episodes. Over an eight-year period, private debt accumulation episodes associated with crises featured weaker output and per capita income (by about 6 percent), consumption (by 8 percent), and investment (by 15 percent; figure 5.5; tables A.5 and A.7). Private debt episodes with crises also saw significantly more pronounced deteriorations in external positions, especially international reserves and external debt, than did noncrisis episodes. Episodes associated with crises featured broadly stable real exchange rates, in contrast to noncrisis episodes, which were accompanied by strong real exchange rate appreciation; this relationship would be consistent with a more productive use of borrowed funds in noncrisis episodes.

Similarities. Regardless of the borrowing sector, rapid debt accumulation episodes with crises featured considerably worse macroeconomic outcomes and vulnerabilities than did those not associated with crises. Both types of episodes associated with crises saw sharp rises in inflation relative to noncrisis episodes, as well as larger falls in international reserves. Fiscal and current account deficits widened in both types of episodes with crises but more in government debt accumulation episodes than in private debt episodes.

Combined government and private debt accumulation episodes with crises were accompanied by significantly weaker investment and consumption growth than were solely private episodes. For episodes in which crises were avoided, combined episodes also featured slower overall growth than did solely private debt accumulation episodes (table A.5).

Differences. Government debt accumulation episodes associated with crises tended to be more costly than private debt episodes associated with crises,

FIGURE 5.4 Macroeconomic developments during government debt accumulation episodes in EMDEs

Eight years after the start of rapid government debt accumulation episodes, those episodes associated with financial crises had lower output, investment, and consumption than episodes without any crisis events. Episodes associated with financial crises featured significantly larger government debt increases, as well as lower international reserves and larger external debt, although with wide heterogeneity.

A. Government debt

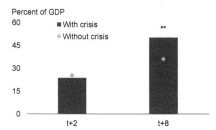

B. Output and per capita output

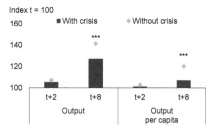

C. Investment and consumption

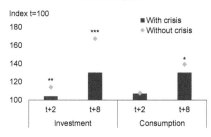

D. International reserves and external debt

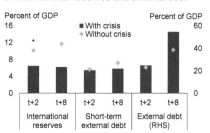

Sources: International Monetary Fund; Laeven and Valencia (2018); World Bank.
Note: Median for episodes with data available for at least eight years from the beginning of the episode. Year "t" refers to the beginning of rapid government debt accumulation episodes. Episodes associated with crises are those that experienced financial crises (banking, currency, and debt crises, as in Laeven and Valencia 2018) during or within two years after the end of episodes. EMDEs = emerging market and developing economies. "*", "***", and "****" denote that medians between episodes associated with crises and those with no crises are statistically different at 10 percent, 5 percent, and 1 percent levels, respectively, based on Wilcoxon rank-sum tests.
A. Government debt in percent of GDP two and eight years after the beginning of the government debt accumulation episode (t).
B.C. Cumulative percent increase from t, based on real growth rates for output (GDP), output (GDP) per capita, investment, and consumption.
D. Series shown as percent of GDP.

with much larger shortfalls in output and investment growth, especially in the early years after a crisis. Government debt accumulation episodes were accompanied by real exchange rate depreciation whereas private debt accumulation episodes were accompanied by an appreciation, in part reflecting domestic demand booms that supported asset prices and real appreciation. The difference may also reflect the fact that most of the government debt accumulation episodes occurred in the first half of the

FIGURE 5.5 Macroeconomic developments during private debt accumulation episodes in EMDEs

Eight years after the start of rapid private debt accumulation episodes, those episodes associated with financial crises had significantly lower output, investment, and consumption than did episodes without any crisis events. Episodes associated with financial crises featured lower international reserves and larger external debt.

A. Private debt

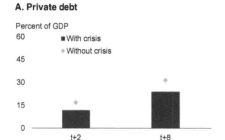

B. Output

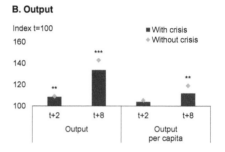

C. Investment and consumption

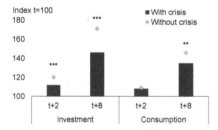

D. International reserves and external debt

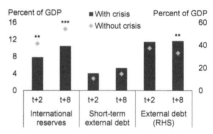

Sources: International Monetary Fund; Laeven and Valencia (2018); World Bank.

Note: Median for episodes with data available for at least eight years from the beginning of the episode. Year "t" refers to the beginning of rapid private debt accumulation episodes. Episodes associated with crises are those that experienced financial crises (banking, currency, and debt crises, as in Laeven and Valencia 2018) during or within two years after the end of episodes. EMDEs = emerging market and developing economies. "*", "**", and "***" denote that medians between episodes associated with crises and those with no crises are statistically different at 10 percent, 5 percent, and 1 percent levels, respectively, based on Wilcoxon rank-sum tests.

A. Cumulative change in private debt in percent of GDP two and eight years after the beginning of the private debt accumulation episode (t).

B.C. Based on real growth rates for output (GDP), output (GDP) per capita, investment and consumption.

D. Series shown as percent of GDP.

sample, when more countries maintained pegged exchange rates, which tended to be abandoned when crises hit.

Debt and financial crises

The preceding section described countries' susceptibility to financial crises during episodes of rapid debt accumulation, with about half of the episodes associated with such crises. This section uses an econometric model to quantify the effect of debt accumulation on the likelihood of financial crises.

Empirical literature. The econometric exercise here builds on an extensive literature on early warning models, as discussed in chapter 2.[12] The first generation of early warning models, in the 1980s and 1990s, aimed at predicting currency crises and largely focused on macroeconomic and financial imbalances. Measures of balance sheet health became more prominent in such models after the Asian financial crisis, especially in predicting banking crises. A combination of government solvency and liquidity indicators has also been used in studies of sovereign debt crises.

Econometric model. In the baseline regression specification, the probability of a financial crisis is estimated as a function of the pace of debt accumulation and several control variables in a panel logit model with random effects (see appendix B for a description of the model). The regression is estimated separately for sovereign debt, banking, and currency crises because these are likely to be associated with different sectoral vulnerabilities. All explanatory variables are lagged because the focus is on preconditions that make crises more likely. In addition, the use of lagged variables attenuates potential endogeneity bias caused by contemporaneous interactions between economic fundamentals and crises. An unbalanced annual panel dataset of 139 EMDEs over the period 1970-2018 is employed.

The correlates of crises are drawn from a rich empirical literature on the determinants of financial crises, or of the vulnerabilities that worsen the impact of crises. This literature has identified the following correlates of higher crisis probabilities:

- *Factors that increase rollover risk.* These factors are particularly relevant during periods of elevated financial stress; they include high short-term external debt and high or rapidly growing total, government, or private debt.

- *Factors that restrict policy room to respond.* These factors include low international reserves, large fiscal or current account deficits, and weak institutions.

---

[12] See Berg, Borensztein, and Patillo (2005); Chamon and Crowe (2012); Frankel and Saravelos (2012); and Kaminsky, Lizondo, and Reinhart (1998) for extensive reviews of the literature on early warning models. For models involving currency crises, see Eichengreen, Rose, and Wyplosz (1995); Frankel and Rose (1996); and Kaminsky and Reinhart (2000). For models involving banking crises, see Borio and Lowe (2002); Demirgüç-Kunt and Detragiache (1998); and Rose and Spiegel (2012). For models involving debt crises, see Dawood, Horsewood, and Strobel (2017) and Manasse, Roubini, and Schimmelpfenning (2003).

• *Factors that suggest overvaluation of assets.* These factors indicate potential for large asset price corrections; they include exchange rate misalignments and credit and asset price booms.

The role of debt

Of these potential correlates, the regression model identifies several that are statistically significant and robust correlates of the probability of financial crises (table A.2).[13] These correlates include higher external vulnerabilities (higher short-term debt, higher debt service, and lower international reserves), adverse shocks (higher U.S. interest rates and lower domestic output growth), and faster debt accumulation—especially if true of both government and private debt. These findings are broadly consistent with the literature on leading indicators of financial crises, particularly with regard to the important roles of the composition of debt and pace of debt accumulation.[14] In addition, the regressions here suggest that *combined* private and government debt buildups significantly increase the probability of a currency crisis.

Debt accumulation. An increase in debt, either government or private, was associated with significantly higher probabilities of crisis in the following year. For example, an increase of 30 percentage points of GDP in *government* debt over the previous year (equivalent to the median buildup during a government debt accumulation episode) increased the probability of entering a sovereign debt crisis to 2.0 percent (from 1.4 percent) and that of entering a currency crisis to 6.6 percent (from 4.1 percent). For *private* debt, an increase of 15 percentage points of GDP in debt (equivalent to the median increase during a private debt accumulation episode) doubled the probability of entering a banking crisis to about 4.8 percent, and the probability of a currency crisis to 7.5 percent, in the following year—probabilities considerably larger than those for a similarly sized buildup in government debt.

Combined government and private debt accumulation. Simultaneous increases in both government and private debt increased the probability of a currency crisis. Thus, an increase of 15 percentage points of GDP in private

---

[13] Appendix A lists the variables used in the baseline model and presents a number of robustness tests, for example, for alternative model specifications (random effects probit model) and twin crises. Twin crises are defined as the simultaneous occurrence of any two types of financial crises (sovereign debt, banking, or currency). Such episodes are usually associated with much larger changes in typical leading indicators. The correlates in the baseline model indeed have higher statistical significance in predicting twin crises than in predicting individual crises.

[14] Relevant empirical regularities are reported in, for example, Manasse, Roubini, and Schimmelpfenning (2003) on sovereign debt crises; Kaminsky, Lizondo, and Reinhart (1998) on currency crises; and Kauko (2014) on banking crises.

debt together with an increase of 30 percentage points of GDP in government debt resulted in a 24 percent probability of entering a currency crisis
the next year—more than six times the probability had debt remained stable
(3.9 percent) and about one-third more than similarly sized government or
private debt buildups separately.

The role of shocks and vulnerabilities

Adverse shocks. Compared to average output growth outside crises (4
percent), growth in EMDE crisis episodes averaged -1 percent. Contractions
of this magnitude increased the probability of entering a sovereign debt crisis
in the subsequent year to 1.9 percent from 1.2 percent outside crisis episodes
(figure 5.6). A 2-percentage-point increase in U.S. real interest rates—half of
the cumulative increase during a typical tightening phase of U.S. monetary
policy—increased the probability of entering a currency crisis by almost one-
half to 6.0 percent from 4.1 percent.

External vulnerabilities. A larger share of short-term debt in external debt,
greater debt service cost, and lower reserve cover were associated with
significantly higher probabilities of financial crises.

- *Short-term debt.* Compared to the probability of a sovereign debt crisis of
  1.2 percent associated with a share of short-term debt of 10 percent of
  external debt (the average during noncrisis episodes), a 30 percent share
  of short-term debt in external debt (Mexico's share before it plunged
  into a twin currency and debt crisis in 1982) raised the probability of
  entering a sovereign debt crisis in the following year to 2.0 percent.

- *Debt service.* A 50 percent ratio of debt service to exports—Mexico's
  average debt service burden in the early 1980s—was associated with
  probabilities of entering a sovereign debt crisis of 2.8 percent and a
  banking crisis of 5.5 percent. This was more than double the probabilities associated with a 15 percent debt service-to-export ratio in the
  average noncrisis episode.

- *Reserve cover.* The probability of a debt or banking crisis exceeded 3
  percent, and that of a currency crisis 5 percent, for a reserve cover of one
  month of imports (which was the case in Mexico in the early 1980s)
  compared to probabilities of 0.6-2.0 percent for banking and debt crises,
  and 3.8 percent for currency crises, when reserve cover amounted to four
  months of imports (the average for noncrisis episodes).

Other shocks and vulnerabilities. Other vulnerabilities identified tended to
be more specific to certain types of crises or borrowing sectors.

FIGURE 5.6 **Predicted crisis probabilities**

Higher U.S. real interest rates, lower GDP growth, and faster debt buildups raise the probability of crises.

A. Probability of financial crisis after adverse shock

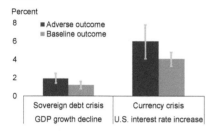

B. Probability of financial crisis after debt buildup

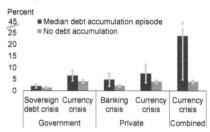

Sources: Laeven and Valencia (2018); World Bank.
Note: Predicted probability of currency, banking, and debt crises (as defined in Laeven and Valencia 2018) based on regression in table B.2 in appendix B. Variable definitions are in table B.1. Whiskers indicate 95 percent confidence intervals. EMDE = emerging market and developing economy.
A. "Adverse outcome" is GDP growth of -1 percent (average EMDE growth during crisis episodes) or U.S. policy interest rate increase of 2 percentage points (cumulative U.S. federal funds rate increase from end-2015 to mid-2018). "Baseline outcome" is GDP growth of 4 percent (average EMDE growth outside crisis episodes) and no U.S. policy interest rate increase.
B. Predicted probabilities assuming government debt buildup of 30 percentage points of GDP or private debt buildup of 15 percentage points of GDP or both in the median debt accumulation episode.

- *Wholesale funding.* Higher wholesale funding by banks, proxied by the ratio of credit to deposits, was associated with a greater probability of a banking crisis but appears to have been largely unrelated to the probabilities of sovereign debt and currency crises.

- *Real exchange rate overvaluation.* Real exchange rate overvaluation was associated with a higher probability of a currency crisis but tended to be largely unrelated to banking and sovereign debt crises (Dornbusch et al. 1995).

- *Concessional debt and foreign direct investment flows.* A higher share of concessional debt, which consists of loans extended on more generous than commercial terms, was associated with a lower probability of a sovereign debt crisis but tended to be largely unrelated to banking and currency crises. Larger foreign direct investment inflows, a more stable form of finance than portfolio inflows, were associated with a lower probability of a currency crisis.

Crisis probabilities: Small or large? In isolation, some of these probabilities may appear small, as is expected because they are associated with individual indicators. These probabilities could cumulate rapidly, however, when multiple indicators deteriorate at the same time as has frequently happened before financial crises. Indeed, as documented in the previous chapters, in a typical financial crisis, an adverse shock is often compounded by elevated debt and multiple other vulnerabilities.

Selected country case studies

The preceding section quantified how shocks and vulnerabilities have affected the likelihood of crises. In addition, beyond measures that can be easily quantified, countries with financial crises during or after a debt accumulation episode shared some structural and institutional weaknesses that made their economies more prone to crises once an adverse shock hit. These structural and institutional weaknesses are explored in this section in a set of selected country case studies of financial crises.

Approach. The case studies focus on 43 crisis episodes in 34 EMDEs that have witnessed rapid government or private debt accumulation since 1970 (for a description of the methodology and sources used in these case studies, see appendix C). Most of these cases (65 percent) involved overlapping private and government debt accumulation episodes. Almost all cases (90 percent) involved two crises, and 40 percent involved three crises. Although nonexhaustive, the case studies were selected by the following criteria. First, they are representative of debt accumulation episodes over the past 50 years. Second, they include a broad range of EMDEs, including both large EMDEs in major regional debt crises episodes and low-income countries. Third, they have been sufficiently examined in earlier studies for a general assessment about their causes and consequences to be reached with confidence.

For each of the cases examined, earlier work—International Monetary Fund (IMF) Article IV consultation reports, academic studies, and policy papers—provides a wealth of information on the structural features and institutional background. This section focuses on macroeconomic policies and structural and institutional features that relate to shortcomings in financial sector supervision and corporate governance, as well as to political uncertainty, balance sheet mismatches, heavily managed exchange rates, state-led growth models, heavy presence of state-owned enterprises, less diversified economies, and implicit sovereign guarantees. Individual aspects of these have been widely discussed in the literature.[15]

---

[15] The main references for the country case studies described in this section are listed in table C.1 in appendix C. For a discussion of some of these macroeconomic, structural, and institutional shortcomings see Balassa (1982), Kaufmann (1989), and Sachs (1985, 1989), on growth strategies and uses of debt; Roubini and Wachtel (1999) on current account sustainability; Daumont, Le Gall, and Leroux (2004) and Kawai, Newfarmer, and Schmukler (2005) on inadequate banking regulation; Brownbridge and Kirkpatrick (2000) on balance sheet mismatch; and Capulong et. al. (2000) for poor corporate governance.

Macroeconomic policies

Inefficient use of debt. In addition to financing import substitution policies, public debt was used in some countries in the first wave to finance current government spending and populist policies that led to overly expansionary macroeconomic policies (Argentina, Brazil, Chile, and Peru). In other countries, rapid private borrowing resulted in debt-fueled domestic demand booms, including property booms (Thailand and Ukraine) or inefficient manufacturing investment (the Republic of Korea).

Inadequate fiscal management. Many countries had severe fiscal weaknesses. These weaknesses included weak revenue collection (Argentina, Brazil, Indonesia, and the Russian Federation), widespread tax evasion (Argentina and Russia), public wage and pension indexing (Argentina, Brazil, Mexico, and Uruguay), monetary financing of fiscal deficits (Argentina and Brazil), and substantial use of energy and food subsidies (the Arab Republic of Egypt and República Bolivariana de Venezuela).

Risky composition of debt. Many of the crisis countries borrowed in foreign currency. They struggled to meet debt service obligations and faced steep jumps in debt ratios following currency depreciations (Indonesia, Mexico, and Thailand). In Uruguay, for example, almost all public debt was denominated in U.S. dollars in the mid-1990s. Several countries relied on short-term borrowing and faced rollover difficulties when investor sentiment deteriorated (Indonesia, Korea, the Philippines, and Russia in the late 1990s). In ECA in the 2000s, countries borrowed cross-border from nonresident lenders and faced a credit crunch once liquidity conditions tightened for global banks that were the source of this lending (Croatia, Hungary, and Kazakhstan in the late 2000s).

Balance sheet mismatches. A substantial number of currency and banking crises and most concurrent currency and banking crises were associated with balance sheet mismatches (Indonesia, Malaysia, Mexico, and Russia in the late 1990s). Sovereign debt crises less frequently involved balance sheet mismatches, except when banking supervision was weak (Indonesia and Turkey in the 1990s).

Managed exchange rates. Many, but far from all, crises were associated with managed exchange rates, which tended to lead to overvaluation of currencies during years of rapid growth, debt buildup, and capital inflows but eventually succumbed to speculative attacks (Brazil, Mexico, and the Slovak Republic).

Structural and institutional features

Poorly designed growth strategies. Many of the case studies of crises in the 1970s and early 1980s showed heavy state intervention through state-led industrialization, state-owned companies, and state-owned banks (Balassa 1982). Industrial policy in countries such as Argentina, Brazil, and República Bolivariana de Venezuela focused on import substitution industrialization, typically financed by external borrowing.

Lack of economic diversification. A number of the crisis countries had undiversified economies, which increased their vulnerability to terms of trade shocks. Several countries in LAC and SSA, in particular, were heavily dependent on both oil and nonoil commodity exports (Bolivia, Niger, Nigeria, Paraguay, and Uruguay in the 1970s and 1980s). When commodity prices fell in the 1980s, the profitability of (often state-owned) corporates in the resource sector, fiscal revenues, and export proceeds collapsed, which triggered financial crises.

Inadequate banking regulation. Poor banking regulation was a common feature in many case studies. Several SSA countries experienced banking crises in the 1980s primarily because of the failure of banks that were typically state-owned and subject to little oversight (Cameroon, Kenya, Niger, and Tanzania). In the East Asia and Pacific (EAP) region, financial deregulation contributed to insufficient regulation and oversight of the financial sector in the second wave (Indonesia, Korea, Malaysia, the Philippines, and Thailand), which resulted in growing weaknesses, including balance sheet mismatches, and excessive risk taking by corporates. In several countries in ECA during the 2000s, cross-border lending was inadequately regulated by domestic regulators (Croatia, Hungary, and Kazakhstan).

Poor corporate governance. Among case studies of the 1980s and 1990s, poor corporate governance was a common shortcoming, notably in some EAP countries (Indonesia, Korea, and Thailand). Along with poor bank regulation, this shortcoming led to inefficient corporate investment, because banks lent to firms without rigorously evaluating their creditworthiness.

Political uncertainty. Many sovereign debt crises were associated with severe political uncertainty (Indonesia, Philippines, Turkey, and República Bolivariana de Venezuela).

Triggers of crises

Case studies suggest that crises were usually triggered by external shocks, although in a small number of countries domestic factors also played a role.

External shocks. The most common triggers of crises were external shocks to the real economy, which included a sudden rise in global interest rates (LAC in the 1980s), a slowdown in global growth (ECA in the 2000s), a fall in commodity prices for commodity exporting economies (LAC and SSA in the 1980s and Russia in the 1990s), and contagion from both global crises (2007-09 global financial crisis) and regional crises (Asian financial and Russian crises in the 1990s), which generated sudden withdrawals of capital inflows.

Natural disasters. Natural disasters such as droughts were a major contributing factor to crises in some countries, typically smaller, less diversified economies (Bangladesh in the 1970s, Nepal in the 1980s, and Zimbabwe in the 2000s).

Other domestic shocks. In a small number of countries, crises were triggered, or exacerbated, by other domestic shocks. Typically, these were episodes of political turmoil (Turkey and Zimbabwe).

Resolution of crises

Many, though not all, crises were resolved by policy programs of adjustment and structural reform supported by financing from the IMF, World Bank, and other multilateral bodies and partner countries.

IMF support. Most countries in these case studies adopted IMF-supported policy programs to overcome their crises. The countries that did not use IMF support typically had stronger fundamentals, including lower public debt and larger international reserves (Colombia, Kazakhstan, and Malaysia).

Debt restructuring. Among the case studies of sovereign debt crises, many ended with default and restructuring of debt (Argentina, Cameroon, Mexico, and Nigeria). These cases were more common in the 1980s, 1990s, and early 2000s. Debt restructuring was often prolonged and occurred well after the initial sovereign debt crisis.

Reforms. IMF support was conditional on the implementation of macroeconomic and structural reforms. For many EMDEs in LAC in the 1980s and in EAP in the 1990s, crises were the trigger for policy changes to allow greater exchange rate flexibility and strengthen monetary policy regimes.

Shifting policy debate

In several cases, crises revealed shortcomings that were mainly recognized ex post but had rarely been flagged before the crises. Following these crises, research (described in academic studies and policy reports) shifted its focus to these issues. For example, the Asian financial crisis propelled the challenges of balance sheet mismatches and weak corporate governance as well as the need for robust bank supervision to the forefront of policy discussions (Brownbridge and Kirkpatrick 2000; IMF 1999). The launch of the Financial Sector Assessment Program in 1999 started systematic assessments of financial sectors (IMF 2000).

The 2007-09 global financial crisis shifted attention to the two-way links between the real economy and financial markets and triggered an intensive research program on macrofinancial links. It also led to a wide range of policy measures to better monitor different segments of financial markets, including credit and housing markets. In addition, the global financial crisis shifted an earlier consensus on the use of capital controls. Before 2008, capital controls were largely considered ineffective and detrimental (Forbes 2004, 2007). After the global financial crisis, the literature shifted to a guarded endorsement of capital controls if appropriately designed and implemented in the "right" circumstances (Forbes, Fratzscher, and Straub 2015; IMF 2012, 2015).

Selected case studies of financial crises

To examine how different macroeconomic policies and institutional features could lead to or prevent financial crises, annex 5A singles out a country pair for each of the first two global waves of debt. For each country pair—Indonesia and Mexico for the first wave and Chile and Thailand for the second—only one country experienced a financial crisis despite debt buildups during each wave. After a period of rapid debt accumulation in the 1970s and 1980s, both Mexico and Indonesia faced rising interest rates and currency pressures as the U.S. Federal Reserve began tightening monetary policy in the late 1970s. Indonesia responded with fiscal and monetary policy tightening, trade liberalization, and privatization. Mexico, in contrast, slid into currency and debt crises amid a timid government response.

During the 1990s, both Chile and Thailand saw rapid private debt buildups. In Chile, the buildup was accompanied by mounting fiscal surpluses, plunging government debt, and the introduction of a floating exchange rate regime that discouraged foreign currency borrowing. In contrast, Thailand's private debt buildup was not fully offset by declining government debt, as had been the case in Chile, and the country maintained a fixed exchange rate that encouraged foreign currency borrowing; both factors made it vulnerable to capital outflows culminating in a crisis.

Conclusion

National episodes of rapid debt accumulation have been common in EMDEs, and about half of these episodes were associated with financial crises. When they occurred, financial crises were typically triggered by external shocks, but in some instances also by domestic political turmoil. When such adverse shocks occurred, larger or more rapidly growing debt constituted a vulnerability that increased the likelihood of a country sliding into crisis. Larger buildups of either government or private debt on the order of that in the median episode were associated with a 50 percent higher likelihood of financial crises. In addition, external vulnerabilities, such as a larger share of short-term debt, higher debt service cost, and lower reserve cover, increased the probability of crisis. Most countries that slid into crises also suffered from inadequate fiscal, monetary, and financial sector policies.

The analysis in this chapter emphasizes the critical role of strong institutional frameworks that can reduce the likelihood and the impact of crises. These include robust financial regulation and supervision, fiscal frameworks that credibly maintain sustainability, and monetary policy frameworks and exchange rate regimes geared toward macroeconomic stability. In addition, the chapter shows that the likelihood of crises can be reduced by ensuring a resilient composition of debt. Debt denominated in local currency and at long maturities is less prone to market disruptions than is foreign currency or short-term debt.

The previous three chapters presented detailed analyses of global and national episodes of debt accumulation. In light of the insights from these chapters, the next chapter examines the likely direction of the current global wave of debt accumulation and summarizes the main lessons and policy messages for EMDEs.

ANNEX 5A **Selected case studies of debt accumulation**

Four country cases illustrate the difference between countries that suffered financial crises and those that did not during the first and second waves of global debt accumulation. Countries that suffered crises had more accommodative policies and greater vulnerabilities to external shocks.

To sharpen the role of different structural and institutional features in driving macroeconomic outcomes during national rapid debt accumulation episodes, this annex focuses on a select set of country case studies in the first two global waves of debt. Two country pairs are singled out—one for each of the first two global waves of debt—of which one country had a financial crisis and the other did not during their national episodes of rapid debt accumulation.

During the first wave of debt accumulation, both Mexico and Indonesia had rapid government debt accumulation episodes but only Mexico suffered a triple crisis in 1982. During the second wave of debt accumulation, both Chile and Thailand witnessed rapid private debt buildups but only Thailand suffered a crisis in 1997.

Two differences feature in both country pairs: first, those with financial crises maintained considerably more accommodative fiscal and monetary policy than those without crises; second, those with financial crises had greater existing vulnerabilities (for example, higher short-term debt or higher total debt).

Mexico in the first global wave

Debt accumulation. Mexico borrowed heavily in foreign currency (mostly U.S. dollars) against future oil revenues in the 1970s. Central government debt rose by almost 20 percentage points of GDP between 1972 and 1982, to 32 percent of GDP in 1982 (figure 5A.1). External debt grew from 19 percent of GDP in 1972 to 30 percent of GDP in 1981. Inflation averaged 24 percent a year during 1979-81, despite a peg to the U.S. dollar, and the current account deficit widened to 5.1 percent of GDP. Mexico pursued an import substitution industrialization policy in the 1970s, which generated economic inefficiencies that would have necessitated fundamental change at some point. It also pursued expansionary fiscal and monetary policies, with widening fiscal and current account deficits. Although a balance of payment crisis briefly struck in 1976, oil discoveries and the oil price shock in the late 1970s delayed necessary structural reforms and allowed another fiscal expansion.

FIGURE 5A.1 **Debt in selected countries**

In the run-up to the sharp increase in global interest rates in the early 1980s, the government debt buildup in Mexico (where it coincided with crises) was larger than in Indonesia (where it did not). In the run-up to a reversal in investor sentiment in the late 1990s, the private debt buildup in Thailand (where it coincided with crises) was larger—and the government debt decline over the same period smaller—than in Chile (where it did not).

A. Debt during the first global wave of debt, Mexico and Indonesia

B. Debt during the second global wave of debt, Chile and Thailand

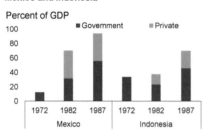

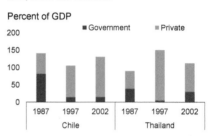

Sources: Mbaye, Moreno-Badia, and Chae (2018); World Bank.
Note: Government and private debt are proxied by central government debt and credit to the private sector, respectively. Private debt data not available for 1972 for Mexico and Indonesia.

Adverse shocks. In October 1979, the U.S. Federal Reserve began to tighten monetary policy, and short-term interest rates rose sharply. This rise coincided with a global economic slowdown and a sharp decline in commodity prices, particularly oil prices. As a result of the twin shocks, compounded by three-quarters of interest payments being tied to variable interest rates, Mexico's debt service payments surged in 1982. In addition, the overvalued exchange rate generated fears of devaluation and a balance of payments crisis, triggering capital flight. The peso was allowed to float freely in early 1982 and depreciated sharply. Mexico's external debt reached 47 percent of GDP (of which one-third was short-term), debt service costs increased to 53 percent of exports, and reserves plunged to less than 1 percent of total debt.

Financial crisis. In August 1982, Mexico defaulted on its sovereign debt. Although Mexico's debt was not the largest, it sparked a series of defaults and systematic collapse in Latin America (Boughton 2001). GDP growth plunged from an average of 9.0 percent in 1980-81 to -0.1 percent during 1982-87. The peso collapsed: between 1981 and 1982 it depreciated by more than half, and by 1987 it had lost 98 percent of its value. Inflation soared and averaged 84 percent a year during 1982-87. The debt crisis also led to a banking crisis, and the government nationalized the entire banking system.

Indonesia in the first global wave

Debt accumulation. During 1972-80, the period during which Mexico's central government debt rose rapidly, Indonesia's central government debt initially declined by almost 20 percentage points of GDP as oil revenues improved fiscal positions. Starting in 1980, however, central government debt climbed rapidly from 14 percent of GDP in 1980 to 46 percent of GDP in 1987. The global recession of the early 1980s widened the current account deficit to 6 percent of GDP in 1983. The authorities responded with fiscal consolidation.

Macroeconomic policies. As with Mexico, U.S. monetary policy tightening and global economic weakness triggered intermittent currency pressures in 1983 and 1986. The rupiah was allowed to depreciate amid tightly enforced capital controls, high reserves (15 percent of total debt), and a small share of short-term debt (15 percent of external debt; Arndt and Hill 1988). Monetary policy was tightened with modest short-term interest rate increases and direction to state-owned enterprises to move funds from state banks into central bank notes. Inflation declined, and capital flight was limited. The government also implemented various reforms from 1983, including deregulation of the banking system, the introduction of a value added tax, trade liberalization, and privatization of the large state enterprise sector. During 1980-87, growth averaged 5.6 percent.

Thailand in the second global wave

Debt accumulation. Private debt grew rapidly to a peak of 146 percent of GDP in 1997 from 51 percent of GDP a decade earlier, whereas central government debt declined by more than 30 percentage points of GDP to 5 percent of GDP in 1997. Following rapid financial sector liberalization in the early 1990s, sizeable interest rate differentials, combined with an exchange rate peg, encouraged large capital inflows. Real estate investment grew rapidly, largely funded with short-term external debt, which exposed corporations and banks to significant exchange rate and rollover risks. Poorly governed privatizations to politically connected entities and government-directed credit toward political allies created moral hazard in the form of expectations of government guarantees to politically connected lending. Although bank deposits were not explicitly insured by the government, political considerations and past practice suggested that the Thai government would bail out failing banks (Burnside, Eichenbaum, and Rebelo 2004).

Financial crisis. By 1996, unsold properties began to accumulate, and investors concerned about defaults started withdrawing capital, putting downward pressure on the baht. The government initially raised interest rates, introduced capital controls, and drew down foreign exchange reserves but eventually allowed the baht to float in July 1997. By the end of 1997, the currency had depreciated by about 40 percent and the stock market had lost 40 percent of its value. Bankruptcies soared, growth plunged from 5.7 percent in 1996 to -2.8 percent in 1997 and -7.6 percent in 1998, and many banks became insolvent. Following widespread nationalizations and bank closures, Thailand's government debt reached 30 percent of GDP in 2002, from 4 percent in 1996. The crisis spread across much of East Asia.

Chile in the second global wave

Debt accumulation. Private debt rose rapidly from 59 percent of GDP in 1987 to 91 percent of GDP in 1997—only one-third as much as the private debt increase in Thailand over the same period—and further to 116 percent of GDP in 2002. The buildup in private debt was more than offset by a marked decline in government debt, from 82 percent of GDP to 15 percent of GDP over 1987-2002. During 1987-97 in the run-up to the Asian financial crisis, Chile's decline in central government debt was twice as steep as that in Thailand.

Macroeconomic policies. During the 1990s, disciplined fiscal, monetary, and financial policy stances were maintained. Since the mid-1980s, fiscal balances had been in surplus, and in 2000 an explicit structural budget surplus rule was introduced. This fiscal rule helped to institutionalize fiscal discipline and to lock in the credibility that had been built up in the past decades. Exchange rate policy had shifted from a semi-fixed regime to a floating regime with an inflation-targeting framework in 1999. Monetary credibility had also been enhanced through an independent central bank, decreed in 1989. Inflation had fallen from almost 30 percent in the early 1990s to less than 3 percent in 2002.

After the collapse of Chilean banks during the Latin American debt crisis in the 1980s, the government made sweeping changes to the banking law and adopted a better regulatory framework to reduce exposure to external shocks (Cowan and de Gregorio 2007). As a result, Chilean banks had an average capital adequacy ratio of 13 percent and nonperforming loans were below 2 percent during 1988-2002.

Conclusion

These cases illustrate two main differences between those countries where rapid debt accumulation coincided with crises and those where it did not.

First, countries without crises had relatively more modest debt buildups. Whereas government debt rose rapidly in Mexico, it declined in Chile in the run-up to the sharp rise in global interest rates in the early 1980s. Government debt in Indonesia and in Chile had declined for a decade before global interest rates began rising sharply in the early 1980s (Indonesia) or risk sentiment turned against EMDEs in the late 1990s (Chile). As a result, both governments were better placed than their counterparts in Mexico and Thailand, respectively, to withstand external shocks. Private debt rose two-thirds less in Chile than in Thailand in the run-up to the Asian financial crisis, adding to Chile's greater financial resilience.

Second, countries without crises had less accommodative policies. Whereas Indonesia's fiscal policy tightened during its government debt run-up in the mid-1980s, Mexico's fiscal policy remained expansionary during its government debt run-up in the 1970s despite double digit inflation and weakening current account balances. In part because of a fiscal rule and flexible exchange rates, Chile maintained fiscal surpluses and discouraged currency mismatches during the 1980s and 1990s whereas Thailand's accommodative monetary policy after financial liberalization and its pegged exchange rate regimes fueled a property boom and encouraged currency mismatches.

References

Abbas, A., A. Pienkowski, and K. Rogoff. 2019. *Sovereign Debt: A Guide for Economists and Practitioners.* New York: Oxford University Press.

Arndt, H. W., and H. Hill. 1988. "The Indonesian Economy: Structural Adjustment after the Oil Boom." *Southeast Asian Affairs* 15: 106-19.

Balassa, B. 1982. *Development Strategies in Semi-Industrial Economies.* Washington, DC: World Bank.

Baldacci, E., I. Petrova, N. Belhocine, G. Dobrescu, and S. Mazraani. 2011. "Assessing Fiscal Stress." IMF Working Paper 11/100, International Monetary Fund, Washington, DC.

Berg, A., E. Borensztein, and C. Pattillo. 2005. "Assessing Early Warning Systems: How Have They Worked in Practice?" *IMF Staff Papers* 52 (3): 462-502.

Borio, C., and P. Lowe. 2002. "Assessing the Risk of Banking Crises." *BIS Quarterly Review* 7 (1): 43-54.

Boughton, J. 2001. *Silent Revolution. The International Monetary Fund 1979-89.* Washington, DC: International Monetary Fund.

Brownbridge, M., and C. Kirkpatrick. 2000. "Financial Regulation in Developing Countries." *The Journal of Development Studies* 31 (1): 1-24.

Burnside, C., M. Eichenbaum, and S. Rebelo. 2004. "Government Guarantees and Self-Fulfilling Speculative Attacks." *Journal of Economic Theory* 119 (1): 31-63.

Chamon, M., and C. Crowe. 2012. "Predictive Indicators of Crises." In *Handbook in Financial Globalization: The Evidence and Impact of Financial Globalization*, edited by G. Caprio, 499-505. London: Elsevier.

Claessens, S., and M. A. Kose. 2018. "Frontiers of Macrofinancial Linkages." BIS Papers 95, Bank for International Settlements, Basel.

Claessens, S., M. A. Kose, and M. Terrones. 2012. "How Do Business and Financial Cycles Interact?" *Journal of International Economics* 87 (1): 178-90.

Cowan, K., and J. De Gregorio. 2007. "International Borrowing, Capital Controls, and the Exchange Rate: Lessons from Chile." In *Capital Controls and Capital Flows in Emerging Economies: Policies, Practices, and Consequences*. Cambridge, MA: National Bureau of Economic Research.

Daumont, R., F. Le Gall, and F. Leroux. 2004. "Banking in Sub-Saharan Africa: What Went Wrong?" IMF Working Paper 04/55, International Monetary Fund, Washington, DC.

Dawood, M., N. Horsewood, and F. Strobel. 2017. "Predicting Sovereign Debt Crises: An Early Warning System Approach." *Journal of Financial Stability* 28: 16-28.

Dell'Ariccia, G, D. Igan, L. Laeven, and H. Tong. 2014. "Policies for Macrofinancial Stability: Dealing with Credit Booms and Busts." In *Financial Crises: Causes, Consequences, and Policy Responses*, edited by S. Claessens, M. A. Kose, L. Laeven, and F. Valencia. Washington, DC: International Monetary Fund.

Dell'Ariccia, G, D. Igan, L. Laeven, and H. Tong. 2016. "Credit Booms and Macrofinancial Stability." *Economic Policy* 31 (86): 299-355.

Demirgüç-Kunt, A., and E. Detragiache. 1998. "The Determinants of Banking Crises in Developing and Developed Countries." *Staff Papers* 45 (1): 81-109.

Dornbusch, R., I. Goldfajn, R. Valdés, S. Edwards, and M. Bruno. 1995. "Currency Crises and Collapses." *Brookings Papers on Economic Activity* 1995 (2): 219-93.

Eichengreen, B., A. K. Rose, and C. Wyplosz. 1995. "Exchange Market Mayhem: The Antecedents and Aftermath of Speculative Attacks." *Economic Policy* 10 (21): 249-312.

Elekdag, S., and Y. Wu. 2013. "Rapid Credit Growth in Emerging Markets: Boon or Boom-Bust?" *Emerging Markets Finance and Trade* 49 (5): 45-62.

Enoch, C., and I. Ötker-Robe. 2007. "Lessons from Country Experiences with Rapid Credit Growth, and Policy Implications." In *Rapid Credit Growth in Central and Eastern Europe*, 349-66. London: Palgrave Macmillan.

Forbes, K. J. 2004. "Capital Controls: Mud in the Wheels of Market Discipline." NBER Working Paper 10284, National Bureau of Economic Research, Cambridge, MA.

Forbes, K. J. 2007. "The Microeconomic Evidence on Capital Controls: No Free Lunch." In *Capital Controls and Capital Flows in Emerging Economies: Policies, Practices and Consequences*, edited by S. Edwards, 171-202. Chicago: University of Chicago Press.

Forbes, K., M. Fratzscher, and R. Straub. 2015. "Capital-Flow Management Measures: What Are They Good For?" *Journal of International Economics* 96 (July): S76-S97.

Frankel, J. A., and A. K. Rose. 1996. "Currency Crashes in Emerging Markets: An Empirical Treatment." *Journal of International Economics* 41 (3-4): 351-66.

Frankel, J. A., and G. Saravelos. 2012. "Can Leading Indicators Assess Country Vulnerability? Evidence from the 2008-09 Global Financial Crisis." *Journal of International Economics* 87 (2): 216-31.

Furceri, D., and A. Zdzienicka. 2012. "How Costly Are Debt Crises?" *Journal of International Money and Finance* 31 (4): 726-42.

Gelpern, A. 2016. "Sovereign Debt: Now What?" *Yale Journal of International Law* 41: 45-95.

Gourinchas, P.-O., R. Valdes, and O. Landerretche. 2001. "Lending Booms: Latin America and the World." NBER Working Paper 8249, National Bureau of Economic Research, Cambridge, MA.

Harding, D., and A. Pagan. 2002. "Dissecting the Cycle: A Methodological Investigation." *Journal of Monetary Economics* 49 (2): 365-81.

IMF (International Monetary Fund). 1999. *Report of the Managing Director to the Interim Committee on Progress in Strengthening the Architecture of the International Financial System.* Washington, DC: International Monetary Fund.

IMF (International Monetary Fund). 2000. *Financial Sector Assessment Program (FSAP) A Review: Lessons from the Pilot and Issues Going Forward.* Washington, DC: International Monetary Fund.

IMF (International Monetary Fund). 2012. *The Liberalization and Management of Capital Flows—An Institutional View.* Washington, DC: International Monetary Fund.

IMF (International Monetary Fund). 2014. *Global Financial Stability Report: Risk Taking, Liquidity, and Shadow Banking.* International Monetary Fund, Washington, DC.

IMF (International Monetary Fund). 2015. *The IMF's Institutional View on Capital Flows in Practice.* Washington, DC: International Monetary Fund.

Jordà, Ò., M. Schularick, and A. M. Taylor. 2011. "Financial Crises, Credit Booms, and External Imbalances: 140 Years of Lessons." *IMF Economic Review* 59 (2): 340-78.

Kaminsky, G. L., S. Lizondo, and C. M. Reinhart. 1998. "Leading Indicators of Currency Crises." *IMF Staff Papers* 45 (1): 1-48.

Kaminsky, G. L., and C. M. Reinhart. 1999. "The Twin Crises: The Causes of Banking and Balance-of-Payments Problems." *American Economic Review* 89 (3): 473-500.

Kaufman, R. R. 1989. "The Politics of Economic Adjustment Policy in Argentina, Brazil, and Mexico: Experiences in the 1980s and Challenges for the Future." *Policy Sciences* 22 (3): 395-413.

Kauko, K. 2014. "How to Foresee Banking Crises? A Survey of the Empirical Literature." *Economic Systems* 38 (3): 289-308.

Kawai, M., R. Newfarmer, and S. Schmukler. 2005. "Crisis and Contagion in East Asia: Nine Lessons." *Eastern Economic Journal* 31 (2): 185-207.

Kindleberger, C. P., and R. Z. Aliber. 2011. *Manias, Panics and Crashes: A History of Financial Crises.* London: Palgrave Macmillan.

Laeven, L., and F. Valencia. 2018. "Systemic Banking Crises Revisited." IMF Working Paper 18/206, International Monetary Fund, Washington, DC.

Manasse, P., N. Roubini, and A. Schimmelpfennig. 2003. "Predicting Sovereign Debt Crises." IMF Working Paper 221, International Monetary Fund, Washington, DC.

Mbaye, S., M. Moreno-Badia, and K. Chae. 2018. "Global Debt Database: Methodology and Sources." IMF Working Paper 18/111, International Monetary Fund, Washington, DC.

Mendoza, E. G., and M. E. Terrones. 2008. "An Anatomy of Credit Booms: Evidence from Macro Aggregates and Micro Data." NBER Working Paper 14049, National Bureau of Economic Research, Cambridge, MA.

Mendoza, E. G., and M. E. Terrones. 2012. "An Anatomy of Credit Booms and Their Demise." NBER Working Paper 18379, National Bureau of Economic Research, Cambridge, MA.

Ohnsorge, F., and S. Yu. 2016. "Recent Credit Surge in Historical Context." Policy Research Working Paper 7704, World Bank, Washington, DC.

Reinhart, C., V. Reinhart, and K. Rogoff. 2012. "Public Debt Overhangs: Advanced-Economy Episodes since 1800." *Journal of Economic Perspectives* 26 (3): 69-86.

Reinhart, C. M., and K. S. Rogoff. 2009. *This Time Is Different. Eight Centuries of Financial Folly.* Princeton, NJ: Princeton University Press.

Reinhart, C. M., and K. S. Rogoff. 2011. "From Financial Crash to Debt Crisis." *American Economic Review* 101 (5): 1676-706.

Romer, C. D., and D. H. Romer. 2017. "New Evidence on the Aftermath of Financial Crises in Advanced Countries." *American Economic Review* 107 (10): 3072-118.

Rose, A. K., and M. M. Spiegel. 2012. "Dollar Illiquidity and Central Bank Swap Arrangements During the Global Financial Crisis." *Journal of International Economics* 88 (2): 326-40.

Roubini, N., and P. Wachtel. 1999. "Current-Account Sustainability in Transition Economies." In *Balance of Payments, Exchange Rates, and Competitiveness in Transition Economies*, edited by M. I. Blejer and M. Škreb. Boston: Kluwer Academic Publishers.

Sachs, J. 1985. "External Debt and Macroeconomic Performance in Latin America and East Asia." *Brookings Papers on Economic Activity* 1985 (2): 523-73.

Sachs, J. 1986. "Managing the LDC Debt Crisis." *Brookings Papers on Economic Activity* 1986 (2): 397-440.

Schularick, M., and A. M. Taylor. 2012. "Credit Booms Gone Bust: Monetary Policy, Leverage Cycles, and Financial Crises, 1870-2008." *American Economic Review* 102 (2): 1029-61.

Tornell, A., and F. Westermann. 2005. *Boom-Bust Cycles and Financial Liberalization.* Cambridge, MA: MIT Press Books.

World Bank. 2019. *Global Economic Prospects: Heightened Tensions, Subdued Investment.* June. Washington, DC: World Bank.

[In the United States], if the future is like the past, this implies that debt rollovers, that is the issuance of debt without a later increase in taxes, may well be feasible. Put bluntly, public debt may have no fiscal cost.

Olivier Blanchard (2019)
Senior Fellow at the Peterson Institute
for International Economics

CHAPTER 6
Policies: Turning Mistakes into Experience

In the current global wave of debt, emerging market and developing economies have already accumulated a record amount of debt. This debt buildup has been accompanied by mounting vulnerabilities. For now, prospects for continued low global interest rates appear to mitigate some of the concerns about these vulnerabilities. Yet the study of global and national debt episodes offers several cautionary lessons. For a country's debt to be benign, it needs to be well-spent to finance output-enhancing purposes and its composition needs to be managed to help ensure resilience in the face of economic and financial disruptions. Once debt distress materializes, prompt resolution is critical to avoid a prolonged period of weak activity. These lessons point to several policy priorities: sound and transparent debt management, robust macroeconomic policy frameworks and financial regulation and supervision that support sustainable debt accumulation in public and private sectors, and business environments and institutions conducive to strong corporate governance.

Introduction

Another wave of debt accumulation has been underway in emerging market and developing economies (EMDEs) since 2010. As documented in chapter 4, this wave of global debt, the fourth during the past 50 years, has already been larger, faster, and more broad-based than the three previous episodes. The preceding three global waves ended with financial crises in many EMDEs, raising the question of whether the current wave will end in a similar way.

Several factors are likely to shape the trajectory of the current wave of debt, including prospects for global interest rates and economic growth. Although EMDEs are not in full control of some of these factors, they would benefit from using the lessons from their own experiences with debt accumulation to avoid the mistakes of the past.

Against this backdrop, this chapter addresses the following questions:

- What forces will shape the evolution of the current debt wave?
- What are the lessons to be drawn from previous episodes of debt accumulation?
- What policies can lower the likelihood and cost of future debt crises?

In the course of answering these questions, the chapter makes three contributions to an already-rich policy debate.

- *Prospects for the current wave.* The chapter discusses the likely evolution of the current wave of debt accumulation from the perspective of EMDEs. It also considers the recent debate about the merits of debt accumulation in the current era of low interest rates.[1] Previous work has mostly focused on the consequences of debt accumulation for advanced economies, as reviewed in chapter 2.

- *Lessons from the global and national episodes of debt accumulation.* The chapter offers a compilation of salient lessons about the consequences of debt buildup based on the analysis of the global and national episodes of debt accumulation presented in the earlier chapters.

- *Policy prescriptions.* The chapter offers a comprehensive set of policy prescriptions that can help lower the likelihood of debt-related financial crises and mitigate their effects when they materialize.

The chapter presents the following findings.

Striking the right balance. In the current debt wave, many EMDEs have both accumulated a record amount of debt and experienced a persistent growth slowdown (figure 6.1). Some of these economies now also share a wide range of external and domestic vulnerabilities that have historically been associated with a higher likelihood of financial crises. In addition, EMDEs are confronted by a wide range of risks in an increasingly fragile global context. As a result, despite currently record-low global interest rates, stronger policy frameworks in some EMDEs, and a strengthened international safety net, the latest wave of debt accumulation could follow the historical pattern and result in financial crises. The study of past waves shows the critical importance of policy choices in reducing the likelihood that the current debt wave will end in crisis and, if crises were to take place, mitigating their impact.

Lessons from experience. Debt accumulation is unlikely to be benign unless it is well-spent to finance truly output-enhancing purposes and it is resilient (in terms of maturity, currency, and creditor composition) to economic and financial market disruptions. Such resilience requires not only prudent

---

[1] Blanchard (2019); Blanchard and Summers (2019); Furman and Summers (2019); and Krugman (2019) argue for increased borrowing, whereas Auerbach, Gale, and Krupkin (2019); CRFB (2019); Mazza (2019); and Riedl (2019) caution against debt accumulation.

FIGURE 6.1 **Debt accumulation and growth in the current wave**

Despite a rapid debt buildup since 2010, global growth has been anemic and EMDE growth has slowed.

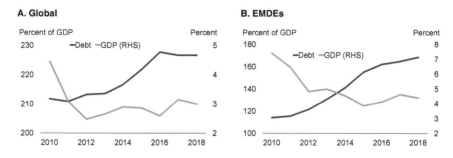

Source: World Bank.
Note: Total debt (in percent of GDP) and real GDP growth (GDP-weighted at 2010 prices and exchange rates). EMDEs = emerging market and developing economies.

government debt management but also robust financial system regulation and supervision and sound corporate governance. It is critical to respond effectively to external shocks especially when there are domestic vulnerabilities. Private debt can quickly turn into public debt during periods of financial stress. Once debt distress materializes, prompt resolution is critical to avoid a prolonged period of weak economic activity.

Policy options. Although specific policy priorities depend on country circumstances, four broad strands of policy options can help contain the risks associated with debt accumulation. *First,* governments need to put in place mechanisms and institutions, including sound debt management and high debt transparency, that help them strike the proper balance between the benefits and costs of additional debt. International creditors can support sustainable borrowing by implementing prudent lending standards (including in terms of transparency), helping build capacity, appropriately distributing risk, and ensuring the productive use of debt. *Second,* the benefits of stability-oriented and resilient fiscal and monetary policy frameworks and exchange rate regimes cannot be overstated. *Third,* financial sector policies need to be designed to foster responsible private sector borrowing. Such policies include robust supervisory and regulatory systems as well as corporate and bank bankruptcy frameworks that allow prompt debt resolution to limit the damage from debt distress. *Fourth,* it is essential to have strong corporate governance practices and effective bankruptcy and insolvency regimes.

The remainder of this chapter is organized as follows. The next section discusses the factors that may determine the likely evolution of the current wave of debt accumulation in light of the challenges confronting EMDEs. The subsequent two sections draw lessons from the analysis of global and national waves of debt accumulation, which yields the policy options discussed in the following section. The chapter concludes with a summary and suggests topics for future research.

The current wave: What next?

The recent buildup of debt has been both large at the country level and broad-based across countries. Although current levels of government or private debt are, on average, still below or near those in the median rapid debt accumulation episode, increases in government or private debt since 2010 have already exceeded those of the typical historical episode in about one-quarter of EMDEs (figure 6.2). In some EMDEs, private debt has risen more than twice as much (30 percentage points of gross domestic product [GDP]) as in the typical previous episode. In several of these economies, elevated private debt has been accompanied by other vulnerabilities that have been identified as correlates of the probability of financial crisis, including elevated foreign-currency-denominated debt, external debt, or short-term external debt.

The current wave of debt, not yet a decade old, has already included the euro area debt crisis and several EMDE currency crises. Capital flows to EMDEs have been volatile since 2010, with episodes of substantial outflows in 2013, 2015, and 2018. During these episodes, many EMDEs experienced large jumps in bond spreads and significant currency depreciation against the U.S. dollar. In 2018, the risks associated with elevated debt were illustrated by the experiences of Argentina and Turkey, which suffered sharp increases in borrowing costs and slowdowns in growth.

Although EMDEs have gone through periods of volatility during the current wave of debt, they have not experienced widespread financial crises. The key question is whether the current wave of debt accumulation will at some point end in financial crises in many EMDEs, as all its predecessors eventually did, or whether such crises will be avoided perhaps because EMDEs have learned and applied their lessons from the past.

A wide range of factors will determine the evolution of the current wave and its consequences for EMDEs. The remainder of this section discusses the implications of low interest rates and weak growth prospects for debt

FIGURE 6.2 **Current EMDE debt accumulation in historical context**

Although current levels of EMDE government or private debt are, on average, still below or near those in the median rapid debt accumulation episode, increases in government or private debt since 2010 have already exceeded those of the typical historical episode in about one-quarter of EMDEs.

A. Current levels of government debt versus previous rapid debt accumulation episodes

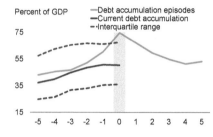

B. Current levels of private debt versus previous rapid debt accumulation episodes

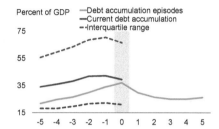

Source: World Bank.
Note: Median levels of debt during debt accumulation episodes, as defined in appendix A. t=0 indicates the peak of debt accumulation episodes that were completed before 2018. For current debt accumulation, t=0 indicates 2018. EMDEs = emerging market and developing economies.

accumulation in EMDEs. It then examines how vulnerabilities have mounted in these economies during the current debt wave. Next, it discusses factors that could lead to a sudden increase in borrowing cost for EMDEs. It concludes with a discussion of improvements in EMDE policy frameworks that could mitigate the risks associated with rapid debt accumulation.

Prolonged period of low interest rates

Low borrowing costs incentivize countries to accumulate debt. For instance, an easing of U.S. financial conditions, a bellwether for global financial conditions, has typically accompanied an increase in capital flows to EMDEs (Feyen et al. 2015). But increased borrowing can also raise vulnerability to a future rebound in interest rates. Historically, rising global interest rates have been a key trigger for financial crises, as documented in previous chapters. EMDE borrowing costs tend to rise sharply during these episodes, and higher debt servicing costs can cause debt dynamics to deteriorate rapidly.

The current environment of low interest rates and persistently low inflation in advanced economies alleviates some risks associated with the latest wave of debt. Policy interest rates in many advanced economies are near historical lows after major central banks recently reverted to an easing stance after winding down tightening cycles in 2018. Moreover, monetary policy in

FIGURE 6.3 **Interest rates and inflation**

The current environment of low interest rates, and expectations that interest rates will remain low, mitigate immediate concerns about rapid debt accumulation.

A. Long-term interest rates

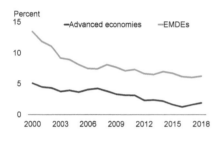

B. Policy rate expectations in major advanced economies

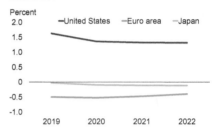

C. Headline inflation

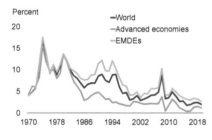

D. Long-term inflation expectations

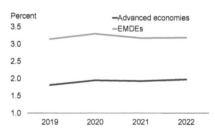

Sources: Bloomberg; Consensus Economics; Ha, Kose, and Ohnsorge (2019); World Bank.
Note: EMDEs = emerging market and developing economies.
A. Average long-term nominal government bond yields (with maturity of 10 years) computed with current U.S. dollar GDP as a weight, based on up to 36 advanced economies and 84 EMDEs.
B. Market-implied policy rates. Expected rates based on overnight index swap (OIS) forward rates.
C. Median annual average inflation.
D. Long-term consensus inflation expectations.

advanced economies is likely to be accommodative for the foreseeable future as growth prospects and inflation expectations remain subdued (figure 6.3). This is reflected in low policy interest rate expectations in 2020-22. In EMDEs, many of which face slowing demand growth, subdued prices for their commodity exports, and disinflationary pressures, policy makers may also cut policy rates further in the near term.

Structural headwinds also seem likely to keep real interest rates low in the longer term. Estimates of the neutral interest rate, the rate consistent with stable inflation and an economy operating at full capacity, have declined markedly across advanced economies over the past decades (Holston, Laubach, and Williams 2017). The structural factors responsible for this decline are likely to persist. They include slowing labor force growth, a product of population aging and declining birth rates; slowing productivity growth since the most recent peak in the late 1990s; and muted prospects for a productivity revival (Eggertsson, Mehrotra, and Robbins 2019; Fernald 2016; Gordon 2012). An increased demand for safe assets, driven in part by the quantitative easing by central banks in major advanced economies, and decreased appetite for capital investments also seem likely to continue weighing on interest rates (Del Negro et al. 2017; Rachel and Summers 2019; Williams 2018).

Low global interest rates have encouraged an aggressive search for yield, bouts of large capital flows to EMDEs, and a sharp narrowing of bond spreads. About one-quarter of sovereign and corporate bonds issued in advanced economies—and some bonds issued by Hungary and Poland— currently trade at negative yields.[2] Negative yields on advanced economy debt already helped compress debt service burdens for EMDE borrowers and nudged debt toward a declining path in the future.[3] Thus, interest payments on EMDE government debt fell from an average of 2.6 percent of GDP in 2000-07, to 1.6 percent of GDP in 2010-18, despite the increase in debt over that period. At current long-term interest rates and nominal GDP growth, debt-to-GDP ratios appear to be on stable or falling trajectory in almost half of EMDEs (figure 6.4).

The debate on the implications of low interest rates for additional debt accumulation has focused on advanced economies, as discussed in chapter 2.[4] Some argue that advanced economies, especially those that issue reserve currencies, should take advantage of low interest rates to borrow more to finance priority expenditures. Others caution that high debt weighs on long-term growth by increasing the risk of crises, limiting the scope for countercyclical fiscal stimulus, and dampening private investment.

---

[2] In the two EMDEs with recent negative-yielding sovereign bond issuances (Hungary and Poland), government, household and corporate debt have risen only moderately (by at most 7 percentage points of GDP) over the past decade. Spreads on emerging market debt both for corporate and sovereign bonds reached all-time lows in 2017, boosting borrowing. Average spreads on corporate bonds have fallen from precrisis levels for all EMDEs, including low-income countries, as well as for lower-rated corporate bonds.

[3] Debt is defined to be on a declining path if the primary balance is larger than the debt-stabilizing primary balance at current growth and interest rates (Kose et al. 2017).

[4] Blanchard (2019); Blanchard and Summers (2019); Blanchard and Tashiro (2019); Blanchard and Ubide (2019); Eichengreen et al. (2019); Furman and Summers (2019); Krugman (2019); and Rachel and Summers (2019) discuss reasons for additional government spending financed by borrowing in advanced economies, and the United States in particular, whereas Alcidi and Gros (2019); Auerbach, Gale, and Krupkin (2019); CRFB (2019); Eichengreen (2019); Mazza (2019); Riedl (2019); Rogoff (2019a, 2019b); and Wyplosz (2019) caution against adding to debt, citing in particular the example of the United States.

FIGURE 6.4 **Debt trajectories**

Growth still exceeds long-term interest rates in more than half of EMDEs. Historically, growth has exceeded long-term interest rates most of the time, but in many cases borrowing was sufficiently large to set debt on a rising trajectory nevertheless.

A. Share of economies with interest rates below growth

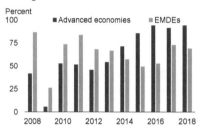

B. Share of economies with interest rates below growth, 1990-2018

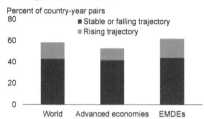

Sources: Haver Analytics; Kose et al. (2017); World Bank.
Note: EMDEs = emerging market and developing economies.
A. Share of country-year pairs in each group when long-term nominal interest rates (represented by 10-year local currency government bond yields) are below nominal GDP growth in up to 34 advanced economies and 83 EMDEs.
B. Share of countries where long-term nominal interest rates (represented by 10-year local currency government bond yields) are below nominal GDP growth. Sample of up to 36 advanced economies and 84 EMDEs over 1990-2018. The remainder to 100 is the share of countries in which long-term nominal interest rates exceeded nominal GDP growth.

For EMDEs, there are additional concerns about debt sustainability even during times of low global interest rates. First, financing costs may be low relative to GDP growth, but they may not be low enough to offset the sheer magnitude of borrowing. Second, both interest rates and growth rates are highly volatile in EMDEs.

- *Interest rate-growth differential versus magnitude of borrowing.* During 1990-2018, the interest rate-growth differential was negative in more than half (58 percent) of country-year pairs.[5] Even in about a quarter of these instances, however, the differential was not large enough to offset the increase in debt from primary balances and maintain the government debt ratio on a stable or declining path. As a result, during 1990-2018, primary balances, long-term interest rates, and nominal GDP growth were such that debt was on a steadily rising trajectory in 43 percent of country-year pairs among 34 advanced economies and 50 percent of country-year pairs among 83 EMDEs.

---

[5] Over the period 1990-2018, 53 percent of country-year pairs among 34 advanced economies and 62 percent of country-year pairs among 83 EMDEs had interest rates lower than growth. Over a longer, 200-year horizon for a smaller sample of 55 mostly advanced economies, average interest rates have also been lower than average growth rates more often than not, but marginal borrowing costs rose steeply during crises (Mauro and Zhou 2019).

- *Stability of interest rate-growth differential.* When borrowing costs rise, they rise more steeply in the average EMDE than in the average advanced economy; when growth declines, it declines more sharply in the average EMDE than in the average advanced economy. On average in those months during 1990-2018 when long-term interest rates increased, they rose by 0.3 percentage point in the average EMDE, two-thirds more than the average advanced-economy. Similarly, when real GDP growth slowed from one year to the next during 1990-2018, it slowed by 3.2 percentage points in the average EMDE, compared with 2.5 percentage points in the average advanced economy.[6]

For these two reasons, in particular, low or falling global interest rates provide no sure protection against financial crises for EMDEs. Indeed, half of all crises during episodes of rapid debt accumulation occurred in years when U.S. long-term (10-year) interest rates were falling and one-eighth occurred in years when U.S. long-term real interest rates were below 1 percent (as they have been since 2016).

Weak growth prospects

In addition to interest rates and fiscal positions, economic growth is another major determinant of debt sustainability. An important reason for rapid debt accumulation has been the sharp growth slowdown over the course of the fourth wave of debt. EMDE growth slowed after 2010 to a trough of 4.1 percent in 2016 before a modest recovery took hold (Kose and Ohnsorge 2020). The growth slowdown during 2011-16 was broad-based (affecting more than three-fifths of EMDEs) and protracted. Amid this broad-based growth weakness, EMDEs have struggled to fully unwind fiscal and monetary stimulus implemented during the global financial crisis, resulting in erosion of EMDE fiscal positions and in additional borrowing to maintain current spending levels.

During the current wave of debt, potential growth in EMDEs has also declined, because of slower productivity growth as well as demographic change (Ruch 2020; figure 6.5). Productivity growth has declined as investment growth has slowed, gains from factor reallocation have faded (including the migration of labor from agriculture to manufacturing and services), and growth in global value chains has moderated. Slower investment growth has tempered capital accumulation. Demographic trends

---

[6] When nominal GDP growth slowed in EMDEs, it slowed by more than 6 percentage points on average during 1990-2018, compared with less than 3 percentage points in advanced economies.

FIGURE 6.5 **Long-term growth prospects**

Long-term growth prospects have slowed substantially from precrisis rates. Potential growth is expected to decline in the next decade.

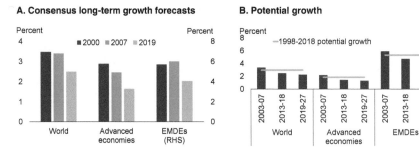

A. Consensus long-term growth forecasts

B. Potential growth

Sources: Consensus Economics; Haver Analytics; Penn World Tables; United Nations Population Prospects; World Bank.
Note: EMDEs = emerging market and developing economies.
A. Bars show long-term (10-year ahead) average annual growth forecasts surveyed in respective years. Sample includes 38 countries—20 advanced economies and 18 EMDEs—for which Consensus forecasts are consistently available from 1998 to 2018. Aggregate growth rates calculated using constant 2010 U.S. dollar GDP weights.
B. Period average of annual GDP-weighted averages. Estimates based on production function approach. Sample includes 50 EMDEs and 30 advanced economies.

have also become less favorable to growth, since the share of working-age populations in EMDEs peaked around 2010.

Current trends in these fundamental drivers of potential growth suggest that it is likely to slow further over the next decade, to a pace about 0.5 percentage point lower than in 2013-17 (World Bank 2018a). For commodity-exporting EMDEs—almost two-thirds of EMDEs—growth prospects will be further dimmed by the expected slowdown in commodity demand growth as major commodity-consuming emerging markets slow and mature (World Bank 2018a). The past decade has been marked by repeated growth disappointments. If these persist into the next decade, they could lead to growing concerns about debt sustainability, even in a world of low interest rates.

Moreover, during the current wave of debt, there have been signs that government debt has been used for "less efficient spending" rather than on productive investment in physical or human capital that could boost potential growth in EMDEs. Public investment in EMDEs fell from an average of 2.1 percent of GDP in 2002-09 to 0.9 percent of GDP in 2010-18 (IMF 2019b). Among commodity exporters, declining tax revenues following the commodity price plunge of 2014-16 widened fiscal deficits and raised debt despite lower investment (World Bank 2018a). Meanwhile, house prices have risen sharply in EMDEs, suggesting that some of the rise in private debt has financed residential construction, which does not yield export earnings.

Mounting vulnerabilities

The previous three debt waves highlighted the risks associated with a sharp buildup of debt. Financial crises typically occurred when external shocks hit EMDEs with domestic vulnerabilities. As discussed in the subsection titled "Better Policy Frameworks," many EMDEs have improved their monetary and fiscal policy frameworks over the past two decades, but elevated debt levels during the current wave of debt accumulation have been accompanied by rising fiscal, corporate, and external vulnerabilities (figures 6.6 and 6.7). These vulnerabilities include lower international reserves and larger shares of EMDEs with current account and fiscal deficits.

- Although still above their 1980s and 1990s averages, international reserves relative to external debt have fallen since 2010 in more than two-thirds of EMDEs, and in one-quarter the ratio has more than halved.

- Current account deficits in EMDEs averaged 4.5 percent of GDP in 2018, compared with 3.1 percent of GDP in 2010. In 2018, 55 percent of EMDEs had weaker current account balances than in 2010; 76 percent ran current account deficits (compared with 69 percent in 2010); and 44 percent had current account deficits in excess of 5 percent of GDP.

- An average cyclically adjusted primary fiscal deficit of 0.6 percent of GDP in 2007 in EMDEs had widened to 0.9 percent of GDP by 2018. About one-half of EMDEs had a larger deficit in 2018 than in 2010. Commodity-exporting EMDEs experienced larger deteriorations in fiscal balances, on average, and were running larger deficits than commodity importers.

As documented in chapter 4, the composition of debt has changed significantly in EMDEs. This shift could generate new vulnerabilities. For example, increasing issuance of foreign-currency-denominated corporate debt has contributed to rising currency exposures and heightened the risks of financial distress in the corporate sector and the banking system in the event of a sharp U.S. dollar appreciation. In some EMDEs, the share of nonresident-held bonds in local currency bond markets has grown to more than 30 percent. In low-income countries (LICs), debt has been increasingly

FIGURE 6.6 **Sovereign and corporate vulnerabilities in EMDEs**

Government debt increased broadly across EMDEs between 2010 and 2018. Corporate debt rose even more rapidly.

A. Government debt

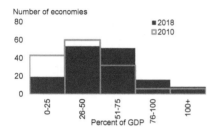

B. Sovereign credit ratings

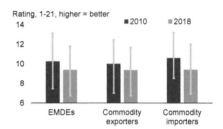

C. Maturity of government debt

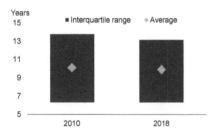

D. Cyclically adjusted primary fiscal balance

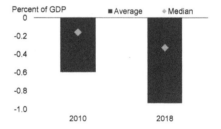

E. Nonfinancial corporate debt

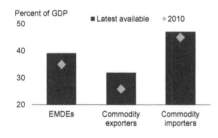

F. Nonfinancial corporate debt

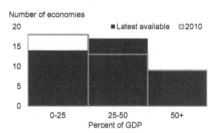

Sources: Institute of International Finance; International Monetary Fund; Kose et al. (2017); World Bank.
Note: EMDEs = emerging market and developing economies.
A. Sample includes 147 EMDEs.
B. Unweighted averages of foreign currency sovereign credit ratings for 49 EMDE commodity exporters and 40 EMDE commodity importers. Whiskers denote interquartile ranges.
C. Unweighted averages of the average maturity of government debt based on 39 EMDEs.
D. Based on data for 151 EMDEs.
E.F. Sample includes 40 EMDEs. Latest available datapoint is 2019Q2 for Argentina, Brazil, Chile, China, Colombia, Hungary, India, Indonesia, Malaysia, Mexico, Poland, the Russian Federation, Saudi Arabia, South Africa, Thailand, and Turkey, and 2017 for the rest.
E. Unweighted average of nonfinancial corporate debt in 21 EMDE commodity exporters and 19 EMDE commodity importers.

FIGURE 6.7 **External vulnerabilities in EMDEs**

Since 2010, external debt has risen in most EMDEs relative to GDP, and current account balances have weakened in commodity exporters. Most EMDEs appear to have adequate foreign reserve coverage to meet balance of payments needs, but significant heterogeneity exists.

A. External debt

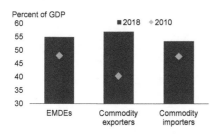

B. Distribution of external debt

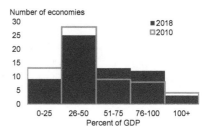

C. Current account balance

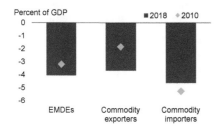

D. Current account balance

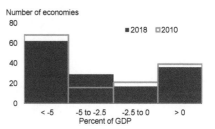

E. Foreign reserves adequacy

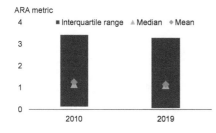

F. Nonresident holdings of local-currency-denominated debt

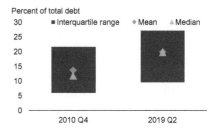

Sources: Ha, Kose, and Ohnsorge (2019); International Monetary Fund; World Bank.
Note: EMDEs = emerging market and developing economies.
A. Unweighted average of total external debt-to-GDP ratios for 31 EMDE commodity exporters and 30 EMDE commodity importers.
B. Sample includes 61 EMDEs.
C. Unweighted average of current account balance-to-GDP ratios for 88 EMDE commodity exporters and 56 EMDE commodity importers.
D. Sample includes 144 EMDEs.
E. Sample includes 48 EMDEs. Dark blue bars show minimum and maximum values. Assessing Reserve Adequacy (ARA) metric is based on IMF (2011), which determines the appropriate reserve cover on a risk-weighted basis covering short-term debt, medium- and long-term debt, and equity liabilities. Risk weights are based on observed outflows during periods of exchange rate pressure. Values above 1 suggest that countries are fully able to meet balance of payments needs using reserves.
F. Sample includes 22 EMDEs.

financed by nonconcessional and private sources. As a result, interest payments have been absorbing a growing share of government revenues (Ruch 2020).

What could make debt expensive?

Debt sustainability in EMDEs could be threatened by an increase in borrowing cost that could be driven by various factors.

Normalization of monetary policy in advanced economies. Although it seems unlikely in the foreseeable future, a return to monetary policy normalization in advanced economies could raise borrowing costs (Ruch 2020). A rapid increase in policy interest rates, as happened in the first global wave of debt accumulation, could be accompanied by large currency depreciations in EMDEs that would sharply increase debt service burdens for foreign-currency-denominated debt (Arteta et al. 2016). It would also be likely to trigger a turn in investor sentiment that would especially affect those EMDEs with large foreign participation in local bond markets, which in some economies now exceeds 30 percent of government bonds.

Disruptions in advanced economy financial markets. The end of the third wave of debt was marked by disruptions in advanced economy financial markets. As documented in chapter 4, in the third wave debt accumulation in advanced economies outpaced that in EMDEs. In contrast, advanced economy debt ratios have been broadly stable in the fourth wave, as pronounced private deleveraging offset government debt increases in advanced economies, whereas in EMDEs the share of private debt has remained broadly stable.

As in the third wave, however, a decade of tightening banking regulation has encouraged the emergence of maturity mismatches and credit risks among institutions in the nonbank financial system (IMF 2019a). Financial stress in nonbank financial institutions could quickly propagate to the rest of the financial system, owing to the interconnectedness between nonbanks and banks. Growing links between nonbank financial systems in advanced economies and EMDEs have increased both the likelihood and the potential magnitude of spillovers from distress in advanced economy nonbanks to EMDE bond markets and broader financial systems.

For example, leveraged loans—defined as loans to firms that are highly indebted, have high debt service costs relative to earnings, and are typically below investment grade—have become an increasingly important part of corporate debt in both advanced economies and EMDEs (BIS 2019). The outstanding stock of leveraged loans has doubled since the global financial crisis (BIS 2018).

Because most leveraged loans are denominated in U.S. dollars, tend to be at variable rates, and are often short term, they are highly vulnerable to rising financing costs. More than half of leveraged loans are packaged into collateralized loan obligations (CLOs), a form of asset-backed security with notable similarities to the collateralized debt obligations (CDOs) based on mortgage loans that played a key role in the global financial crisis.[7] In search for yield, nonbank financial institutions such as pension funds and insurance companies have sought to invest in riskier and less liquid assets in order to meet their nominal return targets. Foreign portfolio investors and global mutual funds have also become more active in EMDE bond markets (IMF 2019a). They have done so, for example, by increasing their issuances of leveraged loans, which have risen significantly in every EMDE region, but especially in East Asia and Pacific.

Commodity price shocks. Many commodity-exporting EMDEs rely heavily on revenues from the resource sector to fund government expenditures and service sovereign debt (Correa and Sapriza 2014). As a result, commodity price shocks have periodically disrupted government finances and been a source of financial instability in EMDEs, culminating in some cases in sovereign debt default or other financial crises (figure 6.8).[8] Indeed, before World War II, commodity price booms often culminated in sovereign defaults in EMDEs (Reinhart and Rogoff 2014). The relationship weakened during the postwar period, but commodity price booms and associated terms of trade movements have remained a major predictor of financial and sovereign debt crises (Caballero 2003). In LICs especially, commodity price shocks have often been associated with financial sector fragility and banking crises (Eberhart and Presbitero 2018; Kinda, Mlachila, and Ouedraogo 2016).

Trade tensions. International trade has been a key engine of growth in EMDEs over the past two decades. An escalation of trade tensions could

---

[7] Both are based on an underlying pool of low-quality loans, structured in tranches of differing seniority on the basis of exposure to credit losses, and are vulnerable to sudden increases in both the magnitude and correlation of losses. However, CLOs are less complex than CDOs, are not commonly used as collateral in repo transactions, and have a better-understood impact on banks' direct exposures.

[8] Even in advanced economies, commodity price swings have sometimes triggered financial crises. For example, the financial crisis of 1837 in the United Kingdom was preceded by a sharp increase in commodity prices (Bordo, Dueker, and Wheelock 2003).

FIGURE 6.8 Debt dynamics in EMDE oil exporters around oil price plunges

Oil price plunges are historically accompanied by deteriorating fiscal debt sustainability in oil exporters, reflecting shrinking oil revenues and weaker growth, but fiscal positions tend to recover quickly after the initial shock.

A. Fiscal sustainability gap

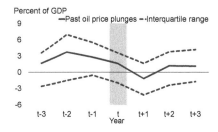

B. Government gross debt

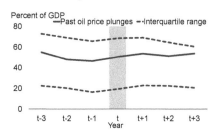

C. Overall fiscal balance

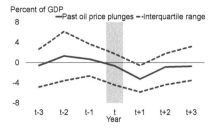

D. Credit to the private sector

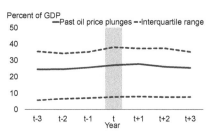

Sources: International Monetary Fund; World Bank (2017a).
Note: Year t refers to the year of oil price plunges. Past oil price plunges include collapses in global oil prices in 1991, 1998, 2001, and 2008 (World Bank 2015). Simple averages of 35 EMDE oil exporters in all episodes. EMDEs = emerging market and developing economies.
C. Samples are restricted to episodes where data on sustainability gaps are available.

depress output in the short term as well as the medium term (Barattieri, Cacciatore, and Ghironi 2018).[9] By increasing investor uncertainty and triggering U.S. dollar appreciation, escalating trade tensions could also cause a significant tightening in global financial conditions (Dizioli and van Roye 2018). Heightened uncertainty could encourage capital flight into safe advanced economy assets, potentially precipitating sudden stops in EMDEs. U.S. dollar appreciations would increase the real value of sovereign and corporate debt denominated in foreign currency and could trigger a retreat of EMDE lending by global banks (Bruno and Shin 2015). To the extent that

---

[9] In addition, EMDEs rely in part on the proceeds from trade taxation to meet spending needs and sovereign debt obligations (van Wijnbergen 1987).

EMDEs' trade is invoiced in U.S. dollars, bilateral depreciation could raise the price of tradeable goods and restrict inventory financing, disrupting global value chains (Boz, Gopinath, and Plagborg-Moller 2017; Bruno, Kim, and Shin 2018).

Corporate debt in China. The large corporate debt buildup in China since 2010 has been primarily to domestic creditors. Its counterpart in the financial system could eventually reveal nonperforming loans and result in a growth slowdown in China (figure 6.9). Concerns also remain about overcapacity in some industries resulting from the debt-fueled rapid investment growth of the past decade (Maliszewski et al. 2016; Wang, Wan and Song 2018; Yu and Shen 2019). Although it has recently declined, high corporate leverage, particularly in state-owned enterprises, has been associated with declining corporate profitability and financial performance (Molnar and Lu 2019; World Bank 2018b). In view of the size of China's economy, adverse spillovers to other EMDEs would likely be significant, including through portfolio reallocation among asset classes (Ahmed et al. 2019; World Bank 2016).

Debt in low-income countries. LICs have accumulated debt rapidly and increasingly from nonconcessional and less transparent sources of finance (Essl et al. 2019). These developments have increased LICs' vulnerability to financing shocks and to the revelation of previously undisclosed debt obligations (Bova et al. 2016; Horn, Reinhart, and Trebesch 2019; Lee and Bachmair 2019). Transparency about contingent liabilities in LICs, such as those stemming from state-owned enterprise debt and public-private partnership transactions, as well as government asset holdings, is also limited. These data limitations are especially acute for debt owed to commercial and non-Paris Club creditors. Poor data coverage can give rise to sudden increases in disclosed debt, for example when debt of loss-making state-owned enterprises migrates to the books of the central government.[10]

Climate events. For some EMDEs, risks related to climate change are substantial. Climate-related risks are particularly pronounced for economies where physical capital and infrastructure are located in high risk areas and for smaller EMDEs that rely heavily on climate-sensitive industries (such as agriculture and tourism) but have limited scope for economic diversification.

---

[10] For example, in the Republic of Congo and in Mozambique, the revelation of unreported debt led to large upward revisions to official debt figures, which resulted in debt distress (IMF 2018b). Only a third of the 59 countries eligible for International Development Association borrowing report private sector external debt statistics (World Bank and IMF 2018).

FIGURE 6.9 **Debt accumulation in China**

Since the global financial crisis, debt in China has increased rapidly while GDP growth has slowed. The increase in the debt ratio over the five years leading up to 2016 was the second largest in the history of emerging market and developing economies. Debt is primarily owed to the private sector and domestically held.

A. GDP growth and total debt

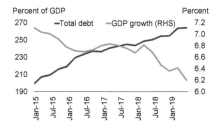

B. Selected economies: Peak five-year change in total debt

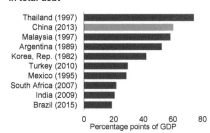

Sources: Haver Analytics; International Monetary Fund; World Bank
A. GDP growth is year-on-year percent change.
B. Largest change in debt in percentage points of GDP over any five-year interval. Data as of December 2019.

The experience of several economies in Latin America and the Caribbean, in particular, shows that debt crises can be triggered by natural disasters. Furthermore, the move to a low-carbon economy could have a material effect for energy-exporting EMDEs. A shift away from the use of carbon-intensive fuels could leave the assets of fossil fuel companies, including state-owned companies, stranded by rules to curb climate change (Carney 2015). Such a shift could have critical implications for debt sustainability both at the firm and the country level.

To the extent that natural disasters are becoming more frequent and persistent as a result of climate change, they are likely to increase macroeconomic volatility and reduce long-term growth prospects, posing a growing risk to debt sustainability in vulnerable EMDEs (Nakatani 2019). EMDEs tend to adopt procyclical policies in the aftermath of natural disasters, which may further deepen the macroeconomic costs of these events (Noy and Nualsri 2011). Political unrest after climate shocks or additional investment needed for climate adaptation may lift government borrowing cost, further increasing the likelihood of debt distress (Klomp 2015). Finally, extreme weather events can lead to a significant deterioration of fiscal and trade balances, which in turn may trigger financial distress and debt crises (Acevedo 2016; Lee, Zhang, and Nguyen 2018; Lis and Nickel 2010).

Domestic vulnerabilities. Elevated debt increases an economy's vulnerability to domestic financing and political shocks even in an environment of benign global financing conditions. Domestic financing shocks can trigger sharp increases in borrowing costs. They may include the sudden emergence of contingent government liabilities, including in state-owned enterprises or public-private partnerships. Policy surprises or sudden bouts of policy uncertainty can also fuel investor concerns about debt repayment causing a spike in borrowing costs.

Economies with unstable political regimes are more prone to financial crises and increased volatility in borrowing costs (Cuadra and Sapriza 2008; Yu 2016). Political instability and unrest often precede debt crises, particularly when a rapid buildup of government debt necessitates policy adjustments that have important distributional consequences (Andreasen, Sandleris, and Van der Ghote 2019). Conversely, political stability tends to be associated with a lower likelihood of sovereign default and quicker resolution of debt crises (Trebesch 2018; Van Rijckeghem and Weder 2009).

Better policy frameworks

Since the 1990s, policy frameworks in many EMDEs have become more resilient. The number of EMDEs with inflation-targeting monetary policy regimes and the number with fiscal rules have risen considerably since the late 1990s, macroprudential tools have been used more proactively, and bankruptcy rights protections have been strengthened.

Monetary and exchange rate policy frameworks. The number of EMDEs with inflation-targeting monetary policy regimes and flexible exchange rates has risen from only 3 and 11, respectively, in 1999 to close to 30 in each case in 2018 (figure 6.10). Many EMDEs also improved the transparency of their central banks over this period, helping to anchor inflation expectations. With improvements in domestic monetary policy frameworks and the global decline in inflation, EMDEs have been able to bring inflation down from double digits in the 1990s to about 3 percent in 2019 (Ha, Kose, and Ohnsorge 2019).

Fiscal policy frameworks. Fiscal rules have been adopted in more than 60 EMDEs. Although their effectiveness has varied, these rules-based policy frameworks facilitated effective countercyclical responses by some of these economies during the last global recession and could help buttress against future shocks (Alfaro and Kanczuk 2016).

Macroprudential policies. Since the global financial crisis, over two-thirds of EMDEs have tightened macroprudential rules—such as standards for bank capital, liquidity buffers, and loan-loss-provisioning—to contain risks from rapid private sector credit growth or house price growth (figure 6.11;

FIGURE 6.10 **Monetary, exchange rate, and fiscal policy frameworks**

Since the 1990s, many EMDEs have introduced fiscal rules and inflation targeting monetary policy regimes, as well as greater exchange rate flexibility and central bank transparency.

A. EMDEs with fiscal rules

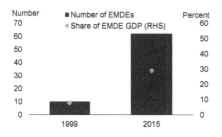

B. EMDEs with inflation-targeting central banks

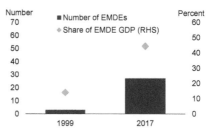

C. EMDEs with flexible exchange rates

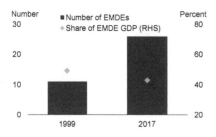

D. Central bank transparency

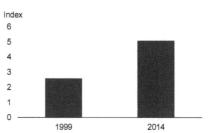

Sources: Dincer and Eichengreen (2014); Ha, Kose, and Ohnsorge (2019); Huidrom et al. (2019); International Monetary Fund; Kose et al. (2017); World Bank.
Note: EMDEs = emerging market and developing economies.
A. An economy is considered to be implementing a fiscal rule if it has one or more fiscal rules on expenditure, revenue, budget balance, or debt.
B. Inflation targeting as classified in the International Monetary Fund's Annual Report of Exchange Arrangements and Exchange Restrictions.
C. An economy is considered to have a flexible exchange rate if it is classified as "Floating" or "Free Floating" in the International Monetary Fund's Annual Report of Exchange Arrangements and Exchange Restrictions.
D. Dincer and Eichengreen Transparency Index (2014). The index ranges from 0 (least independent and transparent) to 15 (most independent and transparent).

Cerutti, Claessens, and Laeven 2017). EMDEs have made efforts to contain risks from volatile capital flows through policies aimed at financial institutions, particularly restrictions on foreign currency exposures, reserve requirements on foreign funding, and liquidity-related measures (Ruch 2020). The overall effectiveness of these policies has depended on how they have interacted with macroeconomic and sector-specific policy measures (Bruno, Shim, and Shin 2017; Claessens 2015).

Structural policies. Since the 2009 global recession, some EMDEs have undertaken reforms to strengthen business climates (although reform

FIGURE 6.11 **Macroprudential policies and bankruptcy procedures**

EMDEs have used macroprudential policy more proactively since the global financial crisis and have improved provisions protecting bankruptcy rights.

A. Macroprudential policy in EMDEs

B. Bankruptcy rights protection in EMDEs

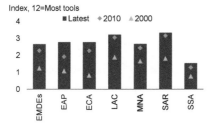

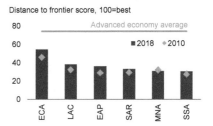

Sources: Cerutti, Claessens, and Laeven (2017); World Bank.
Note: EAP = East Asia and Pacific; ECA = Europe and Central Asia; EMDEs = emerging market and developing economies; LAC = Latin America and the Caribbean; MNA = Middle East and North Africa; SAR = South Asia; SSA = Sub-Saharan Africa.
A. Sample includes 123 EMDEs. Unweighted average of the Macroprudential Policy Index of Cerutti, Claessens, and Laeven (2017). The Macroprudential Policy Index measures the number of tools used by authorities and is based on a simple sum of up to 12 including, but not limited to, countercyclical capital buffers and loan-to-value ratios.
B. Distance to frontier score for strength of insolvency resolution. A higher index indicates reforms that improve the business climate. EAP, ECA, LAC, MNA, SAR, and SSA include 22, 22, 32, 19, 8, and 46 economies, respectively. Advanced economies include 36 economies. Based on World Bank *Doing Business* reports for 2010 and 2019.

momentum slowed after 2010) and reduce trade costs, which can strengthen long-term growth prospects. Recent reforms in bankruptcy procedures include the introduction of new bankruptcy laws in the Arab Republic of Egypt and in India, the strengthening of secured creditors' rights in India, and the establishment of new restructuring mechanisms in Poland. Nevertheless, EMDE bankruptcy protection laws still lag international best practices, with creditors often experiencing long, costly, and weakly enforced debt recovery processes.

Stronger global financial regulation. Since the global recession, EMDEs have enacted reforms to improve access to finance while strengthening financial supervision. Since 2009, several EMDEs that are Financial Stability Board members have established national financial stability councils or committees along Financial Stability Board guidelines (Brazil, China, India, Mexico, the Russian Federation, and Turkey) and given their central banks new mandates to conduct macroprudential supervision (Indonesia, Russia, and South Africa; FSB 2018a, 2019). Most of these EMDEs have made progress in implementing reforms, especially to meet Basel III capital and liquidity requirements and implement over-the-counter derivatives reforms (FSB 2018a). EMDEs that are also members of the Basel Committee on

Banking Supervision, including Brazil, China, Russia, and South Africa, have put in place risk-based capital rules, liquidity coverage ratio regulations, and capital conservation buffers (BCBS 2019).

The crisis led to a rethinking of the role, benefits, and costs of financial and capital account liberalization, especially in light of the role played by cross-border capital flows in financial crises (Reinhart and Rogoff 2008; Ruch 2020). A consensus has emerged that capital flow management measures can play a legitimate role in promoting macroeconomic and financial stability (Koh and Yu 2020). Along these lines, Brazil has reined in large capital flows, and China and India have continued their gradual pace of capital account opening.

Financial sector reforms developed at the global level since the crisis have also increased resilience (Arteta and Kasyanenko 2020; BIS 2018). The Group of Twenty global financial regulatory reform agenda has led to major financial reforms, including the international adoption of the Basel III capital and liquidity standards (FSB 2018b). Global financial safety nets have been expanded significantly, with the volume of resources available in country-specific, regional, and multilateral financial safety nets tripling between 2007 and 2016 including through the creation of regional financing arrangements, expanded International Monetary Fund (IMF) resources, and international reserve holdings (IMF 2018a).[11] There are also now an estimated 160 bilateral swap lines between central banks around the world (Bahaj and Reis 2018).

Striking the right balance

EMDEs need to navigate a difficult terrain during the debt wave that is still underway. They face weaker growth prospects driven by multiple structural factors, yet they have pressing investment needs to achieve development goals and improve people's living standards. A key current challenge for EMDEs is to find the right balance between taking advantage of the present low interest rate environment and avoiding the risks posed by excessive debt accumulation.

On the upside, the current financial environment appears to alleviate some risks associated with debt accumulation. In particular, global interest rates remain at very low levels, and they are expected to remain low for the

---

[11] The global financial safety net has four layers: (1) self-insurance against external shocks using foreign reserves or fiscal space at the national level, (2) bilateral swap lines between countries, (3) regional financing arrangements, and (4) the global financial backstop provided by the IMF (IRC Taskforce on IMF Issues 2018).

foreseeable future. In addition, some EMDEs have better fiscal, monetary, and financial sector policy frameworks now than in previous debt waves. A number of major reforms have been undertaken to make the global financial safety net more secure.

The study of the past three global waves of debt, however, suggests reasons for caution. Despite currently low real interest rates, stronger policy frameworks, and a more secure global safety net, the current wave of debt accumulation could follow the historical pattern and once again lead to financial crises.

In a highly uncertain global environment, EMDEs face a wide range of risks, including the possibility of disruptions in advanced economy financial markets, steep declines in commodity prices, trade tensions, and a sudden deterioration in China's corporate debt market. Materialization of any of these risks could lead to a sharp rise in global interest rates, a spike in risk premiums, or a sharp deterioration in growth prospects and could, in turn, trigger debt distress in EMDEs. In addition to their record debt buildup during the current wave, EMDEs have accumulated other vulnerabilities that could increase the risks and costs of debt distress.

As a result, low or falling global interest rates provide no sure protection against financial crises. Indeed, historically, half of all crises during episodes of rapid debt accumulation occurred in years when U.S. long-term (10-year) interest rates were falling and one-eighth of episodes occurred in years when U.S. long-term real interest rates were below 1 percent (as they have been since 2016).

The study of the past three waves of debt indicates the critical role of policy choices in reducing the likelihood that the current debt wave will end in crises and, if crises do take place, in mitigating their impact. For EMDEs with sound fiscal positions and policy frameworks that provide strong assurance of long-term sustainability, low interest rates may offer an opportunity to undertake debt-financed productive spending to boost growth prospects if the cyclical position is appropriate. For economies with constrained fiscal positions or highly leveraged corporate sectors, however, the lessons from previous waves of debt call for caution.

Seven major lessons

The analysis of the waves of global and national debt accumulation episodes yields several important lessons for EMDEs.

Accumulate debt with care. Borrowing, when well-spent and sustainable, could support growth. Waves of broad-based debt accumulation have typically coincided with global upturns amid accommodative monetary policy and financial market development; however, about half of rapid debt accumulation episodes at the country level were associated with financial crises. Episodes of rapid government debt accumulation were more likely than episodes of rapid private debt to be associated with crisis, and were costlier than crises following rapid buildups of private debt.

Use debt efficiently. The present combination of weak global growth and low interest rates makes government debt accumulation an appealing option for EMDEs to boost growth-friendly spending (World Bank 2019). It is critical, however, that the debt be used for productive purposes to boost potential growth as painfully learned especially from the experience of the first wave. Crises were common in countries that borrowed heavily to finance state-led industrialization or real estate markets (for example, Argentina and Brazil in the first wave and Thailand in the second).

Maintain a resilient debt composition. A debt composition tilted toward foreign-currency-denominated, short-term, or nonresident-held debt makes countries more vulnerable to shifts in market sentiment, currency depreciation, or spikes in global interest rates and risk premiums. Crises have been more likely when the share of short-term external debt was higher (Rodrik and Velasco 2000). The first and second waves showed how a high share of foreign-currency-denominated debt meant that currency depreciations led to an increase in both debt servicing costs and debt ratios.

Regulation and supervision of the financial sector matter. Inadequate regulatory and supervisory regimes can encourage excessively risky lending and debt buildup. This was the case in the Asian financial crisis during the second wave and in several economies in Europe and Central Asia during the third wave. Conversely, a robust regulatory system can temper the incentive to take excessive risks resulting from the public safety net for the financial system (moral hazard).

Beware of external shocks (especially when there are domestic vulnerabilities). Crises typically occurred when external shocks hit countries that had substantial domestic vulnerabilities, including reliance on external and short-term debt in conjunction with a fixed exchange rate and low levels of reserves (Bordo, Meissner, and Stuckler 2010; Claessens et al. 2014; Mishkin 1999). Countries with higher international reserve levels were significantly more resilient to these types of shocks (Gourinchas and Obstfeld 2012). In addition to external shocks, domestic political shocks contributed to crises by increasing policy uncertainty and weakening investor sentiment.

Private debt can rapidly turn into government debt. Large private sector losses, including losses threatening bank solvency, and the materialization of contingent liabilities, including those of state-owned enterprises, can lead governments to provide substantial financial support (Mbaye, Moreno-Badia, and Chae 2018). This situation occurred in the East Asia and Pacific region in the second wave, and in Europe and Central Asia in the third wave, with governments providing substantial support to banks. Although the provision of government support can save a banking system from collapse, it can also lead to a steep jump in public debt (Bova et al. 2016; Claessens et al. 2014; World Bank 2015). Fiscal space can shrink rapidly as a result even though fiscal deficits may have been moderate.

Develop effective mechanisms to recognize losses and restructure debt. Having mechanisms in place to promptly recognize and restructure debt can improve the prospects for recovery from crisis, particularly public debt crises (Haldane et al. 2005; Kroszner 2003) or banking crises (Rutledge et al. 2012). The protracted resolution after the Latin American crises of the 1970s and 1980s and the Sub-Saharan Africa debt distress in the 1980s and 1990s were associated with a period of very low, or even negative, per capita income growth. Growth rebounded only after the Brady plan and the Heavily Indebted Poor Countries initiative and the Multilateral Debt Relief Initiative resolved debt distress and reduced debt overhangs.

Policy implications

As documented earlier in this chapter, policy frameworks in many EMDEs have improved since the first two waves of debt. These improvements played a critical role in mitigating the adverse impact of the global financial crisis on these economies at the end of the third wave of debt accumulation; however, there is still considerable scope for further improvement. Specific policy priorities ultimately depend on country circumstances, but four broad strands of policies can help contain the risks associated with the recent debt accumulation.

Policies for managing debt

Governments need to put in place mechanisms and institutions that help them strike the proper balance between the benefits and costs of additional debt. These policies include sound debt management, high debt transparency, and thorough monitoring of contingent liabilities. Although such policies apply mostly to borrowers, creditors also need to implement measures to mitigate risks associated with excessive debt accumulation.

Sound debt management can help reduce borrowing costs, enhance debt sustainability, and limit fiscal risks.[12] Debt managers are increasingly adopting proactive policies to build buffers and make the composition of debt more resilient, but further progress is needed (World Bank 2013). Prudent debt management favors debt contracted on terms that preserve macroeconomic and financial resilience—preferably at longer maturities, at fixed (and favorable) interest rates, and in local currency. A debt composition that is less vulnerable to market disruptions reduces the likelihood that a decline in market sentiment, sharp depreciations, or interest rate spikes will erode debt sustainability. A well-developed and liquid domestic bond market can reduce the need for foreign-currency-denominated lending and help ensure stability in government financing (Árvai and Heenan 2008; World Bank and IMF 2001a).

Transparent balance sheets are a prerequisite for sound debt management. History shows that public debt spikes can result from the revelation of previously undisclosed liabilities such as those revealed in Mozambique during the fourth wave (Jaramillo, Mulas-Granados, and Jalles 2017; Weber 2012). Greater fiscal transparency is associated with lower borrowing costs, improvements in government effectiveness, and lower government debt (Kemoe and Zhan 2018; Montes, Bastos, and de Oliveira 2019). Improvements in data collection practices for LIC debt would help policy makers undertake better informed borrowing decisions and have been associated with lower borrowing costs (Cady and Pellechio 2006; World Bank and IMF 2018). Principles and guidelines for debt transparency have been created, both by international financial institutions, including the IMF's fiscal transparency code, and by the private sector (IIF 2019; IMF 2019c).

Monitoring and mitigation of contingent government liabilities are integral for sound public debt management. Recent survey evidence suggests that most public debt managers *monitor* risks of contingent liabilities but that only a minority uses risk *mitigation* tools, such as reserve accounts (40 percent of respondents) or risk exposure limits on contingent liabilities (30 percent of respondents; Lee and Bachmair 2019).

---

[12] Recognizing the need for better debt management, the World Bank and IMF have developed guidelines, best practices, and frameworks to assist countries in implementing debt management strategies (World Bank and IMF 2001b, 2009a, 2009b, 2014; see also Abbas, Pienkowski, and Rogoff 2019).

Creditors, including international financial institutions, play an important role in mitigating the risks associated with debt accumulation. They need to ensure that their own lending practices are prudent. More broadly, whereas country authorities have the primary responsibility to transparently report their debt data, international financial institutions work to support such transparency and sustainable lending practices in several ways. The IMF and the World Bank collect and disseminate debt statistics that are used by a wide range of stakeholders; produce reports of public debt data at the country level via joint debt sustainability analyses (DSAs); support countries' efforts to produce medium-term debt management strategies (MTDSs); publish information on countries' borrowing capacity; and directly coordinate with other multilateral, bilateral, and private creditors (World Bank and IMF 2009a, 2009b). All of these efforts promote prudent decision making by borrowers and lenders.

Macroeconomic policies

Notwithstanding substantial improvements since the 1990s, macroeconomic policy frameworks can be strengthened further in many EMDEs (World Bank 2019). Monetary policy frameworks and exchange rate regimes can be strengthened to increase central bank credibility. Fiscal frameworks can ensure that borrowing remains within sustainable limits and borrowed funds are used well.

Monetary and exchange rate policies. The benefits of stability-oriented and resilient monetary policy frameworks cannot be overstated. During episodes of financial stress, when EMDE currencies tend to depreciate sharply, strong monetary policy frameworks will be helpful not least because the exchange rate pass-through to inflation tends to be smaller in countries with more credible, transparent, and independent central banks; inflation-targeting monetary policy regimes; and better-anchored inflation expectations (Kose et al. 2019). With less pass-through from depreciation to inflation, central banks in EMDEs will have more scope to support activity. Flexible exchange rates can provide an effective mechanism for macroeconomic adjustment and help avoid currency overvaluations and buildup of large currency mismatches on balance sheets—a common precursor of crises. A flexible exchange rate regime requires, however, that monetary policy pursue a credible policy of inflation control to provide an effective nominal anchor to the economy. Such a policy framework needs to be complemented by strong institutional arrangements.

Fiscal rules can help prevent fiscal slippages, ensure that revenue windfalls during times of strong growth are prudently managed, and contain and manage risks from contingent liabilities (Cebotari 2008; Currie and Velandia 2002; Romer and Romer 2019; Ülgentürk 2017). Strong fiscal frameworks have also been associated with lower inflation and inflation volatility, supporting the central bank in delivering its mandate (Ha, Kose, and Ohnsorge 2019). EMDEs have made important strides in the adoption and design of fiscal rules (Schaechter et al. 2012).[13] But fiscal rules may be effective only once a certain degree of broader government effectiveness is achieved and sound budgetary institutions are in place.[14]

Alternatives to debt accumulation are available to expand fiscal resources for priority spending. Public spending can be reallocated to uses that are more likely to boost future growth, including education and health spending, as well as to climate-smart infrastructure investment to strengthen economic resilience. Government revenue bases can be broadened by removing special exemptions and strengthening tax administration (Gaspar, Ralyea, and Ture 2019; IMF 2019b; World Bank 2017b). Governments can also take action to foster private sector-led growth. Reform agendas to improve business climates and institutions have resulted in significant gains in investment and productivity in EMDEs (World Bank 2018a). In turn, increased private sector growth could expand the revenue base and, ultimately, strengthen government revenues.

Financial sector policies

Robust financial sector regulation and supervision can help prevent risks from building up. Financial market deepening can help mobilize domestic savings that may provide more stable sources of financing than capital inflows.

Improved financial system regulation and supervision, by acting on systemic exposures and ensuring adequate capital buffers, can help prevent risks from building up. Robust prudential regulation and supervision can help preempt the buildup of systemic financial weaknesses. Macroprudential policies can help moderate lending to households and corporates. The use of

---

[13] Schaechter et al. (2012) create a fiscal rule index that captures both the number and characteristics of fiscal rules in operation in advanced economies and EMDEs and show how EMDEs have played catch-up to advanced economies since 2000. Ardanaz et al. (2019) find that well-designed fiscal rules can help safeguard public investment during downturns.

[14] Calderón, Duncan, and Schmidt-Hebbel (2016) estimate that fiscal and monetary policy procyclicality is greater in countries with weak institutions. Bergman and Hutchison (2015, 2018) show that fiscal rules are effective only when government effectiveness exceeds a minimum threshold. World Bank (2015) discusses the circumstances and features that can make fiscal rules more effective.

living wills for banks and robust bank bankruptcy regimes can help with the orderly winding down of insolvent institutions, including through the bail-in of creditors. Credibility and predictability of bank resolution can help prevent spillovers from the failure of one financial institution to others by reassuring creditors about the continued functioning of the financial system as a whole (Hoshi 2011).

Financial market deepening can help expand the pool of stable long-term domestic savings available for domestic investment. It requires an enabling environment of robust institutions, protection of creditor rights, sound regulatory quality, and macroeconomic stability (Laeven 2014; Sahay et al. 2008). At the same time, however, excessively rapid growth in financial markets can increase financial stability risks. A careful balance between measures to promote financial market deepening and supervision and regulation is therefore critical.

Strengthening institutions

Well-enforced frameworks for sound corporate governance can help ensure that funds borrowed by private corporates are well used. Sound bankruptcy frameworks can help prevent debt overhangs from weighing on investment for prolonged periods.

The promotion of good corporate governance can mitigate risks arising from the corporate sector. Stronger corporate governance can tilt firms' financing toward equity rather than debt (Mande, Park, and Son 2012); increase hedging of foreign currency positions to protect against external shocks (Lel 2012); and encourage more efficient firm operation (Henry 2010). Other measures, such as increased stress testing of listed corporates' balance sheets, can also help contain risks from corporate credit growth.

Effective bankruptcy and insolvency regimes can both help in the resolution of private debt crises and have benefits outside of crises (Leroy and Grandolini 2016). Several EMDEs have recently reformed bankruptcy procedures, but in general, EMDE bankruptcy protection laws lag international best practices.[15] Strengthening bankruptcy protection can boost investment and facilitate responsible corporate risk-taking, helping to relieve the costs of debt overhang. Well-functioning legal, regulatory, and institutional frameworks are crucial for commercial banks and companies to

---

[15] These reforms include a new bankruptcy law in Egypt, a strengthening of secured creditors' rights in India, and the establishment of new restructuring mechanisms in Poland.

resolve nonperforming loans and facilitate business exit and reorganization (Menezes 2014). A robust insolvency regime can improve financial inclusion and increase access to credit by reducing the cost of lending.

Conclusion

This chapter distilled seven lessons from past episodes of debt accumulation and debt-related crises. Debt accumulation is more likely to be benign when debt is well-used for growth-enhancing purposes and when its composition is carefully managed to maintain resilience to financial market disruptions. Such characteristics require not only prudent government debt management but also robust financial system regulation and supervision as well as sound corporate governance. Once debt distress materializes, prompt resolution is critical to avoid a prolonged period of low growth.

These lessons are particularly pertinent at the current juncture as EMDEs enjoy easy financing conditions and have accumulated substantial debt. Although continuing historically low global interest rates mitigate concerns about financing shocks, the record-high debt accumulated in the past decade increases EMDEs' vulnerabilities to such shocks. The next financing shock, when it erupts, will test the ability of EMDEs and their creditors to make the conclusion of this wave of debt different from that of its predecessors.

Against this backdrop, this study suggests three main messages.

- **Unprecedented debt buildup.** The postcrisis wave of global debt buildup has been unprecedented in its size, speed, and reach in EMDEs. Similar waves in the past half-century led to widespread financial crises in these economies. Accordingly, policy makers must remain vigilant about the risks posed by record-high debt levels.

- **Precarious safety of low interest rates.** Continued low global interest rates provide no sure protection against financial crises. The historical record suggests that borrowing costs could increase sharply—or growth could slow steeply—for a wide range of reasons, including heightened risk aversion and rising country risk premiums. A sudden increase in borrowing costs and associated financial pressures would take place against the challenging backdrop of weak growth prospects, mounting vulnerabilities, and elevated global risks.

- **Policies matter.** Robust macroeconomic, financial, and structural policies can help countries strike the right balance between the costs and the benefits of debt accumulation. Such policies are also critical to help reduce the likelihood of financial crises and alleviate their impact if they erupt. Although some EMDEs have better policy frameworks now than during previous debt waves, there remains significant room for improvement.

The evolution of global and national debt accumulation episodes is studied here using an eclectic approach including event studies, econometric methods, and case studies. The study finds a significant stock of existing knowledge about the implications of debt accumulation, and it points to several avenues for future research.

The role of debt transparency. Given growing concern about debt transparency in the current wave, further investigation of its importance in previous crises would be a timely contribution. This investigation would include an in-depth assessment of debt crises triggered by problems related to debt transparency, such as the revelation of hidden debt or the realization of contingent liabilities, including from state-owned enterprises, public-private partnerships, subnational borrowing, collateralized lending, or other explicit and implicit lending guarantees.

The role of non-Paris Club lenders. Future research could usefully investigate the role of non-Paris Club creditors in more detail. Recent literature has sought to uncover the role played by China as a lender to other EMDEs, particularly in the Middle East and North Africa and in Sub-Saharan Africa (Horn, Reinhart, and Trebesch 2019). Further research could build on this and consider how the evolution of debt instruments and the nature of creditors could affect debt sustainability.

LIC debt dynamics. Although the pace of debt buildup in LICs in the fourth wave has been slower than in the first wave, LICs face particular challenges posed by weak debt management and lack of transparency. Future research could examine more closely the role of debt transparency and debt management in weak institutional environments and identify policy solutions most relevant to these countries.

The role of political processes. To address apparent political cycles in borrowing, future research could aim to identify institutional arrangements that prevent, or build resilience against, politically driven unproductive debt buildups. Such arrangements would weigh the incentives of borrowing governments and creditors against the need for borrowing to achieve sustainable and equitable growth.

Institutional frameworks. A large literature explores the role of various vulnerabilities, including debt composition, in financial crises but offers limited analysis of the role of institutional weakness. Future research could examine in greater depth how specific institutional frameworks, such as fiscal rules, inflation targeting, or robust financial supervision and regulation, can reduce the frequency and impact of crises.

Benefits of debt. Whereas much of the literature on the cost of debt has examined the experience of EMDEs, most of the literature on the benefits of debt has examined only advanced economies. Less is therefore known about the benefits of debt in environments with limited financial market development, short-lived governments, poor public expenditure management, and fragile investor confidence.

Debt, productivity, and investment growth. The exceptionally fast and broad-based debt buildup in EMDEs since the global financial crisis has coincided with a period of slowing investment and productivity growth, which raises concerns about the productive use of the funds raised through debt accumulation. At the firm or sectoral level, future research could further explore the link between debt accumulation and productivity growth; at the aggregate level, it could examine more closely the link between debt accumulation and public investment.

References

Abbas, A., A. Pienkowski, and K. Rogoff. 2019. *Sovereign Debt: A Guide for Economists and Practitioners.* New York: Oxford University Press.

Acevedo, S. 2016. "Gone with the Wind: Estimating Hurricane and Climate Change Costs in the Caribbean." IMF Working Paper 16/199, International Monetary Fund, Washington, DC.

Alfaro, L., and F. Kanczuc. 2016. "Fiscal Rules and Sovereign Debt." NBER Working Paper 23370, National Bureau of Economic Research, Cambridge, MA.

Alcidi, C., and D. Gros. 2019. "Public Debt and the Risk Premium: A Dangerous Doom Loop." VoxEU.org, May 22, 2019. https://voxeu.org/article/public-debt-and -risk-premium.

Andreasen, E., G. Sandleris, and A. Van der Ghote. 2019. "The Political Economy of Sovereign Defaults." *Journal of Monetary Economics* 104 (June): 23-36.

Ardanaz, M., E. Cavallo, A. Izquierdo, and J. Puig. 2019. "Growth-Friendly Fiscal Rules? Protecting Public Investment from Budget Cuts Through Fiscal Rule Design." IDB Discussion Paper 698, Inter-American Development Bank, Washington, DC.

Arteta, C., and S. Kasyanenko. 2020. "Financial Sector Developments." In *A Deca-de After the Global Recession: Lessons and Challenges for Emerging and Developing Economies*, edited by M. A. Kose and F. Ohnsorge. Washington, DC: World Bank.

Arteta, C., M. A. Kose, M. Stocker, and T. Taskin. 2016. "Negative Interest Rate Policies: Sources and Implications." Policy Research Working Paper 7791, World Bank, Washington, DC.

Árvai, Z., and G. Heenan. 2008. "A Framework for Developing Secondary Markets for Government Securities." IMF Working Paper 8/174, International Monetary Fund, Washington, DC.

Auerbach, A. J., W. G. Gale, and A. Krupkin. 2019. "If Not Now, When? New Estimates of the Federal Budget Outlook." Brookings Report, February 11, Brookings Institution, Washington, DC.

Bahaj, S., and R. Reis. 2018. "Central Bank Swap Lines." CESifo Working Paper 7124, Centre for Economic Policy Research, Munich.

Barattieri, A., M. Cacciatore, and F. Ghironi. 2018. "Protectionism and the Business Cycle." NBER Working Paper 24353, National Bureau of Economic Research, Cambridge, MA.

BCBS (Basel Committee on Banking Supervision). 2019. *Sixteenth Progress Report on Adoption of the Basel Regulatory Framework*. Basel: Basel Committee on Banking Supervision.

Bergman, U. M., and M. Hutchison. 2015. "Economic Stabilization in the Post-Crisis World: Are Fiscal Rules the Answer?" *Journal of International Money and Finance* 52 (April): 82-101.

Bergman, U. M., and M. Hutchison. 2018. "Fiscal Procyclicality in Developing Economies: The Role of Fiscal Rules, Institutions and Economic Conditions." Unpublished manuscript. https://www.researchgate.net/publication/325820923_Fiscal_Procyclicality_in_Developing_Economics_The_Role_of_Fiscal_Rules_Institutions_and_Economic_Conditions.

BIS (Bank for International Settlements). 2018. "Structural Changes in Banking After the Crisis." CGFS Papers 60, Committee on the Global Financial System, Bank for International Settlements, Basel.

BIS (Bank for International Settlements). 2019. *Credit to the Nonfinancial Sector Statistics*. Basel: Bank for International Settlements.

Blanchard, O. J. 2019. "Public Debt and Low Interest Rates." *American Economic Review* 109 (4): 1197-229.

Blanchard, O. J., and L. H. Summers. 2019. *Evolution or Revolution? Rethinking Macroeconomic Policy after the Great Recession*. Cambridge: MIT Press.

Blanchard, O. J., and T. Tashiro. 2019. "Fiscal Policy Options for Japan." PIIE Policy Brief 19-7, Peterson Institute for International Economics, Washington, DC.

Blanchard, O. J., and A. Ubide. 2019. "Why Critics of a More Relaxed Attitude on Public Debt Are Wrong." PIIE Realtime Economic Issues Watch (blog), July 15, 2019. https://www.piie.com/blogs/realtime-economic-issues-watch/why-critics-more-relaxed-attitude-public-debt-are-wrong.

Bordo, M., M. Dueker, and D. Wheelock. 2003. "Aggregate Price Shocks and Financial Stability: The United Kingdom 1796-1999." *Explorations in Economic History* 40 (2): 143-69.

Bordo, M., C. Meissner, and D. Stuckler. 2010. "Foreign Currency Debt, Financial Crises and Economic Growth: A Long-Run View." *Journal of International Money and Finance* 29 (4): 642-65.

Bova, E., M. Ruiz-Arranz, F. Toscani, and H. E. Ture. 2016. "The Fiscal Costs of Contingent Liabilities; A New Dataset." IMF Working Paper 16/14, International Monetary Fund, Washington, DC.

Boz, E., G. Gopinath, and M. Plagborg-Moller. 2017. "Global Trade and the Dollar." NBER Working Paper 23988, National Bureau of Economic Research, Cambridge, MA.

Bruno, V., S. Kim, and H. Shin. 2018. "Exchange Rates and the Working Capital Channel of Trade Fluctuations." BIS Working Paper 694, Bank for International Settlements, Basel.

Bruno, V., I. Shim, and H. S. Shin. 2017. "Comparative Assessment of Macroprudential Policies." *Journal of Financial Stability* 28 (February): 183-202.

Bruno, V., and H. S. Shin. 2015. "Capital Flows and the Risk-Taking Channel of Monetary Policy." *Journal of Monetary Economics* 71 (April): 119-32.

Caballero, R. 2003. "The Future of the IMF." *American Economic Review, Papers and Proceedings* 93 (2): 31-38.

Cady, J., and A. Pellechio. 2006. "Sovereign Borrowing Cost and the IMF's Data Standards Initiatives." IMF Working Paper 06/78, International Monetary Fund, Washington, DC.

Calderón, C., R. Duncan, and K. Schmidt-Hebbel. 2016. "Do Good Institutions Promote Countercyclical Macroeconomic Policies?" *Oxford Bulletin of Economics and Statistics* 78 (5): 650-70.

Carney, M. 2015. "Breaking the Tragedy on the Horizon—Climate Change and Financial Stability." Speech at Lloyd's of London, September 29, London.

Cebotari, A. 2008. "Contingent Liabilities: Issues and Practice." IMF Working Paper 245, International Monetary Fund, Washington, DC.

Cerutti, E., S. Claessens, and L. Laeven. 2017. "The Use and Effectiveness of Macroprudential Policies: New Evidence." *Journal of Financial Stability* 28 (February): 203-24.

Claessens, S. 2015. "An Overview of Macroprudential Policy Tools." *Annual Review of Financial Economics* 7 (December): 397-422.

Claessens, S., M. A. Kose, L. Laeven, and F. Valencia. 2014. *Financial Crises: Causes, Consequences, and Policy Responses.* Washington, DC: International Monetary Fund.

Correa, R., and H. Sapriza. 2014. "Sovereign Debt Crises." International Finance Discussion Paper 1104, May, Board of Governors of the Federal Reserve System, Washington, DC.

CRFB (Committee for a Responsible Federal Budget). 2019. "Why Should We Worry About the National Debt?" Budgets & Projections Paper, April 16, Committee for a Responsible Federal Budget, Washington, DC.

Cuadra, G., and H. Sapriza. 2008. "Sovereign Default, Interest Rates and Political Uncertainty in Emerging Markets." *Journal of International Economics* 76 (1): 78-88.

Currie, E., and A. Velandia. 2002. "Risk Management of Contingent Liabilities Within a Sovereign Asset-Liability Framework." World Bank, Washington, DC.

Del Negro, M., D. Giannone, M. P. Giannoni, and A. Tambalotti. 2017. "Safety, Liquidity, and the Natural Rate of Interest." *Brookings Papers on Economic Activity* 2017 (Spring): 235-316.

Dincer, N., and B. Eichengreen. 2014. "Central Bank Transparency and Independence: Updates and New Measures." *International Journal of Central Bank-ing* 10 (1): 189-259.

Dizioli, A., and B. van Roye. 2018. "The Resurgence of Protectionism: Potential Implications for Global Financial Stability." In *Financial Stability Review*, November. Frankfurt: European Central Bank.

Eberhardt, M., and A. Presbitero. 2018. "Commodity Price Movements and Banking Crises." IMF Working Paper 18/153, International Monetary Fund, Washington, DC.

Eggertsson, G. B., N. R. Mehrotra, and J. A. Robbins. 2019. "A Model of Secular Stagnation: Theory and Quantitative Evaluation." *American Economic Journal: Macroeconomics* 11 (1): 1-48.

Eichengreen, B. 2019. "The Return of Fiscal Policy." *Project Syndicate*, May 13, 2019. https://www.project-syndicate.org/commentary/return-of-fiscal-policy-by-barry-eichengr een-2019-05.

Eichengreen, B., A. El-Ganainy, R. Esteves, and K. J. Mitchener. 2019. "Public Debt through the Ages." NBER Working Paper 25494, National Bureau of Economic Research, Cambridge, MA.

Essl, S., S. Kilic Celik, P. Kirby, and A. Proite. 2019. "Debt in Low-Income Countries: Evolution, Implications, Remedies." Policy Research Working Paper 8794, World Bank, Washington, DC.

Fernald, J. 2016. "What Is the New Normal for U.S. Growth?" FRBSF Economic Letter 2016-30, Federal Reserve Bank of San Francisco.

Feyen, E., S. Ghosh, K. Kibuuka, and S. Farazi. 2015. "Global Liquidity and External Bond Issuance in Emerging Markets and Developing Economies." Policy Research Working Paper 7373, World Bank, Washington, DC.

FSB (Financial Stability Board). 2018a. *Evaluation of the Effects of Financial Regulatory Reforms on Infrastructure Finance.* Basel: Financial Stability Board.

FSB (Financial Stability Board). 2018b. *Implementation and Effects of the G20 Financial Regulatory Reforms.* Basel: Financial Stability Board.

FSB (Financial Stability Board). 2019. "Implementation of G20/FSB Financial Reforms in Other Areas: Summary of Key Findings Based on the 2018 FSB Implementation Monitoring Network (IMN) Survey." Financial Stability Board, Basel, Switzerland.

Furman, J., and L. H. Summers. 2019. "Who's Afraid of Budget Deficits? How Washington Should End Its Debt Obsession." *Foreign Affairs* 98: 82-94.

Gaspar, V., J. Ralyea, and E. Ture. 2019. "High Debt Hampers Countries' Response to a Fast-Changing Global Economy." *IMFBlog; Insights & Analysis on Economics & Finance* (blog), April 10, 2019. https://blogs.imf.org/2019/04/10/high-debt-hampers-countries -response-to-a-fast-changing-global-economy/.

Gordon, R. J. 2012. "Is U.S. Economic Growth Over? Faltering Innovation Confronts the Six Headwinds." NBER Working Paper 18315, National Bureau of Economic Research, Cambridge, MA.

Gourinchas, P.-O., and M. Obstfeld. 2012. "Stories of the Twentieth Century for the Twenty-First." *American Economic Journal: Macroeconomics* 4 (1): 226-65.

Ha, J., M. A. Kose, and F. Ohnsorge. 2019. *Inflation in Emerging and Developing Economies: Evolution, Drivers and Policies.* Washington, DC: World Bank.

Haldane, A. G., A. Penalver, V. Saporta, and H. S. Shin. 2005. "Analytics of Sovereign Debt Restructuring." *Journal of International Economics* 65 (2): 315-33.

Henry, D. 2010. "Agency Costs, Ownership Structure and Corporate Governance Compliance: A Private Contracting Perspective." *Pacific-Basin Finance Journal* 18 (1): 24-46.

Holston, K., T. Laubach, and J. C. Williams. 2017. "Measuring the Natural Rate of Interest: International Trends and Determinants." *Journal of International Economics* 108 (Supplement 1): S59-S75.

Horn, S., C. M. Reinhart, and C. Trebesch. 2019. "China's Overseas Lending." NBER Working Paper 26050, National Bureau of Economic Research, Cambridge, MA.

Hoshi, T. 2011. "Financial Regulation: Lessons from the Recent Financial Crises." *Journal of Economic Literature* 49 (1): 120-8.

Huidrom, R., M. A. Kose, J. J. Lim, and F. Ohnsorge. 2019. "Why Do Fiscal Multipliers Depend on Fiscal Positions?" *Journal of Monetary Economics.* Advance online publication. https://doi.org/10.1016/.

IIF (Institute of International Finance). 2019. "Voluntary Principles for Debt Transparency." Institute of International Finance, Washington, DC.

IMF (International Monetary Fund). 2011. "Assessing Reserve Adequacy." IMF Policy Paper, International Monetary Fund, Washington, DC.

IMF (International Monetary Fund). 2018a. *Global Financial Stability Report. A Decade after the Global Financial Crisis: Are We Safer?* Washington, DC: International Monetary Fund.

IMF (International Monetary Fund). 2018b. *Macroeconomic Developments and Prospects in Low-Income Developing Countries.* Washington, DC: International Monetary Fund.

IMF (International Monetary Fund). 2019a. *Global Financial Stability Report. Lower for Longer.* October. Washington, DC: International Monetary Fund.

IMF (International Monetary Fund). 2019b. *Fiscal Monitor: Curbing Corruption.* April. Washington, DC: International Monetary Fund.

IMF (International Monetary Fund). 2019c. "Fiscal Transparency Initiative: Integration of Natural Resource Management Issues." IMF Policy Paper, International Monetary Fund, Washington, DC.

IRC Taskforce on IMF Issues. 2018. "Strengthening the Global Financial Safety Net." Occasional Paper 207, European Central Bank, Frankfurt.

Jaramillo, L., C. Mulas-Granados, and J. T. Jalles. 2017. "Debt Spikes, Blind Spots, and Financial Stress." *International Journal of Finance & Economics* 22 (4): 421-37.

Kemoe, L., and Z. Zhan. 2018. "Fiscal Transparency, Borrowing Costs, and Foreign Holdings of Sovereign Debt." IMF Working Paper 18/189, International Monetary Fund, Washington, DC.

Kinda, T., M. Mlachila, and R. Ouedraogo. 2016. "Commodity Price Shocks and Financial Sector Fragility." IMF Working Paper 16/12, International Monetary Fund, Washington, DC.

Klomp, J. 2015. "Sovereign Risk and Natural Disasters in Emerging Markets." *Emerging Markets Finance and Trade* 51 (6): 1326-41.

Koh, W. C., and S. Yu. 2020. "Macroeconomic and Financial Policies." In *A Decade after the Global Recession: Lessons and Challenges for Emerging and Developing Economies,* edited by M. A. Kose and F. Ohnsorge. Washington, DC: World Bank.

Kose, M. A., S. Kurlat, F. Ohnsorge, and N. Sugawara. 2017. "A Cross-Country Database of Fiscal Space." Policy Research Working Paper 8157, World Bank, Washington, DC.

Kose, M. A., H. Matsuoka, U. Panizza, and D. Vorisek. 2019. "Inflation Expectations: Review and Evidence." Policy Research Working Paper 8785, World Bank, Washington, DC.

Kose, M. A., and F. Ohnsorge, eds. 2020. *A Decade after the Global Recession: Lessons and Challenges for Emerging and Developing Economies.* Washington, DC: World Bank.

Kroszner, R. S. 2003. "Sovereign Debt Restructuring." *American Economic Review* 93 (2): 75-9.

Krugman, P. 2019. "Perspectives on Debt and Deficits." *Business Economics* 54 (3): 157-59.

Laeven, L. 2014. "The Development of Local Capital Markets: Rationale and Challenges." IMF Working Paper 14/234, International Monetary Fund, Washington, DC.

Lee, A., and F. Bachmair. 2019. "A Look Inside the Mind of Debt Managers: A Survey on Contingent Liabilities Risk Management." World Bank Treasury Public Debt Management, World Bank, Washington, DC.

Lee, D., H. Zhang, and C. Nguyen. 2018. "The Economic Impact of Natural Disasters in Pacific Island Countries: Adaptation and Preparedness." IMF Working Paper 18/108, International Monetary Fund, Washington, DC.

Lel, U. 2012. "Currency Hedging and Corporate Governance: A Cross-Country Analysis." *Journal of Corporate Finance* 18 (2): 221-37.

Leroy, A., and G. Grandolini. 2016. *Principles for Effective Insolvency and Creditor and Debtor Regimes*. Washington, DC: World Bank.

Lis, E., and C. Nickel. 2010. "The Impact of Extreme Weather Events on Budget Balances." *International Tax and Public Finance* 17 (4): 378-99.

Maliszewski, W., S. Arslanalp, J. Caparusso, J. Garrido, S. Guo, J. Kang, W. Lam, T. D. Law, W. Liao, N. Rendak, P. Wingender, J. Yu, and L. Zhang. 2016. "Resolving China's Corporate Debt Problem." IMF Working Paper 16/203, International Monetary Fund, Washington, DC.

Mande, V., Y. K. Park, and M. Son. 2012. "Equity or Debt Financing: Does Good Corporate Governance Matter?" *Corporate Governance: An International Review* 20 (2): 195-211.

Mauro, P., and J. Zhou. 2019. "Can We Sleep More Soundly?" Prepared for the Twentieth Jacques Polak Annual Research Conference, Washington, DC, November 7-8.

Mazza, J. 2019. "Is Public Debt a Cheap Lunch?" *Bruegel* (blog), January 21, 2019. https://bruegel.org/2019/01/is-public-debt-a-cheap-lunch/.

Mbaye, S., M. Moreno-Badia, and K. Chae. 2018. "Bailing Out the People? When Private Debt Becomes Public." IMF Working Paper 18/141, International Monetary Fund, Washington, DC.

Menezes, A. 2014. "Debt Resolution and Business Exit: Insolvency Reform for Credit, Entrepreneurship, and Growth." *Viewpoint: Public Policy for the Private Sector*, No. 343, World Bank, Washington, DC.

Mishkin, F. 1999. "Global Financial Instability: Framework, Events, Issues." *Journal of Economic Perspectives* 13 (4): 3-20.

Molnar, M., and J. Lu. 2019. "State-Owned Firms behind China's Corporate Debt." OECD Economics Department Working Paper 1536, Organisation for Economic Co-operation and Development, Paris.

Montes, G. C., J. C. A. Bastos, and A. J. de Oliveira. 2019. "Fiscal Transparency, Government Effectiveness and Government Spending Efficiency: Some Internation-al Evidence Based on Panel Data Approach." *Economic Modelling* 79 (June): 211-25.

Nakatani, R. 2019. "A Possible Approach to Fiscal Rules in Small Islands—Incorporating Natural Disasters and Climate Change." IMF Working Paper 19/186, International Monetary Fund, Washington, DC.

Noy, I., and A. Nualsri. 2011. "Fiscal Storms: Public Spending and Revenues in the Aftermath of Natural Disasters." *Environment and Development Economics* 16 (1): 113-28.

Rachel, L., and L. H. Summers. 2019. "On Falling Neutral Real Rates, Fiscal Policy, and the Risk of Secular Stagnation." BPEA Conference Draft, March 7-8, Brookings Institution, Washington, DC.

Reinhart, C. M., and K. S. Rogoff. 2008. "Is the 2007 U.S. Sub-Prime Financial Crisis So Different? An International Historical Comparison." *American Economic Review: Papers & Proceedings* 98 (2): 339-44.

Reinhart, C. M., and K. S. Rogoff. 2014. "This Time Is Different: A Panoramic View of Eight Centuries of Financial Crises." *Annals of Economics and Finance* 15 (2): 215-68.

Riedl, B. 2019. "Yes, We Should Fear Budget Deficits." *Economics 21* (blog), February 8, 2019. https://economics21.org/yes-we-should-fear-budget-deficits.

Rodrik, D., and A. Velasco. 2000. "Short-Term Capital Flows." In *Annual World Bank Conference on Development Economics 1999*, edited by B. Pleskovic and J. E. Stiglitz, 59-90. Washington, DC: World Bank.

Rogoff, K. 2019a. "Risks to the Global Economy in 2019." *Project Syndicate*, January 11, 2019. https://www.project-syndicate.org/commentary/global-economy-main-risks-in-2019-by-kenneth-rogoff-2019-01.

Rogoff, K. 2019b. "Government Debt Is Not A Free Lunch." *Project Syndicate*, December 6, 2019. https://www.project-syndicate.org/commentary/government-debt-low-interest-rates-no-free-lunch-by-kenneth-rogoff-2019-11.

Romer, C. D., and D. H. Romer. 2019. "Fiscal Space and the Aftermath of Financial Crises: How It Matters and Why." NBER Working Paper 25768, National Bureau of Economic Research, Cambridge, MA.

Ruch, F. U. 2020. "Prospects, Risks and Vulnerabilities." In *A Decade after the Global Recession: Lessons and Challenges for Emerging and Developing Economies,* edited by M. A. Kose and F. Ohnsorge. Washington, DC: World Bank.

Rutledge, V., M. Moore, M. Dobler, W. Bossu, N. Jassaud, and J. Zhou. 2012. "From Bail-Out to Bail-In: Mandatory Debt Restructuring of Systemic Financial Institutions." Staff Discussion Note 2012/03, International Monetary Fund, Washington, DC.

Sahay, R., M. Čihák, P. N'Diaye, A. Barajas, R. Bi, D. Ayala, Y. Gao, A. Kyobe, L. Nguyen, C. Saborowski, K. Svirydzenka, and S. R. Yousefi. 2008. "Rethinking Financial Deepening: Stability and Growth in Emerging Markets." Staff Discussion Note 5/08, International Monetary Fund, Washington, DC.

Schaechter, A., T. Kinda,, N. T. Budina, and A. Weber. 2012. "Fiscal Rules in Response to the Crisis-Toward the 'Next-Generation' Rules: A New Dataset." IMF Working Paper 12/187, International Monetary Fund, Washington, DC.

Trebesch, C. 2018. "Resolving Sovereign Debt Crises: The Role of Political Risk." CESifo Working Paper Series 7161, Kiel Institute for the World Economy; Centre for Economic Policy Research, Kiel, Germany.

Ülgentürk, L. 2017. "The Role of Public Debt Managers in Contingent Liability Management." OECD Working Paper on Sovereign Borrowing and Public Debt Management 8, Organisation for Economic Co-operation and Development, Paris.

Van Rijckeghem, C., and B. Weder. 2009. "Political Institutions and Debt Crises." *Public Choice* 138 (3/4): 387-408.

Van Wijnbergen, S. 1987. "Protectionism and the Debt Crisis." DRD Discussion Paper 266, Development Research Department, World Bank, Washington, DC.

Wang, D., K. Wan, and X. Song. 2018. "Quota Allocation of Coal Overcapacity Reduction among Provinces in China." *Energy Policy* 116 (May): 170-81.

Weber, A. 2012. "Stock-Flow Adjustments and Fiscal Transparency: A Cross-Country Comparison." IMF Working Paper 12/39, International Monetary Fund, Washington, DC.

Williams, J. C. 2018. "The Future Fortunes of R-star: Are They Really Rising?" FRBSF Economic Letter 2018-13, Federal Reserve Bank of San Francisco.

World Bank. 2013. *Europe and Central Asia: Sovereign Debt Management in Crisis: A Toolkit for Policymakers.* Washington, DC: World Bank.

World Bank. 2015. *Global Economic Prospects Report: Having Fiscal Space and Using It.* January. Washington, DC: World Bank.

World Bank. 2016. *Global Economic Prospects: Spillovers amid Weak Growth.* January. Washington, DC: World Bank.

World Bank. 2017a. *Global Economic Prospects: A Fragile Recovery.* June. Washington, DC: World Bank.

World Bank. 2017b. *Tax Revenue Mobilization: Lessons from World Bank Group Support for Tax Reform.* Washington, DC: World Bank.

World Bank. 2018a. *Global Economic Prospects: Broad-Based Upturn, but for How Long?* January. Washington, DC: World Bank.

World Bank. 2018b. *Global Economic Prospects: The Turning of the Tide.* June. Washington, DC: World Bank.

World Bank. 2019. *Global Economic Prospects: Heightened Tensions, Subdued Investment.* June. Washington, DC: World Bank.

World Bank and IMF (International Monetary Fund). 2001a. *Developing Government Bond Markets: A Handbook.* Washington, DC: World Bank.

World Bank and IMF (International Monetary Fund). 2001b. "Guidelines for Public Debt Management." World Bank, Washington, DC.

World Bank and IMF (International Monetary Fund). 2009a. "Developing a Medium-Term Debt Management Strategy (MTDS): Guidance Note for Country Authorities." World Bank, Washington, DC.

World Bank and IMF (International Monetary Fund). 2009b. "Managing Public Debt: Formulating Strategies and Strengthening Institutional Capacity." World Bank, Washington, DC.

World Bank and IMF (International Monetary Fund). 2014. "Revised Guidelines for Public Debt Management." World Bank, Washington, DC.

World Bank and IMF (International Monetary Fund). 2018. "G-20 Note: Improving Public Debt Recording, Monitoring and Reporting Capacity in Low and Lower Middle-Income Countries: Proposed Reforms." World Bank, Washington, DC.

Wyplosz, C. 2019. "Olivier in Wonderland." Vox CEPR Policy Portal, June 17, 2019. https://voxeu.org/content/olivier-wonderland.

Yu, B., and C. Shen. 2019. "Environmental Regulation and Industrial Capacity Utilization: An Empirical Study of China." *Journal of Cleaner Production.* Advance online publication. https://www.sciencedirect.com/science/article/pii/S0959652619338569.

Yu, S. 2016. "The Effect of Political Factors on Sovereign Default." *Review of Political Economy* 28 (3): 397-416.

APPENDIX A **Event study methodology**

The list of completed events using the baseline methodology presented in the text is shown for government debt accumulation episodes in table A.1, for private debt accumulation episodes in table A.2, and for crisis events in table A.3. Median durations and amplitudes of these episodes are shown in table A.4, and for combined government and private debt accumulation episodes in table A.5. The results are robust to using mean or subsamples of countries (tables A.6 and A.7).

An alternative dating algorithm is used as robustness test. The alternative definition of debt accumulation episodes is in line with the literature on credit booms. To control for financial development, the literature on private credit booms identifies credit booms as sizable deviations of the ratios of credit to gross domestic product (GDP) from their trend (Mendoza and Terrones 2008). Applying this approach here, a debt accumulation is identified as the period between the trough and the peak in the government or private debt-to-GDP ratio provided at some point during the period the deviation of the debt-to-GDP ratio exceeds one standard deviation from its Hodrick-Prescott-filtered trend.

Although this approach identifies a larger number of episodes, three-quarters of these episodes have overlapping peaks or troughs (two-thirds have overlapping peaks) and most results are robust to the use of this alternative definition (table A.8). The median episode extends for seven (government) to eight (private) years; the median episode features a debt buildup of 11 (private) to 30 (government) percent; and more than half or government debt episodes and about one-half of all debt episodes are associated with crises.

TABLE A.1 **Completed episodes of rapid accumulation of government debt**

Country	1st episode	2nd episode	3rd episode	4th episode	5th episode
Albania	2007-2015				
Algeria	1970-1978	1982-1988 [a b]	1992-1995 [b]		
Angola	1997-1999				
Argentina	1968-1975 [b]	1980-1989 [a b c]	1992-2002 [a b c]		
Aruba	2000-2002				
Azerbaijan	1994-1999 [a]				
Bangladesh	1973-1977 [b]	1980-1987 [a]	1989-1994	1997-2002	
Belarus	2005-2011 [b]	2013-2016 [b]			
Benin	1972-1983	1992-1994 [b]	2006-2011		
Bolivia	1970-1985 [a b c]	2001-2004			
Bosnia and Herzegovina	2007-2014				
Brazil	1967-1987 [b c]	1989-1992 [a b]	1995-2002 [b]		
Bulgaria	1981-1993 [c]				
Burkina Faso	1970-1987	1989-1994 [a b]			
Burundi	1971-1999 [a]	2001-2004			
Cambodia	1995-2003				
Cameroon	1970-1979	1984-1995 [a b c]			
Central African Republic	1970-1974 [a]	1979-1984	1990-1994 [a b]	1999-2005	2009-2014
Chad	1972-1979	1986-1994 [a b]	1998-2000		
Chile	1962-1970	1972-1975 [a b]	1981-1986 [a b c]		
China	1997-2003 [a]	2006-2009			
Colombia	1960-1972	1978-1986 [a b]	1995-2002 [a]		
Congo, Dem. Rep.	1970-1976 [b c]	1979-1983 [a b]	1993-1998 [a b]		
Congo, Rep.	1973-1985 [c]	1992-1994 [a b]	2011-2016		
Costa Rica	1958-1973	1975-1978	1988-2002 [a b]		
Côte d'Ivoire	1970-1994 [a b c]				
Croatia	1998-2005 [a]	2007-2014			
Dominican Republic	1997-2003 [a b c]	2007-2013			
Ecuador	1997-1999 [a b c]				
Egypt, Arab Rep.	1970-1982 [a b c]	1989-1992 [b]	2000-2005		
El Salvador	1977-1985 [b]				
Eritrea	1995-2003				
Ethiopia	1974-1994 [b]				
Georgia	2007-2010				
Ghana	1982-1987 [a b]	1990-1994 [b]	1998-2000 [b]		
Guatemala	1954-1972	1975-1985 [b]	2008-2013		

TABLE A.1 **Completed episodes of rapid accumulation of government debt** *(continued)*

Country	1st episode	2nd episode	3rd episode	4th episode
Guinea	1992-1999 [a]	2003-2005 [b]		
Haiti	1973-1983	1985-1992 [a b]	2011-2016	
Honduras	1950-1986 [c]			
Hungary	1989-1993 [a]	2001-2011 [a]		
India	1974-1992 [a]	1996-2003		
Indonesia	1980-1987	1997-2000 [a b c]		
Iran, Islamic Rep.	1974-1981	1985-1988 [b]	2011-2016 [b]	
Jordan	1969-1990 [a b c]			
Kazakhstan	1996-1999 [b]	2007-2015 [a b]		
Kenya	1963-1982	1984-1987 [a]	1989-1993 [a b]	
Kuwait	1987-1991			
Kyrgyz Republic	1994-2000 [a b]	2013-2015		
Lao PDR	1976-1982 [b]	1985-1988 [b]		1996-1998 [b]
Lebanon	1972-1983 [b]	1987-1990 [a]	1993-2006	
Libya	1977-1990			
Madagascar	1976-1988 [a b c]			
Malawi	1975-1987 [c]	1991-1994 [b]	1997-2002	
Malaysia	1955-1972	1974-1977	1980-1987	2007-2015
Mali	1973-1985 [a]	1990-1994 [b]		
Mauritania	1970-1987 [a]	1992-2000 [b]		
Mexico	1971-1977 [b]	1980-1987 [a b c]	1993-1995 [a b]	2007-2016
Moldova	2008-2015 [a]			
Mongolia	1992-1999 [b]			
Morocco	1974-1985 [a b c]			
Mozambique	2007-2016 [b]			
Nepal	1970-1994 [a b]	1997-1999		
Niger	1970-1974	1977-1985 [a c]	1989-1994 [b]	1996-2000
Nigeria	1975-1991 [a b c]			
North Macedonia	2008-2016			
Oman	1990-1994			
Pakistan	1962-1972 [b]	1981-2001	2007-2013	
Panama	1975-1983 [c]	1985-1990 [a]		
Papua New Guinea	1970-1976	1978-2001 [b]	2011-2016	
Paraguay	1981-1987 [b c]	1996-2002 [b]		
Peru	2001-2003			

TABLE A.1 Completed episodes of rapid accumulation of government debt *(continued)*

Country	1st episode	2nd episode	3rd episode	4th episode	5th episode
Philippines	1963-1972	1974-1987 [a b c]	1998-2003 [b]		
Poland	1990-1994 [a]	2000-2013			
Romania	1995-2000 [a b]	2007-2014			
Russian Federation	1996-1999 [a b c]				
Rwanda	1975-1995 [b]	1998-2002			
Saudi Arabia	1989-1999				
Senegal	1972-1985 [c]	1992-1994 [b]			
Sierra Leone	1970-1994 [a b c]				
South Africa	1964-1972	1974-1978	1990-1995		
Sri Lanka	1970-1982 [b]	1984-1989 [a]	1997-2002		
Sudan	2007-2012 [b]				
Syrian Arab Republic	1975-1989 [b]				
Tanzania	1970-1980	1982-1993 [a b c]			
Thailand	1963-1972	1975-1986 [a]	1996-2000 [a b]		
Togo	1972-1985 [c]	1990-1994 [a b]	1997-2000	2004-2007	2010-2016
Tunisia	1975-1978	1980-1997 [a]			
Turkey	1958-1970	1974-1985 [a b c]	1990-1994 [b]	1998-2001 [a b]	
Ukraine	1995-1999 [a b c]	2007-2016 [a b c]			
United Arab Emirates	1973-1979	1981-1988	1990-1993	2001-2009	
Uruguay	1970-1976 [b]	1979-1984 [a b c]	1996-2003 [a b c]		
Uzbekistan	1997-2001 [b]				
Venezuela, RB	1964-1972	1975-1994 [a b c]	2000-2003 [b]	2008-2013 [b]	
Vietnam	2005-2016				
West Bank and Gaza	2000-2005	2010-2015			
Yemen, Rep.	1994-1996 [a b]				
Zambia	1970-1982 [b c]	1987-1991 [b]	1997-2000		
Zimbabwe	1975-1987 [b]	1989-1998 [a b]	2001-2009 [b]	2012-2016	

Source: World Bank.
Note: Superscripts a, b, and c mean that rapid accumulation episodes are associated with banking, currency, and debt crises, respectively.

TABLE A.2 **Completed episodes of rapid accumulation of private debt**

Country	1st episode	2nd episode	3rd episode	4th episode
Algeria	1997-2002	2004-2009		
Angola	2000-2009			
Argentina	1965-1974 [b]	1976-1982 [a b c]	1985-1989 [a b]	1991-2002 [a b c]
Aruba	1986-1990	1993-1996	1998-2003	
Azerbaijan	1996-2009	2011-2015 [b]		
Bangladesh	1974-1990 [a b]			
Belarus	1994-1998 [a b]	2001-2010 [b]		
Benin	1966-1975	1981-1983	2002-2016	
Bolivia	1986-1999 [a]			
Bosnia and Herzegovina	2001-2008			
Brazil	2004-2015 [b]			
Bulgaria	1994-2009 [a b]			
Burkina Faso	1960-1978	1984-1990 [a]	1995-1997	2002-2009
Burundi	1969-1981	1985-1994 [a]	1997-2002	2008-2011
Cameroon	1997-2016			
Central African Republic	1994-2004 [a b]	2006-2013		
Chile	1980-1984 [a b c]	1988-2002	2006-2015	
China	1980-1993	1995-2003 [a]		
Colombia	1990-1998 [a]	2005-2015		
Congo, Rep.	1996-1999	2006-2016		
Costa Rica	1991-2008 [a b]			
Croatia	2000-2012			
Dominican Republic	1985-1987 [b]	1991-2002 [a b c]		
Ecuador	1974-1978	1980-1984 [a b c]	1989-2000 [a b c]	
Egypt, Arab Rep.	1973-1986 [a b c]	1992-2001	2014-2016 [b]	
El Salvador	1990-2000	2002-2007		
Ethiopia	1962-1978	1991-1999 [b]	2004-2006	
Ghana	1967-1971	1981-1989 [a b]	1991-2008 [b]	2011-2015 [b]
Guatemala	1973-1984 [b]	1991-2006	2011-2015	
Guinea	1991-1995 [a]	1999-2006 [b]	2009-2015	
Haiti	1992-2002 [a b]	2007-2014		
Honduras	1950-1978	1981-1987 [c]	1995-2007	
Hungary	1969-1987	1995-2009 [a]		

TABLE A.2 Completed episodes of rapid accumulation of private debt (*continued*)

Country	1st episode	2nd episode	3rd episode	4th episode	5th episode
India	1967-1989	1994-2013			
Indonesia	1980-1990	1993-1997 [abc]	2009-2015		
Iran, Islamic Republic	1955-1970	1974-1980	1984-1986 [b]	1996-2016 [b]	
Jordan	1972-1989 [abc]	1992-2001	2003-2006		
Kazakhstan	1997-2007 [ab]				
Kenya	1966-1980	1987-2004 [ab]	2006-2015		
Kosovo	2001-2011	2013-2018			
Kuwait	1971-1990 [a]	1993-1998	2006-2009	2012-2016	
Kyrgyz Republic	1997-2008 [b]	2011-2018			
Lao PDR	1989-1998 [b]	2006-2010			
Lebanon	1970-1982 [b]	1993-2000	2005-2017		
Liberia	1988-1996 [a]	2000-2016			
Libya	1980-1988	1991-1995	2007-2015		
Madagascar	1975-1980 [c]	1983-1986 [ab]	1989-1991	2002-2015 [b]	
Malawi	1965-1971	1973-1979	1988-1992 [b]	1997-2012 [b]	1997-2012 [b]
Malaysia	1955-1986	1988-1991	1993-1997 [ab]	2008-2016	2008-2016
Mali	1966-1976	1994-1999 [b]	2001-2004		
Mauritania	2006-2009				
Mexico	1983-1986	1988-1995 [ab]	2010-2016		
Moldova	1994-2007 [bc]				
Mongolia	1997-2007 [ab]	2010-2013			
Morocco	1990-2000	2003-2012			
Mozambique	1996-2000	2004-2015 [b]			
Myanmar	1965-1972	1974-1978 [b]	1989-1992 [b]	1994-2001 [b]	
Nepal	1963-1981	1983-2009 [ab]			
Nicaragua	1975-1982 [bc]	1996-2007 [a]			
Niger	1971-1975	1977-1981 [ac]			
Nigeria	1970-1980	1990-1992 [a]	1996-200 [ab]	2006-2009 [a]	
North Macedonia	2001-2015				
Oman	1972-1978	1981-1988	1990-1998	2005-2009	2011-2017
Pakistan	1957-1972 [b]	1975-1979	1984-1986	1991-2000	2002-2008
Panama	1990-2001				
Papua New Guinea	1978-1987	1996-1998	2004-2013		
Paraguay	1961-1971	1987-1997 [ab]	2006-2015		
Peru	1969-1973	1978-1983 [abc]	1989-1999	2006-2015	

TABLE A.2 **Completed episodes of rapid accumulation of private debt (***continued***)**

Country	1st episode	2nd episode	3rd episode	4th episode	5th episode
Philippines	1971-1983 a b c	1986-1997 a b			
Poland	1995-2002	2004-2016			
Romania	2000-2011				
Russian Federation	1996-2015 a b c				
Rwanda	1968-1978	1983-1988	1991-1994 b	1996-2015	
Saudi Arabia	1973-1988	1990-1998	2000-2009	2012-2016	
Senegal	1967-1979 c				
Serbia	2002-2010				
Sierra Leone	1971-1978 c	1999-2009			
South Africa	1967-1973	1980-1985 b c	1993-2008		
Sri Lanka	1973-1979 b	1991-1995	2009-2017		
Sudan	1974-1980 b c	1999-2012 b			
Syrian Arab Republic	1980-1984	1988-1995 b	2002-2010		
Tajikistan	2004-2008	2010-2015 b			
Tanzania	2000-2008	2013-2015			
Thailand	1950-1997 a b	2007-2015			
Togo	1965-1980 c	1985-1987	1990-1993 a b	2002-2016	
Tunisia	1980-1986	1988-2002 a	2006-2017		
Turkey	1989-1997 b				
Uganda	1979-1981 b c	1987-2015 a b			
Ukraine	1996-2009 a b c				
United Arab Emirates	1973-1978	1980-1988	1990-1998	2000-2009	2013-2016
Uruguay	1974-1982 a b c	1994-2002 a b c			
Venezuela, RB	1963-1978	2003-2013 2			
Vietnam	1992-2010 a				
West Bank and Gaza	1998-2006	2008-2016			
Yemen, Rep.	1996-2007 a				
Zambia	1965-1974	1978-1982 b c	1992-1996 a b	2002-2008 b	2010-2015 b
Zimbabwe	1982-1989 b	1994-1997 a b	1999-2002 b		

Source: World Bank.
Note: Superscripts a, b, and c mean that rapid accumulation episodes are associated with banking, currency, and debt crises, respectively.

TABLE A.3 List of financial crises

Economy	Systemic banking crisis (starting date)	Currency crisis (year)	Sovereign debt crisis (year)
Albania	1994	1997	1990
Algeria	1990	1988, 1994	
Angola		1991, 1996, 2015	1988
Argentina	1980, 1989, 1995, 2001	1975, 1981, 1987, 2002, 2013	1982, 2001, 2014
Armenia	1994		
Austria	2008		
Azerbaijan	1995	2015	
Bangladesh	1987	1976	
Belarus	1995	1997, 2009, 2015	
Belgium	2008		
Belize			2007, 2012, 2017
Benin	1988	1994	
Bolivia	1986, 1994	1973, 1981	1980
Bosnia and Herzegovina	1992		
Botswana		1984	
Brazil	1990, 1994	1976, 1982, 1987, 1992, 1999, 2015	1983
Bulgaria	1996	1996	1990
Burkina Faso	1990	1994	
Burundi	1994		
Cambodia		1971, 1992	
Cameroon	1987, 1995	1994	1989
Cabo Verde	1993		
Central African Republic	1976, 1995	1994	
Chad	1983, 1992	1994	
Chile	1976, 1981	1972, 1982	1983
China	1998		
Colombia	1982, 1998	1985	
Comoros		1994	
Congo, Dem. Rep.	1983, 1991, 1994	1976, 1983, 1989, 1994, 1999, 2009, 2016	1976
Congo, Rep.	1992	1994	1986
Costa Rica	1987, 1994	1981, 1991	1981
Côte d'Ivoire	1988	1994	1984, 2001, 2010
Croatia	1998		
Czech Republic	1996		
Cyprus	2011		2013
Denmark	2008		
Djibouti	1991		
Dominica			2002
Dominican Republic	2003	1985, 1990, 2003	1982, 2003
Ecuador	1982, 1998	1982, 1999	1982, 1999, 2008
Egypt, Arab Rep.	1980	1979, 1990, 2016	1984

TABLE A.3 **List of financial crises** *(continued)*

Economy	Systemic banking crisis (starting date)	Currency crisis (year)	Sovereign debt crisis (year)
El Salvador	1989	1986	
Equatorial Guinea	1983	1980, 1994	
Eritrea	1993		
Estonia	1992	1992	
Eswatini	1995	1985, 2015	
Ethiopia		1993	
Fiji		1998	
Finland	1991	1993	
France	2008		
Gabon		1994	1986, 2002
Gambia, The		1985, 2003	1986
Georgia	1991	1992, 1999	
Germany	2008		
Ghana	1982	1978, 1983, 1993, 2000, 2009, 2014	
Greece	2008	1983	2012
Grenada			2004
Guatemala		1986	
Guinea	1985, 1993	1982, 2005	1985
Guinea-Bissau	1995, 2014	1980, 1994	
Guyana	1993	1987	1982
Haiti	1994	1992, 2003	
Honduras		1990	1981
Hungary	1991, 2008		
Iceland	2008	1975, 1981, 1989, 2008	
India	1993		
Indonesia	1997	1979, 1998	1999
Iran, Islamic Rep.		1985, 1993, 2000, 2013	1992
Ireland	2008		
Israel	1983	1975, 1980, 1985	
Italy	2008	1981	
Jamaica	1996	1978, 1983, 1991	1978, 2010
Japan	1997		
Jordan	1989	1989	1989
Kazakhstan	2008	1999, 2015	
Kenya	1985, 1992	1993	
Korea, Rep.	1997	1998	
Kuwait	1982		
Kyrgyz Republic	1995	1997	
Lao PDR		1972, 1978, 1986, 1997	
Latvia	1995, 2008	1992	
Lebanon	1990	1984, 1990	
Lesotho		1985, 2015	
Liberia	1991		1980

TABLE A.3 **List of financial crises** *(continued)*

Economy	Systemic banking crisis (starting date)	Currency crisis (year)	Sovereign debt crisis (year)
Libya		2002	
Lithuania	1995	1992	
Luxembourg	2008		
Madagascar	1988	1984, 1994, 2004	1981
Malawi		1994, 2012	1982
Malaysia	1997	1998	
Maldives		1975	
Mali	1987	1994	
Mauritania	1984	1993	
Mexico	1981, 1994	1977, 1982, 1995	1982
Moldova	2014	1999	2002
Mongolia	2008	1990, 1997	
Morocco	1980	1981	1983
Mozambique	1987	1987, 2015	1984
Myanmar		1975, 1990, 1996, 2001, 2007, 2012	
Namibia		1984, 2015	
Nepal	1988	1984, 1992	
Netherlands	2008		
New Caledonia		1981	
New Zealand		1984	
Nicaragua	1990, 2000	1979, 1985, 1990	1980
Niger	1983	1994	1983
Nigeria	1991, 2009	1983, 1989, 1997, 2016	1983
North Macedonia	1993		
Norway	1991		
Pakistan		1972	
Panama	1988		1983
Papua New Guinea		1995	
Paraguay	1995	1984, 1989, 2002	1982
Peru	1983	1976, 1981, 1988	1978
Philippines	1983, 1997	1983, 1998	1983
Poland	1992		1981
Portugal	2008	1983	
Romania	1998	1996	1982
Russian Federation	1998, 2008	1998, 2014	1998
Rwanda		1991	
São Tomé and Príncipe	1992	1987, 1992, 1997	
Senegal	1988	1994	1981
Serbia		2000	
Seychelles		2008	2008
Sierra Leone	1990	1983, 1989, 1998	1977
Slovak Republic	1998		
Slovenia	1992, 2008		
South Africa		1984, 2015	1985

TABLE A.3 **List of financial crises** *(continued)*

Economy	Systemic banking crisis (starting date)	Currency crisis (year)	Sovereign debt crisis (year)
South Sudan		2015	
Spain	1977, 2008	1983	
Sri Lanka	1989	1978	
Sudan		1981, 1988, 1993, 2012	1979
Suriname		1990, 1995, 2001, 2016	
Sweden	1991, 2008	1993	
Syrian Arab Republic		1988	
Switzerland	2008		
Tajikistan		1999, 2015	
Tanzania	1987	1985, 1990	1984
Thailand	1983, 1997	1998	
Togo	1993	1994	1979
Trinidad and Tobago		1986	1989
Tunisia	1991		
Turkey	1982, 2000	1978, 1984, 1991, 1996, 2001	1978
Turkmenistan		2008	
Uganda	1994	1980, 1988	1981
Ukraine	1998, 2008, 2014	1998, 2009, 2014	1998, 2015
United Kingdom	2007		
United States	1988, 2007		
Uruguay	1981, 2002	1972, 1983, 1990, 2002	1983, 2002
Uzbekistan		2000	
Venezuela, RB	1994	1984, 1989, 1994, 2002, 2010	1982, 2017
Vietnam	1997	1972, 1981, 1987	1985
Yemen, Rep.	1996	1985, 1995	
Yugoslavia, former			1983
Zambia	1995	1983, 1989, 1996, 2009, 2015	1983
Zimbabwe	1995	1983, 1991, 1998, 2003	

Source: World Bank.
Note: Years of crises are taken from Laeven and Valencia (2018).

TABLE A.4 Duration and amplitude of rapid debt accumulation episodes

A. Duration

	Number of episodes, by duration (years)					
	Associated with crises			No crises		
Years:	**2-4**	**5-10**	**11-**	**2-4**	**5-10**	**11-**
Government debt	41	59	37	27	74	18
Private debt	28	39	39	38	83	38
Total debt	32	40	35	29	78	24

B. Amplitude

	Number of episodes, by amplitude (percentage points of GDP)							
	Associated with crises				No crises			
Percentage points of GDP	**-20**	**20-40**	**40-60**	**60-**	**-20**	**20-40**	**40-60**	**60-**
Government debt	24	41	24	48	53	40	16	10
Private debt	66	17	13	10	98	48	11	2
Total debt	9	32	26	40	33	57	20	21

Source: World Bank.
Note: Total debt refers to a sum of government debt and private debt. A period of debt accumulation is identified with the algorithm in Harding and Pagan (2002). When a change in debt-to-GDP ratios over an accumulation period is above the maximum of 10-year moving standard deviation of the ratios during the period, it is considered as a rapid debt accumulation.

TABLE A.5 **Comparison of combined episodes with single episodes**

	Rapid accumulation with crises			Rapid accumulation without crises		
	Government debt	Private debt	Both (combined)	Government debt	Private debt	Both (combined)
Duration (years)	**7**	**8**	3	**7**	**8**	4
Amplitude (percentage points of GDP)	**42.6**	**13.1**	35.3	**21.6**	**14.8**	26.0
Growth (percent)	2.2	3.7	2.7	4.1	**4.6**	4.2
Per capita growth (percent)	**0.1**	1.9	0.9	2.0	**2.5**	2.0
Investment growth (percent)	1.9	**5.7**	2.2	6.3	**7.2**	6.1
Private consumption growth (percent)	2.5	**4.0**	2.9	4.1	**4.8**	4.2
Reserves (percent of GDP)	7.2	7.2	6.6	12.9	13.2	12.9
Short-term external debt (percent of GDP)	4.4	4.8	4.3	3.9	3.7	3.8

Source: World Bank.
Note: A combined episode covers years with concurrent government and private debt accumulation episodes. Single episodes cover years with a solely government debt accumulation episode or a solely private debt accumulation episode. Amplitude for "Both (combined)" is measured as an average of amplitudes of government debt and private debt during a combined government and private debt accumulation episode. Bold numbers indicate statistically significant difference from combined episodes.

TABLE A.6 **Robustness exercises: Government debt**

	Cumulative change in eight years from the beginning of rapid government debt accumulation							
	Baseline		Baseline (mean)		Advanced economies		All countries	
	Crises	No crises	Crises	No crises	Crises	No crises	Crises	No crises
Output	**127**	141	**127**	140	**112**	120	**125**	129
Per capita output	**107**	120	**108**	116	**106**	116	**107**	117
Investment	**130**	167	154	183	**102**	111	**118**	129
Private consumption	130	139	131	138	**111**	119	125	126
Consumer price	**198**	141	626	171	116	123	**186**	133
REER	**88**	101	100	103	95	100	**92**	100
Current account balance	-28	-25	-30	-28	-7	-7	-26	-19
Fiscal balance	**-37**	-27	-39	-28	**-34**	-22	**-35**	-23
Reserves	**60**	105	**89**	128	60	91	**60**	102
Total external debt	402	365	460	458	-	-	402	365
Short-term external debt	**48**	33	**65**	42	-	-	**48**	33

Source: World Bank.
Note: Table shows cumulative levels or shares of GDP in eight years since the beginning of rapid accumulation episodes (year "t") of government debt. Output, per capita output, investment, private consumption, consumer price, REER, and debt-to-GDP ratio are presented as an index equal to 100 in year "t" whereas current account balance, fiscal balance, reserves, total external debt, and short-term external debt are in percent of GDP. "Baseline" shows medians; "Mean" shows average results; "Advanced economies" uses data for advanced economies. The numbers in bold show that differences between crises and noncrises are statistically significant at least at the 10 percent level. REER = real effective exchange rate.

TABLE A.7 **Robustness exercises: Private debt**

	Cumulative change in eight years from the beginning of rapid private debt accumulation							
	Baseline		Baseline (mean)		Advanced economies		All countries	
	Crises	No crises	Crises	No crises	Crises	No crises	Crises	No crises
Output	**133**	143	**135**	147	123	128	**130**	139
Per capita output	112	119	115	119	121	119	115	119
Investment	**146**	171	**174**	245	139	132	142	156
Private consumption	**135**	146	140	161	124	128	134	139
Consumer price	**211**	145	**440**	163	138	132	**195**	141
REER	**99**	109	105	112	106	104	**102**	108
Current account balance	-28	-32	-27	-8	-4	-5	-21	-23
Fiscal balance	**-28**	-18	**-33**	-10	-26	-18	**-27**	-18
Reserves	**65**	112	**82**	173	55	71	**61**	105
Total external debt	**509**	367	569	458	-	-	**509**	367
Short-term external debt	**50**	38	70	54	-	-	**50**	38

Source: World Bank.
Note: Table shows cumulative levels or shares of GDP in eight years since the beginning of rapid accumulation episodes (year "t") of private debt. Output, per capita output, investment, private consumption, consumer price, REER, and debt-to-GDP ratio are presented as an index equal to 100 in year "t" while current account balance, fiscal balance, reserves, total external debt, and short-term external debt are in percent of GDP. "Baseline" shows medians; "Mean" shows average results; "Advanced economies" uses data for advanced economies. The numbers in bold show that differences between crises and non-crises are statistically significant at least at the 10 percent level. REER = real effective exchange rate.

TABLE A.8 Robustness to alternative definition of episodes

	Government debt episodes	Private debt episodes
Number of episodes (count)		
Baseline definition	256	265
Alternative definition	325	362
Share of episodes in baseline and alternative definition (percent)		
With same start or end year	71.1	75.5
With same end year	64.5	63.0
Median duration of episode (years)		
Baseline definition	7	8
Alternative definition	7	8
Median amplitude of episode (percentage points of GDP)		
Baseline definition	30.0	14.5
Alternative definition	29.5	10.6

Source: World Bank.
Note: In the baseline definition, an episode is defined as the increase in debt-to-GDP ratio from peak to trough, if the peak-to-trough increase exceeds one country-specific, 10-year rolling standard deviation. In the alternative definition, an episode is defined as the increase in debt-to-GDP ratio from peak to trough if, during this period, the debt-to-GDP ratio exceeds its Hodrick-Prescott-filtered trend by one standard deviation at some point during the period from trough to peak debt-to-GDP ratio.

Reference

Mendoza, E. G., and M. E. Terrones. 2008. "An Anatomy of Credit Booms: Evidence from Macro Aggregates and Micro Data." NBER Working Paper 14049, National Bureau of Economic Research, Cambridge, MA.

Sources

Boughton, J. 2001. *Silent Revolution. The International Monetary Fund 1979-89.* Washington, DC: International Monetary Fund.

Boughton, J. 2012. *Tearing Down Walls: The International Monetary Fund 1990-1999.* Washington, DC: International Monetary Fund.

Daumont, R., F. Le Gall, and F. Leroux. 2004. "Banking in Sub-Saharan Africa: What Went Wrong?" IMF Working Paper 04/55, International Monetary Fund, Washington, DC.

Fischer, S. 1989. "Resolving the International Debt Crisis." In *Developing Country Debt and Economic Performance* 1: *The International Financial System,* 359-386. Chicago: University of Chicago Press.

Hornbeck, J. 2013. "Argentina's Defaulted Sovereign Debt: Dealing with the 'Hold-outs.'" CRS Report for Congress, Congressional Research Service, Washington, DC.

IMF (International Monetary Fund). 1974. *Bangladesh—Staff Report and Proposed Decision for the 1974 Article XIV Consultation.* Washington, DC: International Monetary Fund.

IMF (International Monetary Fund). 1978a. Bolivia: Staff Report for the 1978 Article IV Consultation. Washington, DC: International Monetary Fund.

IMF (International Monetary Fund). 1978b. *Chile: Staff Report for the 1978 Article IV Consultation*. Washington, DC: International Monetary Fund.

IMF (International Monetary Fund). 1978c. *Uruguay: Staff Report for the 1978 Article IV Consultation*. Washington, DC: International Monetary Fund.

IMF (International Monetary Fund). 1978d. *Venezuela: Staff Report for the 1978 Article IV Consultation*. Washington, DC: International Monetary Fund.

IMF (International Monetary Fund). 1981a. *Brazil: Staff Report for the 1981 Article IV Consultation*. Washington, DC: International Monetary Fund.

IMF (International Monetary Fund). 1981b. *Uruguay: Staff Report for the 1981 Article IV Consultation*. Washington, DC: International Monetary Fund.

IMF (International Monetary Fund). 1982. *Chile: Staff Report for the 1982 Article IV Consultation*. Washington, DC: International Monetary Fund.

IMF (International Monetary Fund). 1984a. *Nepal: Staff Report for the 1984 Article IV Consultation*. Washington, DC: International Monetary Fund.

IMF (International Monetary Fund). 1984b. *Paraguay: Staff Report for the 1984 Article IV Consultation*. Washington, DC: International Monetary Fund.

IMF (International Monetary Fund). 1985. *Chile: Staff Report for the 1985 Article IV Consultation*. Washington, DC: International Monetary Fund.

IMF (International Monetary Fund). 1989. *Argentina—Staff Report for the 1989 Article IV Consultation and Request for Stand-By Arrangement*. Washington, DC: International Monetary Fund.

IMF (International Monetary Fund). 1995. *Uruguay: Staff Report for the 1995 Article IV Consultation*. Washington, DC: International Monetary Fund.

IMF (International Monetary Fund). 1997. *Philippines: Staff Report for the 1997 Article IV Consultation*. Washington, DC: International Monetary Fund.

IMF (International Monetary Fund). 1998a. "External Debt Histories of Ten Low-Income Developing Countries: Lessons From their Experience." IMF Working Paper 72, International Monetary Fund, Washington, DC.

IMF (International Monetary Fund). 1998b. *Niger: Staff Report for the 1998 Article IV Consultation*. Washington, DC: International Monetary Fund.

IMF (International Monetary Fund). 1999a. *Nigeria: Staff Report for the 1999 Article IV Consultation*. Washington, DC: International Monetary Fund.

IMF (International Monetary Fund). 1999b. *Philippines—Staff Report for the 1999 Article IV Consultation, Fourth Review Under the Stand-By Arrangement, and Request for Waiver and Modification of Performance Criteria*. Washington, DC: International Monetary Fund.

IMF (International Monetary Fund). 1999c. *Zimbabwe: Staff Report for the 1999 Article IV Consultation*. Washington, DC: International Monetary Fund.

IMF (International Monetary Fund). 2001a. *Argentina: 2001 Article IV Consultation Staff Report*. Washington, DC: International Monetary Fund.

IMF (International Monetary Fund). 2001b. *IMF-Supported Programs in Indonesia, Korea, Thailand: A Preliminary Assessment*. Washington, DC: International Monetary Fund.

IMF (International Monetary Fund). 2001c. *Uruguay: Staff Report for the 2001 Article IV Consultation*. Washington, DC: International Monetary Fund.

IMF (International Monetary Fund). 2001d. *Zimbabwe: Staff Report for the 2001 Article IV Consultation*. Washington, DC: International Monetary Fund.

IMF (International Monetary Fund). 2003a. *The IMF and Recent Capital Account Crises: Indonesia, Korea, Brazil*. Washington, DC: International Monetary Fund.

IMF (International Monetary Fund). 2003b. *Uruguay: Staff Report for the 2003 Article IV Consultation*. Washington, DC: International Monetary Fund.

IMF (International Monetary Fund). 2012. *The Liberalization and Management of Capital Flows—An Institutional View*. Washington, DC: International Monetary Fund.

IMF (International Monetary Fund). 2016. *Argentina: 2016 Article IV Consultation Staff Report*. Washington, DC: International Monetary Fund.

Kaufmann, D., M. Mastruzzi, and D. Zavaleta. 2003. "Sustained Macroeconomic Reforms, Tepid Growth: A Governance Puzzle in Bolivia?" In *Search of Prosperity: Analytic Narratives on Economic Growth*, edited by D. Rodrik. Princeton, NJ: Princeton University Press.

Kaufman, R. R. 1989. "The Politics of Economic Adjustment Policy in Argentina, Brazil, and Mexico: Experiences in the 1980s and Challenges for the Future." *Policy Sciences* 22 (3): 395-413.

Kawai, M., R. Newfarmer, and S. Schmukler. 2005. "Crisis and Contagion in East Asia: Nine Lessons." *Eastern Economic Journal* 31 (2): 185-207.

Larrain, C. 1998. *Banking Supervision in Developing. Regulatory and Supervisory Challenges in a New Era of Global Finance*. The Hague: Fondad.

Leone, A. M., and J. Pérez-Campanero. 1991. "Liberalization and Financial Crisis in Uruguay (1974-1987)." Working Paper 91/30, International Monetary Fund. Washington, DC.

Radelet, S., J. Sachs, R. Cooper, and B. Bosworth. 1998. "The East Asian Financial Crisis: Diagnosis, Remedies, Prospects." *Brookings Papers on Economic Activity* 1998 (1): 1-90.

Sachs, J. 1985. "External Debt and Macroeconomic Performance in Latin America and East Asia." *Brookings Papers on Economic Activity* 1985 (2): 523-73.

World Bank. 1996. *Bank Restructuring. Lessons from the 1980s*. Washington, DC: World Bank.

APPENDIX B **Regression methodology**

The most common estimation methods used in the empirical literature on predicting crises are logit and probit models. The baseline specification used in this study is a panel logit model with random effects, but for robustness purposes, a random effects probit model and a fixed effects logit model are also used. The Hausman test suggests that the random effects model is appropriate for debt and banking crises but not for currency crises. However, even for currency crises, the coefficient estimates and their statistical significance remain similar in fixed effects and random effects models.

To exploit the time and cross-sectional dimensions, a panel dataset of 139 emerging market and developing economies with annual data over the period 1970–2018 is constructed. The basic structure of the model takes the form:

$$Y_{i,t} = \beta' X_{i,t-1} + \mu_i + \varepsilon_{i,t}$$

where $Y_{i,t}$ is a crisis indicator (either sovereign debt, banking, or currency crisis) for country i in year t, and takes the value of 1 if it is in a crisis, and 0 otherwise; $X_{i,t-1}$ is the vector of determinants of a crisis; β is the vector of coefficient estimates common across all countries; μ_i captures the unobserved country heterogeneity; and $\varepsilon_{i,t}$ is the stochastic error term.

The probability of a crisis is given by

$$\Pr(Y_{i,t} = 1 \mid X_{i,t-1}, \beta, \mu_i) = \Psi(\mu_i + \beta' X_{i,t})$$

where assumptions about the distribution of the error terms, that is, the form of $\varepsilon_{i,t}$, render the estimation of the logit (logistic distribution) or probit (normal distribution) discrete choice panel data model. The parameters can be estimated by maximizing the panel-level likelihood function.

Selection of explanatory variables. The variables are chosen from a close examination of the empirical findings from the early warning crisis literature (see Chamon and Crowe 2012; Frankel and Saravelos 2012; and Kaminsky, Lizondo, and Reinhart 1998 for an extensive review). We include a large number of variables (and various data transformations, such as levels, growth rate, percentage point change, and deviation from trend) that can be characterized into several groups:

- Debt profile: public debt, private debt, short-term debt, variable interest rate debt, concessional debt, multilateral debt, commercial debt, International Monetary Fund credit, and debt service

- Capital account: international reserves, currency mismatch, portfolio flows, and foreign direct investment

- Current account: current account balance, exchange rate overvaluation, exchange rate regime, and terms of trade

- Foreign: U.S. interest rate and advanced economies' gross domestic product (GDP) growth

- Domestic macro: GDP growth, inflation, unemployment, and fiscal balance

- Financial sector: credit to private sector, money supply, and interest rate

- Banking sector: liquidity, leverage, banking concentration, and nonperforming loans

- Structural: trade openness, export diversification, and capital account openness

- Institutional: governance, conflict, and political stability

Some variables had low cross-country coverage and/or limited time series availability (especially banking sector variables and institutional quality indicators) and thus had to be dropped. To attenuate potential endogeneity bias caused by contemporaneous interaction between economic fundamentals and crises, lagged values of the explanatory variables are used, except for U.S. interest rate. The variables used in the baseline model (panel logit random effects model) are listed in table B.1 and the estimation results are summarized in table B.2. Robustness checks using alternative model specifications are provided in tables B.3 and B.4.

Probability of crises. The probability of crises occurring is evaluated at specific points of interest for illustration (while keeping all other variables at their average values), which include crisis episodes such as Mexico's 1982 twin crises. The findings are summarized in table B.5.

Twin crises. The probability of the occurrence of twin crises (any two of sovereign debt, banking, and currency crises) is lower than single crisis events.[1] However, the explanatory variables in the baseline model have better predictive ability in predicting a twin crisis one year ahead.[2] An adverse GDP

---

[1] A twin crisis is defined as the occurrence of any two of sovereign debt, banking, or currency crises within two immediate years.

[2] A triple crisis model (all three types of crisis happening within two immediate years) could not be reliably estimated as there are only seven such episodes with available data for the explanatory variables.

growth shock, a larger share of short-term debt, higher debt service burden, lower reserve cover, and larger changes in government and private debt significantly increase the probability of a twin crisis, although the interaction term of government and private debt is insignificant. The estimation results are shown in table B.6.

Robustness. Several additional correlates were added to the baseline empirical specification to test the robustness of the results. The baseline results are robust to these alternative specifications.[3]

First, the quality of institutions may affect the incidence of crises. However, data for meaningful cross-country and over-time comparison, such as the Worldwide Governance Indicators (WDI; Kaufmann, Kraay, and Mastruzzi 2010), is available starting only in the early 1990s.[4] As a result, most sovereign debt and banking crises as well as many currency crises, which mainly occurred during the first two waves of debt accumulation, will be omitted from the estimation sample. Indeed, the use of WDI data reduces the number of observations by almost a half. Furthermore, most measures of institutional quality are insignificant, whereas the results on other variables are broadly of the same magnitude, signs, and significance as in the baseline specification. Several statistically significant results are counterintuitive and may reflect other omitted factors.

Second, to account for possible nonlinearity of the impact of debt increases on the probability of crises and its dependence on the level of debt, baseline regressions were augmented with squared changes in debt and interactions between a change in debt and the initial level of debt. In most specifications, these new variables are not statistically significant, whereas other coefficients remain consistent with the findings of the baseline model.

Third, the foreign exchange regime or a shift in foreign currency regime influences the probability of financial distress but in different ways for different types of crises. An EMDE with a fixed exchange rate is more likely to suffer a sovereign debt crisis, whereas a shift to a flexible exchange rate increases the likelihood of a banking crisis. A currency crisis is more likely if a shift to a flexible exchange rate regime occurred the year before the crisis. Other regression coefficients remain consistent with the baseline specification regardless of the exchange rate regime.

---

[3] Detailed results are available upon request.
[4] WDI data are available from 1996 to 2017, but with gaps in 1996-2001.

TABLE B.1 Definitions of variables and data sources

Variables	Definition	Source
Crisis	Sovereign debt, banking, or currency crisis	Laeven and Valencia (2018)
Change in U.S. real interest rate	Percentage point change in U.S. real lending interest rate (deflated by GDP deflator)	WDI
GDP growth	Annual percentage growth rate of GDP at market prices based on constant local currency	WDI
Short-term debt	Share of short-term debt (with a maturity of one year or less) in external debt	IDS
Debt service	Ratio of debt service on external debt to exports	IDS
Reserve cover	International reserves in months of imports	IDS
Change in government debt	Percentage point change in public debt to GDP ratio	GDD
Change in private debt	Percentage point change in private debt to GDP ratio	GDD
Concessional debt	Share of concessional debt in external debt	IDS
Funding ratio	Ratio of credit provided to private sector to total deposits	GFDD
Currency overvaluation	Percentage deviation of real effective exchange rate from Hodrick-Prescott-	Darvas (2012); World Bank
Currency mismatch	Ratio of foreign liabilities to foreign assets	Lane and Milesi-Ferretti (2018)
Foreign direct investment	Net inflows of foreign direct investment as a share of GNI	IDS

Source: World Bank.
Note: GDD = Global Debt Database; GFDD = Global Financial Development Database;
IDS = International Debt Statistics; WDI = World Development Indicators.

TABLE B.2 **Random effects logit model**

Dependent variable: Crisis indicator (1 = crisis, 0 = no crisis)

Explanatory variables	Debt crisis	Banking crisis	Currency crisis
Change in U.S. real interest rate	-0.067	0.015	0.253**
	(0.132)	(0.106)	(0.100)
GDP growth	-0.095***	-0.020	-0.006
	(0.025)	(0.025)	(0.020)
Short-term debt	0.026*	0.012	0.006
	(0.015)	(0.012)	(0.011)
Debt service	0.028***	0.029***	0.010
	(0.009)	(0.007)	(0.008)
Reserves cover	-0.573***	-0.163***	-0.115*
	(0.116)	(0.063)	(0.062)
Change in government debt	0.014*		0.016**
	(0.008)		(0.007)
Change in private debt		0.055**	0.052**
		(0.023)	(0.026)
Change in government debt x Change in private debt			0.003***
			(0.001)
Concessional debt	-0.033***		
	(0.009)		
Funding ratio		0.002*	
		(0.001)	
Currency overvaluation			0.165***
			(0.015)
Currency mismatch			0.014
			(0.033)
Foreign direct investment			-0.101**
			(0.046)
Constant	-2.678***	-4.161***	-3.617***
	(0.616)	(0.371)	(0.395)
No. of observations	3,089	2,797	2,395
No. of countries	106	106	99

Source: World Bank.
Note: ***, **, * denote statistical significance at the 1 percent, 5 percent, and 10 percent levels, respectively. Standard errors are in parentheses.

TABLE B.3 Random effects probit model

Dependent variable: Crisis indicator (1 = crisis, 0 = no crisis)

Explanatory variables	Debt crisis	Banking crisis	Currency crisis
Change in U.S. real interest rate	-0.027	0.007	0.118**
	(0.057)	(0.046)	(0.048)
GDP growth	-0.044***	-0.011	-0.006
	(0.012)	(0.011)	(0.010)
Short-term debt	0.010	0.005	0.002
	(0.006)	(0.005)	(0.005)
Debt service	0.012***	0.013***	0.004
	(0.004)	(0.003)	(0.004)
Reserves cover	-0.215***	-0.063***	-0.060**
	(0.045)	(0.025)	(0.028)
Change in government debt	0.007*		0.008*
	(0.004)		(0.004)
Change in private debt		0.021**	0.024*
		(0.010)	(0.013)
Change in government debt x Change in private debt			0.001***
			(0.000)
Concessional debt	-0.014***		
	(0.004)		
Funding ratio		0.001*	
		(0.001)	
Currency overvaluation			0.079***
			(0.007)
Currency mismatch			0.004
			(0.016)
Foreign direct investment			-0.047**
			(0.020)
Constant	-1.537***	-2.186***	-1.861***
	(0.264)	(0.157)	(0.182)
No. of observations	3,089	2,797	2,395
No. of countries	106	106	99

Source: World Bank.
Note: ***, **, * denote statistical significance at the 1 percent, 5 percent, and 10 percent levels, respectively. Standard errors are in parentheses.

TABLE B.4 **Fixed effects logit model**

Dependent variable: Crisis indicator (1 = crisis, 0 = no crisis)

Explanatory variables	Debt crisis	Banking crisis	Currency crisis
Change in U.S. real interest rate	-0.121	-0.021	0.257**
	(0.130)	(0.106)	(0.104)
GDP growth	-0.095***	-0.013	-0.008
	(0.034)	(0.026)	(0.022)
Short-term debt	0.056***	0.012	-0.015
	(0.020)	(0.017)	(0.016)
Debt service	0.032**	0.026***	0.001
	(0.015)	(0.010)	(0.011)
Reserves cover	-0.586***	-0.256***	-0.219***
	(0.154)	(0.082)	(0.085)
Change in government debt	0.018*		0.013**
	(0.010)		(0.007)
Change in private debt		0.055**	0.067**
		(0.027)	(0.029)
Change in government debt x Change in private debt			0.003***
			(0.001)
Concessional debt	-0.059**		
	(0.023)		
Funding ratio		-0.001	
		(0.003)	
Currency overvaluation			0.131***
			(0.016)
Currency mismatch			0.037
			(0.049)
Foreign direct investment			-0.087
			(0.059)
No. of observations	1,186	1,705	1,688
No. of countries	35	55	63

Source: World Bank.
Note: ***, **, * denote statistical significance at the 1 percent, 5 percent, and 10 percent levels, respectively. Standard errors are in parentheses.

TABLE B.5 **Probability of crises**

Dependent variable: Crisis indicator (1 = crisis, 0 = no crisis)

Explanatory variable	Points of interest	Probability of debt crisis	Probability of banking crisis	Probability of currency crisis	Reference
Change in U.S. real interest rate	2 percentage points vs. unchanged			6.0 percent vs. 4.1 percent	Cumulative increase in U.S. Federal Funds rate from end-2015 to mid-2018 vs. no change in interest rate
GDP growth	-1 percent vs. 4 percent	1.9 percent vs. 1.2 percent			Average EMDE growth during crisis vs. noncrisis episodes
Short-term debt	30 percent vs. 10 percent	2.0 percent vs. 1.2 percent			Mexico's 1982 episode vs. EMDE noncrisis episodes
Debt service	50 percent vs. 15 percent	2.8 percent vs. 1.1 percent	5.5 percent vs. 2.1 percent		Mexico's 1982 episode vs. EMDE noncrisis episodes
Reserves cover	1 month vs. 4 months	3.1 percent vs. 0.6 percent	3.3 percent vs. 2.0 percent	5.0 percent vs. 3.8 percent	Mexico's 1982 episode vs. EMDE noncrisis episodes
Change in government debt	30 percentage points of GDP vs. unchanged	2.0 percent vs. 1.4 percent		6.6 percent vs. 3.9 percent	Median government debt accumulation episode vs. no accumulation
Change in private debt	15 percentage points of GDP vs. unchanged		4.8 percent vs. 2.2 percent	7.5 percent vs. 3.9 percent	Median private debt accumulation episode vs no accumulation
Concessional debt	50 percent vs. 25 percent	0.8 percent vs. 1.6 percent			Average EMDE crisis vs. noncrisis episodes
Funding ratio	200 percent vs. 90 percent		3.0 percent vs. 2.3 percent		Ukraine's 2008-09 share vs. EMDE noncrisis episodes
Currency overvaluation	15 percent vs. 0 percent			19.5 percent vs. 2.2 percent	Thailand's real appreciation 1994-97

Source: World Bank.
Note: The table shows the predicted probability of crises in the following year evaluated at various points of interest for each explanatory variable (with the other variables held at their average values). These probabilities are included for variables that are statistically significant at the 10 percent level or below in the baseline regressions (see table B.2).

TABLE B.6 **Logit and probit models for twin crisis**

Dependent variable: Crisis indicator (1 = crisis, 0 = no crisis)

Explanatory variables	Random effects logit	Random effects probit	Fixed effects logit
Change in U.S. real interest rate	0.158	0.068	0.096
	(0.177)	(0.073)	(0.184)
GDP growth	-0.075**	-0.035**	-0.146***
	(0.030)	(0.014)	(0.049)
Short-term debt	0.056***	0.022***	0.073***
	(0.015)	(0.007)	(0.026)
Debt service	0.038***	0.015***	0.026
	(0.012)	(0.005)	(0.017)
Reserves cover	-0.277**	-0.107**	-0.391**
	(0.120)	(0.046)	(0.188)
Change in government debt	0.016*	0.007	0.018**
	(0.009)	(0.005)	(0.010)
Change in private debt	0.088***	0.040***	0.161***
	(0.031)	(0.015)	(0.060)
Change in government debt x Change in private debt	-0.001	-0.000	-0.004
	(0.001)	(0.001)	(0.005)
Constant	-5.639***	-2.716***	
	(0.584)	(0.228)	
No. of observations	2,908	2,908	696
No. of countries	107	107	21

Source: World Bank.
Note: ***, **, * denote statistical significance at the 1 percent, 5 percent, and 10 percent levels, respectively. Standard errors are in parentheses.

References

Chamon, M., and C. Crowe. 2012. "Predictive Indicators of Crises." In *Handbook in Financial Globalization: The Evidence and Impact of Financial Globalization*, edited by G. Caprio, 499-505. London: Elsevier.

Darvas, Z. 2012. "Real Effective Exchange Rates for 178 Countries: A New Database." Bruegel Working Paper 2012/06, Bruegel, Brussels, Belgium.

Frankel, J. A., and G. Saravelos. 2012. "Can Leading Indicators Assess Country Vulnerability? Evidence from the 2008-09 Global Financial Crisis." *Journal of International Economics* 87 (2): 216-31.

Kaminsky, G. L., S. Lizondo, and C. M. Reinhart. 1998. "Leading Indicators of Currency Crises." *IMF Staff Papers* 45 (1): 1-48.

Kaufmann, D., A. Kraay, and M. Mastruzzi. 2010. "The Worldwide Governance Indicators: Methodology and Analytical Issues." Policy Research Working Paper 5430, World Bank, Washington, DC.

Laeven, L., and F. Valencia. 2010. Policy Responses to Systemic Banking Crises." In *Macrofinancial Linkages: Trends, Crises, and Policies*, edited by C. Crowe, S. Johnson, J. Ostry, and J. Zettelmeyer. Washington, DC: International Monetary Fund.

Laeven, L., and F. Valencia. 2018. "Systemic Banking Crises Revisited." IMF Working Paper 18/206, International Monetary Fund, Washington, DC.

Lane, P., and G. Milesi-Ferretti. 2018. "The External Wealth of Nations Revisited: International Financial Integration in the Aftermath of the Global Financial Crisis," *IMF Economic Review* 66 (1): 189-222.

APPENDIX C **Case studies**

An in-depth literature review covered 43 crisis case studies for 30 emerging market and developing economies (EMDEs) with financial crises and rapid debt accumulation episodes since 1970. Although nonexhaustive, the case studies were chosen to (i) be representative of debt accumulation episodes over the past 50 years; (ii) include the large EMDEs in major regional debt crises episodes; (iii) represent crises in low-income countries; and (iv) provide a sufficiently comprehensive literature to base an assessment on. The main sources for in-depth literature reviews are summarized in table C.1.

The search covered all publicly available country reports and flagship publications of international financial institutions (Asian Development Bank, African Development Bank, European Bank for Reconstruction and Development, Inter-American Development Bank, International Monetary Fund, and World Bank) and academic publications published during 1970-2018. Publications were found on the institutions' websites and, especially before 1997, in the EconLit database.

Some caution is required when interpreting results. First, not all topics received equal attention. For example, literature on the role of financial supervision during crisis episodes of the 1970s and 80s is limited (for Chile, Larrain 1998; for Uruguay, Leone and Pérez-Campanero 1991; for the Philippines, Nascimento 1990 and World Bank 1996). However, the decade following the global financial crisis has seen an explosion of financial supervision work and the role of macroprudential policy, reflecting in part the nature of these crises. Second, much of the literature during the 1980s focused on the economies of Latin America that held most of the U.S. banks' liabilities (Fischer 1989). Sub-Saharan African countries, because of their small liability positions, received much less focus, even though the economic impacts on individual economies were equally severe.

TABLE C.1 **Information sources**

Episode	Main sources
Argentina	Hornbeck 2013; IMF 1989, 2001a, 2016; Kaufman 1989; Kawai, Newfarmer and Schmukler 2005
Bangladesh	IMF 1974
Brazil	Boughton 2001; IMF 1981a, 2003a
Bolivia	Boughton 2001; IMF 1978a; Kaufmann, Mastruzzi, and Zavaleta 2003; Sachs 1988b; Morales and Sachs 1999
Cameroon	Daumont, Le Gall, and Leroux 2004; IMF 1998a, 2004b
Chile	Boughton 2001; IMF 1978b, 1982, 1985
Colombia	World Bank 1996
Indonesia	Boughton 2012; IMF 2001b, 2003a
Korea	Boughton 2012; IMF 2001b, 2003a
Malaysia	Boughton 2012; Radelet et al. 1998
Mexico	Boughton 2001, 2012
Nepal	IMF 1984a
Niger	IMF 1998a, 1998b
Nigeria	Daumont, Le Gall, and Leroux 2004; IMF 1999a, 2012
Paraguay	IMF 1984b
Peru	Boughton 2001; Sachs 1985
Philippines	IMF 1997; 1999b; Kawai, Newfarmer and Schmukler 2005
Thailand	Boughton 2012; IMF 2001b; Radelet et al. 1998
Uruguay	IMF 1978c, 1981b, 1995, 2001c, 2003b
Venezuela	Boughton 2001, 2012; IMF 1978d
Zimbabwe	Boughton 2012; IMF 1999c, 2001d

Source: World Bank.
Note: Unless otherwise specified, IMF references refer to Article IV staff reports.

References

Boughton, J. 2001. *Silent Revolution. The International Monetary Fund 1979-89.* Washington, DC: International Monetary Fund.

Boughton, J. 2012. *Tearing Down Walls: The International Monetary Fund 1990-1999.* Washington, DC: International Monetary Fund.

Daumont, R., F. Le Gall, and F. Leroux. 2004. "Banking in Sub-Saharan Africa: What Went Wrong?" IMF Working Paper 04/55, International Monetary Fund, Washington, DC.

Fischer, S. 1989. "Resolving the International Debt Crisis." In *Developing Country Debt and Economic Performance* 1: *The International Financial System,* 359-86. Chicago: University of Chicago Press.

Hornbeck, J. 2013. "Argentina's Defaulted Sovereign Debt: Dealing with the 'Holdouts.'" CRS Report for Congress, Congressional Research Service, Washington, DC.

IMF (International Monetary Fund). 1974. *Bangladesh—Staff Report and Proposed Decision for the 1974 Article XIV Consultation.* Washington, DC: International Monetary Fund.

IMF (International Monetary Fund). 1978a. *Bolivia: Staff Report for the 1978 Article IV Consultation.* Washington, DC: International Monetary Fund.

IMF (International Monetary Fund). 1978b. *Chile: Staff Report for the 1978 Article IV Consultation.* Washington, DC: International Monetary Fund.

IMF (International Monetary Fund). 1978c. *Uruguay: Staff Report for the 1978 Article IV Consultation.* Washington, DC: International Monetary Fund.

IMF (International Monetary Fund). 1978d. *Venezuela: Staff Report for the 1978 Article IV Consultation.* Washington, DC: International Monetary Fund.

IMF (International Monetary Fund). 1981a. *Brazil: Staff Report for the 1981 Article IV Consultation.* Washington, DC: International Monetary Fund.

IMF (International Monetary Fund). 1981b. *Uruguay: Staff Report for the 1981 Article IV Consultation.* Washington, DC: International Monetary Fund.

IMF (International Monetary Fund). 1982. *Chile: Staff Report for the 1982 Article IV Consultation.* Washington, DC: International Monetary Fund.

IMF (International Monetary Fund). 1984a. *Nepal: Staff Report for the 1984 Article IV Consultation.* Washington, DC: International Monetary Fund.

IMF (International Monetary Fund). 1984b. *Paraguay: Staff Report for the 1984 Article IV Consultation.* Washington, DC: International Monetary Fund.

IMF (International Monetary Fund). 1985. *Chile: Staff Report for the 1985 Article IV Consultation.* Washington, DC: International Monetary Fund.

IMF (International Monetary Fund). 1989. *Argentina—Staff Report for the 1989 Article IV Consultation and Request for Stand-By Arrangement*. Washington, DC: International Monetary Fund.

IMF (International Monetary Fund). 1995. *Uruguay: Staff Report for the 1995 Article IV Consultation*. Washington, DC: International Monetary Fund.

IMF (International Monetary Fund). 1997. *Philippines: Staff Report for the 1997 Article IV Consultation*. Washington, DC: International Monetary Fund.

IMF (International Monetary Fund). 1998a. "External Debt Histories of Ten Low-Income Developing Countries: Lessons From their Experience." IMF Working Paper 72, International Monetary Fund, Washington, DC.

IMF (International Monetary Fund). 1998b. *Niger: Staff Report for the 1998 Article IV Consultation*. Washington, DC: International Monetary Fund.

IMF (International Monetary Fund). 1999a. *Nigeria: Staff Report for the 1999 Article IV Consultation*. Washington, DC: International Monetary Fund.

IMF (International Monetary Fund). 1999b. *Philippines - Staff Report for the 1999 Article IV Consultation, Fourth Review Under the Stand-By Arrangement, and Request for Waiver and Modification of Performance Criteria*. Washington, DC: International Monetary Fund.

IMF (International Monetary Fund). 1999c. *Zimbabwe: Staff Report for the 1999 Article IV Consultation*. Washington, DC: International Monetary Fund.

IMF (International Monetary Fund). 2001a. *Argentina: 2001 Article IV Consultation Staff Report*. Washington, DC: International Monetary Fund.

IMF (International Monetary Fund). 2001b. *IMF-Supported Programs in Indonesia, Korea, Thailand: A Preliminary Assessment*. Washington, DC: International Monetary Fund.

IMF (International Monetary Fund). 2001c. *Uruguay: Staff Report for the 2001 Article IV Consultation*. Washington, DC: International Monetary Fund.

IMF (International Monetary Fund). 2001d. *Zimbabwe: Staff Report for the 2001 Article IV Consultation*. Washington, DC: International Monetary Fund.

IMF (International Monetary Fund). 2003a. *The IMF and Recent Capital Account Crises: Indonesia, Korea, Brazil*. Washington, DC: International Monetary Fund.

IMF (International Monetary Fund). 2003b. *Uruguay: Staff Report for the 2003 Article IV Consultation*. Washington, DC: International Monetary Fund.

IMF (International Monetary Fund). 2012. *The Liberalization and Management of Capital Flows—An Institutional View*. Washington, DC: International Monetary Fund.

IMF (International Monetary Fund). 2016. *Argentina: 2016 Article IV Consultation Staff Report*. Washington, DC: International Monetary Fund.

Kaufmann, D., M. Mastruzzi, and D. Zavaleta. 2003. "Sustained Macroeconomic Reforms, Tepid Growth: A Governance Puzzle in Bolivia?" In *Search of Prosperity: Analytic Narratives on Economic Growth*, edited by D. Rodrik. Princeton, NJ: Princeton University Press.

Kaufman, R. R. 1989. "The Politics of Economic Adjustment Policy in Argentina, Brazil, and Mexico: Experiences in the 1980s and Challenges for the Future." *Policy Sciences* 22 (3): 395-413.

Kawai, M., R. Newfarmer, and S. Schmukler. 2005. "Crisis and Contagion in East Asia: Nine Lessons." *Eastern Economic Journal* 31 (2): 185-207.

Larrain, C. 1998. *Banking Supervision in Developing. Regulatory and Supervisory Challenges in a New Era of Global Finance.* The Hague: Fondad.

Leone, A. M., and J. Pérez-Campanero. 1991. "Liberalization and Financial Crisis in Uruguay (1974-1987)." Working Paper 91/30, International Monetary Fund, Washington, DC.

Morales, J., and J. Sachs. 1999. "Bolivia's Economic Crisis." NBER Working Paper 2620, National Bureau of Economic Research, Cambridge, MA.

Nascimento, J. 1990. "The Crisis in the Financial Sector and the Authorities` Reaction: The Case of the Philippines." IMF Working Paper 90/26, International Monetary Fund, Washington, DC.

Radelet, S., J. Sachs, R. Cooper, and B. Bosworth. 1998. "The East Asian Financial Crisis: Diagnosis, Remedies, Prospects." *Brookings Papers on Economic Activity* 1998 (1): 1-90.

Sachs, J. 1985. "External Debt and Macroeconomic Performance in Latin America and East Asia." *Brookings Papers on Economic Activity* 1985 (2): 523-73.

World Bank. 1996. *Bank Restructuring. Lessons from the 1980s.* Washington, DC: World Bank.

APPENDIX D Income classifications

TABLE D.1 Income classification of low-income countries

Low-income countries	Fiscal year 1990	Fiscal year 2020
Afghanistan	L	L
Bangladesh	L	LM
Benin	L	L
Bhutan	L	LM
Burkina Faso	L	L
Burundi	L	L
Cambodia	L	LM
Central African Republic	L	L
Chad	L	L
China	L	UM
Comoros	L	LM
Congo, Dem. Rep.	L	L
Equatorial Guinea	L	UM
Ethiopia	L	L
Gambia, The	L	L
Ghana	L	LM
Guinea	L	L
Guinea-Bissau	L	L
Guyana	L	UM
Haiti	L	L
India	L	LM
Indonesia	L	LM
Kenya	L	LM
Lao PDR	L	LM
Lesotho	L	LM
Liberia	L	L
Madagascar	L	L
Malawi	L	L
Maldives	L	UM
Mali	L	L
Mauritania	L	LM
Mozambique	L	L
Myanmar	L	LM
Nepal	L	L
Niger	L	L
Nigeria	L	LM
Pakistan	L	LM
Rwanda	L	L
São Tomé and Príncipe	L	LM
Sierra Leone	L	L
Somalia	L	L
Sri Lanka	L	UM
Sudan	L	LM
Tanzania	L	L
Togo	L	L
Uganda	L	L
Vietnam	L	LM
Zambia	L	LM

Source: World Bank.
Note: List includes all World Bank Group member countries that were classified as low-income countries in Fiscal Year1990. L stands for low-income country, LM for lower-middle-income country, and UM for upper-middle-income country.

TABLE D.2 Income classification of countries that have received HIPC or MDRI debt relief

HIPC recipients	Fiscal year 1996	Fiscal year 2020
Afghanistan	L	L
Benin	L	L
Bolivia	LM	LM
Burkina Faso	L	L
Burundi	L	L
Cameroon	L	LM
Central African Republic	L	L
Chad	L	L
Comoros	L	L
Congo, Rep.	L	LM
Congo, Dem. Rep.	L	L
Côte d'Ivoire	L	LM
Ethiopia	L	L
Gambia, The	L	L
Ghana	L	LM
Guinea	L	L
Guinea-Bissau	L	L
Guyana	L	UM
Haiti	L	L
Honduras	L	LM
Liberia	L	L
Madagascar	L	L
Malawi	L	L
Mali	L	L
Mauritania	L	LM
Mozambique	L	L
Nicaragua	L	LM
Niger	L	L
Rwanda	L	L
São Tomé and Príncipe	L	LM
Senegal	L	L
Sierra Leone	L	L
Tanzania	L	L
Togo	L	L
Uganda	L	L
Zambia	L	LM

Source: World Bank.
Note: HIPC stands for Highly Indebted Poor Countries; MDRI stands for Multilateral Debt Relief Initiative. HIPC initiative was launched in 1996; MDRI initiative in 2005. List includes all HIPC and MDRI debt relief recipients. L stands for low-income country, LM for lower-middle-income country, and UM for upper-middle-income country.